A FAMILY MAN AT SEA

"My Dearest Margaret…"

Letters Home from a
Mediterranean Flagship
1837-1841

*Edited by
Barbara McDowell*

The Chaucer Head
22 Mill Street
Ludlow
SY8 1BG

First published by The Chaucer Head 2013

Copyright © Barbara McDowell, 2013
Copyright illustrations © as acknowledged 2013

All rights reserved. No part of this publication may be reproduced, stored in a retrieval system, or transmitted, in any form or by any means, electronic, mechanical, photocopying, recording or otherwise, without the prior written consent of the publisher.

Cover illustration:
'Princess Charlotte. Senglea Point Malta' by J.Schranz
© Crown copyright UK Government Art Collection.

ISBN 978-0-9576377-0-2

Printed by the Orphans Press
Leominster, Herefordshire
HR6 0LD

for Daniel

CONTENTS

List of Illustrations　vii
Introduction: Background to the letters　ix
Editors Note and Acknowledgements　xv

THE LETTERS

1.　**1837**
Leaving home - the Admiral and his family - Captain Fanshawe - ship routine - cholera in Malta - disembarking in Malta - Willoughby fails to win the Exhibition - Eliza's engagement to Captain Errington - a Ball - social life in Malta.　1

2.　**1838**
Eliza's wedding - a picnic - a drowning - planning Willoughby's tour - visit to Vesuvius and Herculaneum - Coronation Ball - Toulon - Willoughby's letter - meeting with Willoughby - Carthage and Troy - with the Turkish Fleet - Queen Dowager's arrival - Christmas　37

3.　**1839**
Fancy Dress Ball - Regatta - departure of the Queen Dowager - two weddings - Gozo - Palermo - set sail for Syria - political affairs - family expenditure - Constantinople - Turkish affairs - Basika Bay - court martial - St. Andrew's Day - more courts martial - last Christmas away from home?　83

4.　**1840**
Quarantine in Malta again - Captain Napier - Palmer leaves - waiting for orders - sulphur mines - Napier - problems in Syria - Isle of Thasos - Alexandria - landing in Beyrout - the Mountaineers - attack on Acre - Captain Napier makes terms with Mehemet Ali - birth of grandson　143

5.　**1841**
The new grandson - Malta - letter from Lottie - Napier's honours - Willoughby's extravagance - Malta – the future.　187

Postscript　203

LIST OF ILLUSTRATIONS

Cover illustration:
Princess Charlotte off Senglea Point, Malta by J.Schranz
© Crown copyright UK Government Art Collection.

Overleaf:
Sketch map of the Mediterranean in 1840 showing Packet routes.

In central pages:
1. Admiral Sir Robert Stopford. Portrait by unknown artist, 1840. By permission of the National Portrait Gallery.

2. The Princess Charlotte. Engraving by permission of the National Maritime Museum, Greenwich.

3. Photograph postcard of Durnford Street, Plymouth, late 19th century. By permission of Derek Tait.

4. Loudon's family house in 2013 (previously numbered 44). By permission of Sara McMahon, The Family History Company, Plymouth

5. Letter from John Loudon to his wife in Plymouth, July 1837.

6. Letter from the Princess Charlotte off Palermo, June 1839.

7. Plan of the bombardment of Acre, November 1840: showing the ships and the town. From Clowes 'The Royal Navy' Volume 6, first published 1901.

8. Attack of St. Jean d'Acre showing the ships *Pique, Bellerophon, Thunderer, Princess Charlotte, Powerfull, Revenge, Gorgon and Phoenix*, dedicated to the Admiral Sir Robert Stopford and officers of the Mediterranean Fleet. Lithograph by permission of the National Museum of the Royal Navy, Portsmouth.

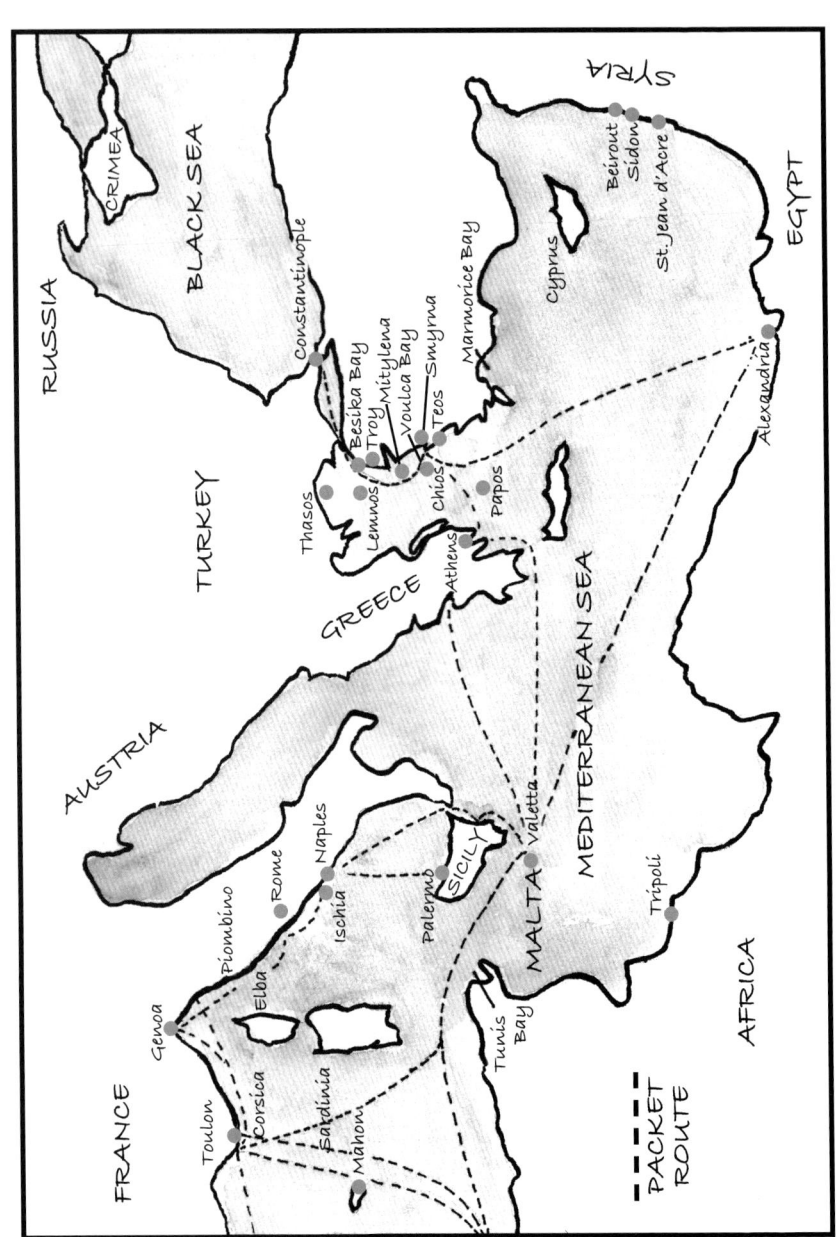

THE BACKGROUND TO THE LETTERS

Events in the Mediterranean

The period between the Battle of Waterloo and the Crimean War is usually thought to have been a peaceful time for the British Navy; in fact 'scarcely a year of it passed without seeing the Navy actively engaged in some corner of the World[1]'. The Mediterranean was one such corner, and in 1837 a British Fleet, led by Admiral Sir Robert Stopford in his flagship the *Princess Charlotte*[2], set sail from Portsmouth as part of an Anglo-French fleet whose purpose, in a three-year tour of duty, was to observe events in the eastern Mediterranean. The fear of Russian dominance in the area due to the declining power of the Ottoman Empire was threatening the stability of Europe.

Egypt had been a province of the Ottoman Empire for over three hundred years but since 1805, under Mehemet Ali, the Pasha of Egypt, it had enjoyed a great deal of autonomy with a strong, well-trained, well-supplied army and a fleet superior to that of the Sultan. In the early 1830s, Mehemet Ali, having decided that the time was ripe to seize full independence, invaded Turkish-controlled Syria, which by 1839 provoked the Western Powers (Britain, Austria, Prussia and Russia but not France - a supporter of Egypt) into action in support of Turkey. At the battle of Nezib in January 1839 the Turkish army was heavily defeated by the Egyptians and the situation was almost immediately exacerbated by the death of the Sultan and his succession by his 16 year-old son. Turkey was further weakened by the remarkable action of the Turkish 'Admiral' Achmet who, believing that Khosrev, the Grand Vizier, and other courtiers in Constantinople, were in the pay of the Russians, took his entire fleet to Alexandria and placed it at the service of Mehemet Ali.

---

1 Clowes 'The Royal Navy' Vol.6, Introduction.
2 The Princess Charlotte, 1st. Rate, 104 guns, 198.5 x 54 feet, 2443 beam, launched on September 14, 1825, from Portsmouth Dockyard.

ix

It soon became clear that the *Princess Charlotte* could not return to England, as originally intended. In August, 1840, the 'Four Powers' delivered a joint ultimatum to Mehemet Ali, demanding his withdrawal from the newly conquered lands – Syria, Crete and others – in return for the guaranteed role of hereditary Viceroy of Egypt; if he refused, the Four Powers threatened the loss of all his possessions. Stopford ordered Admiral Sir Charles Napier, Stopford's second-in-command in the Powerful, together with five other warships, to Beyrout, at that time occupied by over 11,000 Egyptian soldiers plus 4,000 deserting Turkish soldiers.

The *Princess Charlotte,* together with 30 other ships, accompanied the remnants of the Turkish Fleet and 8 Austrian ships, to patrol the Syrian coast, effectively stopping the northwards advance of the 70,000 strong Egyptian army by cutting off supplies. After rejection of the ultimatum by Mehemet Ali, Napier persuaded Stopford to allow him to take charge of the land operation. On Sept 9th, Beyrout was bombarded by 33 warships, destroying the town's defences, and the troops, under Napier, were landed to the north of the town. Napier then led an attack on Sidon and, ignoring Stopford's instruction to return to sea, pressed on, taking 700 prisoners. Napier should have been court-martialled for insubordination, but the kind-hearted Stopford wrote in his support. On orders from the Admiralty in London, on Oct 31st, the *Princess Charlotte* with five of the warships, led a general bombardment of St Jean d'Acre. The Egyptians were hampered by the smoke created by the bombardment and after the grand magazine had been blown up, killing more than 1200 people and destroying much of the town, the Egyptians fled southwards. Napier continued to annoy Stopford by persisting with intermittent fire and without any official authority, then entered into direct negotiations with Mehemet Ali, negotiations which resulted in the signing of a convention in which Egypt evacuated Syria, the Turkish Fleet was returned to Turkey, and Mehemet Ali was guaranteed hereditary government of Egypt. As a result of this convention, France, irritated by events, 'not only held aloof, but also assumed a sulky and threatening attitude[3]'.

---

3   W.L.Clowes 'The Royal Navy', London, Chatham Publishing, 1997, vol. 6, p.310.

The uneasy relationship between Britain and France is shown by comments in the letters.

Thus 'The Syrian War' conflict was resolved and the *Princess Charlotte* returned to England, the three-year tour of duty having become four.

The writer of the letters, Mr. John Loudon

On board the flagship the *Princess Charlotte,* with over 700 men on board, was a Mr John Loudon, aged 61, the Secretary to the Admiral, Sir Robert Stopford. Secretaries to Admirals were often former pursers nominated by the Admiral. In the Navy List, John Loudon appears as a purser from 1799, but he had also been Secretary to Admiral Eyre in South America. In March 1837, he accepted the appointment as Secretary to Admiral Stopford, which paid him an extra £400 per year, income needed to support his son Willoughby, at The King's School, Canterbury, and planning to read Law at Corpus Christi College, Cambridge.

The Secretary's administrative duties were extensive, including the everyday organisation of the ship, communications with other ships in the squadron, and correspondence with the Foreign Office in London. Several clerks worked under the Secretary, writing and copying diplomatic letters, instructions and reports sent by the mailboat (the Packet), which also carried personal letters such as those published here to Loudon's wife, Margaret.

During his four years in the Mediterranean, Loudon's wife Margaret lived in Durnford Street, Plymouth, with three daughters, Eliza (Lizzie) aged 29, Charlotte (Lottie) aged 25, Frances (Fan) aged 21, and a son, Willoughby aged 18. John Loudon wrote to his wife on average once a week and these letters, 220 in all, have survived, though letters from England, apart from a few from his children, have not. Letters from wives to their husbands rarely survive, as it was usual for seamen 'to destroy wives' letters before a battle in case personal or perhaps even political exchanges fell into the wrong hands. We know that Nelson, for example, sorted through his wife's letters and burnt them before the action at

Tenerife...[4]' Letters from husbands at sea, however, were read out to family and friends at home and were more likely to be preserved.

Loudon's descriptions of naval life are on the whole reassuring, with details of the daily life on board, the social life in Malta in the winter months, the lavish banquets, the ladies on the ship and the dancing on the deck, his friendly relationship with the Admiral and other officers such as Captain Arthur Fanshawe (brother-in-law of the Admiral) and Charles Austen (Jane Austen's brother and Captain of the Bellerophon). He enjoys his land excursions to Vesuvius and elsewhere, and describes the sights of Naples, Toulon, Beyrout, Rome and, of course, Malta. He doesn't, however, avoid expressing his feelings of despair at the delay in returning home and his regret at unpleasant duties such as officiating at courts martial, in one court martial successfully petitioning for the reduction of the punishment of an insubordinate midshipman from hanging to transportation. The letters referring to the most important naval incident of the four years, the bombardment of St Jean d'Acre, perhaps understandably do not fully convey to his wife the drama of the event.

Loudon's predominant concerns shown in his letters are about his family and in particular the burden of responsibility borne by his wife; most sailor's wives 'stayed at home, enduring years of separation and anxiety, bringing up small children, managing domestic affairs.... often crossing the boundaries of what was understood to be conventional female activity[5]'. He gives advice and support to his family on running the home, educating his lazy son, saving money and so on. 'The wives of seaman, left alone for long periods to run households and oversee family finances, needed to be adept at accounts...'[6]. Margaret sent regular financial accounts to her husband for his approval and comments - 'Willoughby (must) examine all his Bills & avoid employing the Cambridge tradesmen who look upon the students as their game. He should get all clothes in Plymouth and London & even his groceries - who would think of his consuming £3.14.9 for Sugar and Tea in the 6 weeks...' (July 27th, 1839)

---

4 Margarette Lincoln 'Naval Wives and Mistresses', London, National Maritime Museum, 2007, p.30.
5 Ibid. p.15
6 Ibid. p.107

Loudon bitterly regrets missing the engagement and wedding of his eldest daughter, fretting about the pressures on his wife of wedding arrangements and even the difficulties of Eliza in breastfeeding his grandson but when his son travelled around Europe from July1838 to January 1839, Loudon clearly delights in the time they were able to spend together. 'We are showing him the lions in great style and this is a chance he is not likely to have again for there is every probability of his visiting Asia and Greece and then returning by Italy and France in time for his term at Cambridge.' (August 13th, 1838)

Despite Loudon's occasional worries there is much well-written and detailed description, often joyful, and the letters give a picture of an extraordinary man with a good sense of humour, very dutiful, very loving and much loved by his children, a few of whose letters are included here. He enjoys sending home presents to his family - 'I send a small Frail of Smyrna figs as I know you like them and they are good for you' (4th January 1838) and 'I have written to Eliza and sent her a Bedside Rug - a little coffee and a few anchovies' (9th March 1840). He also takes commissions – Fan asks for 'some small size black silk gloves and mittens, from one I believe to 2 shillings a pair. We have seen some sent to Augusta Foot by her brother and they appear so beautiful and cheap that we should like to have some' (27th March 1841). He also requests goods to be sent to the ship – 'Captain Fanshawe tells me I must really have a new pair of Epaulettes and a new Undress Coat. If my Tailor in Fore Street is sure of my measure I wish him to send me one of good cloth made in his neatest way and a pair of real good Epaulettes they are so apt to tarnish here' (24th June 1839).

Loudon doesn't hesitate to comment on the political situation – 'we shall have no finger in it unless Russia begins her insidious policy of helping the Sultan by way of getting Constantinople the Key of the Dardanelles and encroaching by degrees upon our possessions in India' (23rd July 1839) and 'I fear from the wrongheadedness of some of our diplomatics there will in the end be a fracas between us and the French who evidently favour Mehemet Ali and wish him to reform Syria' (29th July 1840).

Every letter starts 'My Dearest Margaret' and ends 'Your ever affectionate husband John Loudon' and they are all addressed to 44 Durnford Street, Plymouth. A tourist's companion of 1823 describes Durnford Street as 'mostly occupied with genteel families, chiefly those of naval and military officers'. At one time Durnford Street alone boasted an R. N. captain, a Baronet, 2 colonels, 1 major and 9 professional men. In 1847, Capt Arthur Fanshawe lived at no. 4, Lower Durnford Street, Capt Lawrence at no. 31. The impressive Barracks on the Eastern side were built in 1781[7].

The letters provide a fascinating insight into four years in the life of a family man at a time when communications were limited to hand-written letters, letters sometimes going astray, often delayed, taking two to six weeks to arrive. Insight also into the routines of life on a warship, life on shore at Malta, and, throughout, the longing for the pleasures of home and family.

---

7   Plymouth's Street Directories, Local Studies Library.

Editor's Note

John Loudon's 220 letters to his wife were acquired many years ago and in good condition, though a number are cut around the margins in order to show that they had been 'smoked' as a protection against cholera. As was often the practice in the nineteenth century, when letters became charged by weight, some are written across and down, making them difficult to read; otherwise, Loudon's writing is very legible and his original spelling and punctuation have been retained.

Transcribing them was such an enjoyable experience, watching the characters develop in a situation set in a world so different to that of today yet with such recognisable emotions, that I felt they deserved publication. In the 96,000 words of the letters, there was inevitably some duplication of news and comment, which have been omitted in this book. For example, many of the letters include inquiries about the health of neighbours in Plymouth, and events such as Mrs Duckworth's fall from a donkey and Loudon's climb up Vesuvius were repeated. The weather was frequently reported, obviously a very important matter for a sailing ship, but this can make tedious reading so has only been included where appropriate. The letters published here are reduced to about 83,000 words, without, I hope, loss of interest or dramatic content.

Barbara McDowell
Ludlow
2013

Acknowledgements

Illustrations by permission of the Royal Naval Museum, Portsmouth (8), the National Maritime Museum (2), the National Portrait Gallery (1), the Government Art Collection (cover) and Sara McMahon (4).

Many thanks to Margarette Lincoln, Deputy Director of the National Maritime Museum, for permission to quote from 'Naval Wives and Mistresses'. Thanks also for the help of Sara McMahon, Roger Bragger, Derek Tait, David Burnett, Valerie Thomas and, of course, my family for their encouragement and advice.

A FAMILY MAN AT SEA

1837

Leaving home - the Admiral and his family - Captain Fanshawe - ship routine - cholera in Malta - disembarking in Malta - Willoughby fails to win the Exhibition - Eliza's engagement to Captain Errington - a Ball - social life in Malta.

From Admiral Sir Robert Stopford, 8th. March, 1837, Upper Harley Street, London to Mr. John Loudon, 44 Durnford Street, Plymouth.

Sir,
Upon my appointment to the Mediterranean Command,... hearing from several persons your fitness for the important office of Secretary, I beg to know whether I may look forward to your accepting it. I have the honor to be Sir, Your very obedient servant Robert Stopford.

My Dearest Margaret. 27 March, Dorset Square
I wrote you on my landing at Portsmouth whence I set off in the Rocket at 9 and arrived here at 5 just in time for Robert's[8] dinner and very kindly was I received. My companions in the coach were very pleasant respectable people - one, a young lady who had been

---
8   Robert is Margaret's brother, Eliza his wife.

My Dearest Margaret...

2 years at school at St. Dennis and had travelled through Flanders and lived at Strasburg with her family - her Grandfather was a German Clergyman and all the family, though English, spoke German. This morning after breakfast I called upon my Admiral and found him every thing I could wish and he received me most kindly. We had a long chat and I cannot say even to you the many kind things he said - among others that now he considered himself afloat he has promised to take Jeffrey if I like. I said I might write him, but I told him it would perhaps be better to wait till I returned to Plymouth when I could see how he was. I then called on Sir Wm Burnett and the family whom I dine with tomorrow - from them I went to the Admiralty where I had a long chat with Sir Wm Parker and very kind he was - I am however to see him again and get my lesson. He has already let me in to a good many secrets as to the management of the Station - but I shall have my full lesson from all the boards in the Course of a day or two.

I am My Dearest Margaret your affectionate husband John Loudon.

No cough whatever.

1 June, Fountain Inn Portsmouth

Nothing could be finer than our passage up at 7 o'clock on Tuesday morning we were inside the Needles and at 9 at Spithead. I went on Board Princess Charlotte - neither Captain Fanshawe nor Sainthill were on Board but the latter soon came and was very civil and obliging. My cabin has much to do to it and I had every assistance from Sainthill in making alterations which they did not like to meddle with till I came. After managing things as well as I could I lunched with the Officers and came on shore with my Desk and Carpet Bag, and on my way to the Dockyard left a card for Capt Fanshawe who lodges just opposite, as he was out with Mrs Fanshawe, and met Mr Henville who asked me immediately to meet a small party at Dinner, but not having a Dinner Dress I excused myself, promising to give him a call tomorrow - at the Dock Gates however I met Rosenberg who pressed me so warmly to dine with him on Board where they had a few friends that I slipt into the Boat and in five minutes was in the Britannia. Nobody could be kinder than Rosenberg and altogether I passed a pleasant evening till 9 o'clock when I returned to my Inn. Here I found a card from Capt

2

1837

Fanshawe who had called immediately and invited me to Dine en famille at half past 6. Yesterday morning I breakfasted with him and had a very comfortable chat. We walked to the Port arms together and there I passed two good hours with Edge who really received me warmly and gave me all the information he could. He introduced me to Sir Philip, who though called a Humbug, was at least very civil to me. I then saw Sir Frederic Maitland who was very friendly and nice. I dined with Capt and Mrs Fanshawe and like then more and more. I had a very nice letter from Sir Robert saying he expected to be here the end of the week and touching upon many preparatory points which 'tis as well I am on the spot to attend to as I find my signature is as good as his for drawing our supplies of Books and Stationary. Jeffrey is on shore and so far useful at the Dockyard - Inch is on Board - Palmer is entered as a Landsman which gives him £15 a year and if he behaves himself, which I have little doubt of, he will be put on the Retinue List as an Able Seaman. I have a very good letter from Willoughby who has had a kind one from Beatson[9]. His letter is principally taken up with his books and tasks for the examination.

    I am again on Board getting all put right - May I have my old striped sofa cover I had at Deal? It would be just the thing now for my Bed is a Sofa by day and I should not require to buy a cover. I am getting into comfortable condition thanks to Capt Fanshawe who has come off with me and has been planning and working like a horse with the Carpenters. He is indeed a noble fellow. I have 3 joiners at work cleaning off my Bureau and I hope to write you tomorrow again by Capt Blythe - at present I am hardly quiet enough - with love to dear Liz Charl and Fan and kind regards to dear Mrs Crayke, Mrs Scobell and Party, I assure you My Dearest Margaret, Your affectionate Husband John Loudon. A very nice band is now playing over my head while I write.

5 o'clock

    I am just come on shore with Capt Fanshawe who would be much obliged if you will send for Ross and tell him that as Edge does not answer if Ross chooses to come up by the Brunswick he will give him a fair trial. I think myself he will do best it rests with

---

9   Willoughby's tutor

My Dearest Margaret...

himself. Capt Fanshawe recollects him quite well and is in hopes he will be active enough for the situation. But he must come at once or say he declines that Capt Fanshawe may look out for another. Ross lives in a cottage opposite the Victualling Office Inn as you go to the Victualling Yard - you can send my Dressing Case by him. God Bless you all. Young Palmer answers well.

{Letter with black seal in mourning for the King}   *24 June,*
42 Penny Street

You will see by this My Dearest Margaret that the Admiral's arrival is again a false alarm - but he is now certainly, he says, to be here on Monday Evening or Tuesday morning and I have after due vexation on the circumstance taken up my quarters on here to find a great improvement in their cleanliness, having had a thorough scrubbing in my absence - the Bed taken down and very nicely put up with another mattress and quite to my liking - so much so that I found myself at 6 this morning on the same side I laid down on and perfectly refreshed. We arrived late having been detained towing a poor Emigrant Vessel bound to Van Dieman's Land as far as the breakwater and delayed by a fog which prevented us putting on all our power for fear of accidents - but it was moderate and smooth and no sea sickness even among the Ladies. I had an opportunity of rubbing up my Portuguese among four of that Nation from Rio de Janeyro, one of whom understood me perfectly and I thought would have kissed me for he did not know a word of English. He came over to put his son to an English school being an enthusiast for England and is to make a tour through our manufacturing towns before he returns to the Brazils. Mr Fownes was a passenger and a most pleasant fellow he is - you will say I ought to profit by such an example as him, for he passed the whole evening from Tea till Bedtime rummaging in his Carpet Bag and shewing me his toilette apparatus and all kind of nick-nackery, so minute and in apple-pie order that I told him I believed he must travel, for such things as an end not a means of travel - but so long as it procured him satisfaction it was all the same. One thing I posed him in however he had not a Glass to shave by as he pretended to be independent wherever he went and this you know I have in my twopence halfpenny little case. He is the same natty man on shore, he says, and will not permit his wife or anyone to lay a finger on any of his things. We are now 28 short and I really think we shall be moving about the end of next week - a story has got round that Sir Thomas Hardy is very ill and that Sir Robert is to have Greenwich in which case you will soon have your hard bargain back upon your hands, but Capt. Fanshawe says tis all stuff[10].

3 o'clock
I did not go off, wishing to see the procession and hear the Proclamation of our gracious Queen[11]. I sat an hour for my picture which will be finished on Tuesday - broiling hot and I am keeping indoors where I am cool and comfortable. Rosenberg has left his card - the first who has called. God Bless You My Dearest Margaret, Your Ever Affectionate Husband John Loudon.

Write by Pike the Carpenter who comes by the Brunswick and is to be found at Miss Bedfords - if not, by Post. It would be hard to begrudge our own postage.

To Fanny Loudon. *29 June*
My first employment after getting up and bathing at South Sea is to pray for Many Happy Returns of the Day to my Dearest Fan. It was a happy day to her Mamma and me that gave her to us and she has much added to that every year of her life by her good conduct and dutiful behaviour in every respect which must ever endear her to our warmest and best affections. I say nothing of a Young Ladys age, but if my reckoning be right you are better entitled to be called 'of age' than our gracious Queen who makes it out you know at 18 - and I <u>must</u> say that you are fairly entitled to be considered at the age of discretion, that having been your distinctive character ever since the time I brought you to <u>disgrace</u> for stamping and calling names to poor old Sarah. It is said 'discretion' is the better part of valour - I think it so of everything else. How many broils and bickerings all saved by it and how quiet and comfortable both home and abroad are by its means. I only hope you and old Jack[12] will keep good friends.

---

10   Stopford was expected to be appointed Governor of the Naval Hospital at Greenwich after the death of Hardy, in which case Loudon would return to England with Stopford. In fact, much to Loudon's disgust, Admiral Fleeming was chosen instead.
11   Queen Victoria acceded the throne on June 20th 1837
12   The family pony

My Dearest Margaret…

30th. *June*

I have just received your dear letter of Wednesday with the other precious dispatches by Boynton Creyke, only one hour after your dear Mamma's by the Post and am hurrying through the answers to them if I can in time for Dr.Thomas who goes by the Brunswick at 6. All morning I have been with my worthy Admiral then at the Dockyard with Mr.Edge where I met Admiral Ross - he walked with me to my Lodgings and on our way we met Capt. Falcon who came in both together and had a chat over a Glass of Wine and Water and a Biscuit. Tomorrow we all go on Board and sail on Sunday. God Bless you Dearest Fan I wish I had been at your party on the strawberry occasion would you believe it I have not eaten one this season!. You will see Georgie the week after next. I shall write from Gib.

Meantime I am Dearest Fan Your affectionate Father John Loudon.

My Dearest Margaret.   30 June, 42 Penny Street

We are all begun and in good train. I go every morning at 10 to the Admiral and about 12 we finish when I go about other matters. The Ladies like my cabin much of which is laid with green cloth and very neat and the Admiral is much pleased with it and sat in it sometimes. Yesterday we mustered the people in great state and an excellent appearance they made - we are now full[13]. Dear Will! It would have done your heart good to have seen him, so manly and healthy a fellow and looking the Gentleman in every way. I am not surprised at his making friends. He set off with young Robert Baker a fine young man on the Rocket on Wednesday so as to be with Mr Beatson[14] on Thursday according to promise. I have sent him a cheque for Mr Wallace's account £56 to take back with him and shall arrange for his drawing a certain sum from the Bankers when he goes to Corpus - a better college I hear than Pembroke so that you need not give yourself any trouble on that score. You must now draw and pay the poor girls quarters and any other little things you want and send your Bankers Book to be marked up for we made a terrible pull upon them lately. I shall have an opportunity of writing you from Gibraltar where we touch and I may tell you

---

13   The full complement of the Princess Charlotte was 738 men
14   Willoughby's tutor

1837

but it must not yet go further we are to go along the East Coast of Spain to Barcelona to communicate with the Ships there on our way to Malta. This bustle quite agrees with me. I get up at 6, go down to South Sea Beach, launch a machine and bathe, then walk on the common in the midst of drumming and fifing bugling and soldiering till 8, come home, dress and Breakfast at 9 and go to the Bush at 10 when the days work begins. I like my dear Admiral and Lady Stopford[15] more and more indeed we promise to be very happy but I must conclude - Adieu - God Bless You - If we do not sail on Sunday I will write you again. Sir George Cockburn is here and his brother Col.Cockburn. I am recommended by Lady Stopford to get myself a pair of blue gauze spectacles which they all have for the glare of Malta - and as soon as I dispatch this I shall look for a pair. Palmer behaves very well and my cabin in nice order. Jeffrey is still on Shore, but very ready and always looks in about Breakfast time - he never names his wife nor I to him[16]. Inch is a very fine young man indeed and writes an excellent hand - and young Couch a very fine young man but will require a little time to bring him in[17] - so I am very well off. Again God Bless you. Your Affectionate Husband John Loudon.

1 July, Portsmouth. Saturday

It is now 5 p.m. and we are going on Board at half past 6. We talk of sailing tomorrow but our men are not yet arrived from the River and I think myself we shall be detained till Monday because they have to be paid their advance. We are to look in off Plymouth to be joined by the Wolverine, but I fear a sight of us at a distance will be your share unless you could persuade Williams or the Admiral through Mr and Miss Whimper to come out in the Tender I think Tuesday or Wednesday will be the day - I have been a good deal with Adml.Ross, Capt and Mrs Falcon and one Mr Renny, who returns to Town tomorrow and asked very kindly for you all. I embrace the opportunity of Capt Couch to send you my picture and the Lady says if you think it too much marked on I have been lately ill and not quite so full as I could wish, she

---

15 Lady Stopford, the daughter of Capt. Robert Fanshawe, married Robert Stopford in 1808
16 Palmer and Jeffrey are stewards who look after Loudon.
17 Inch and Couch are clerks who work for Loudon, copying letters which carried diplomatic instructions and all the other communications regarding the administration of the Squadron.

My Dearest Margaret...

could very easily mend it and she can make a small copy of it for 2 Guineas. You know I am not so young as I was - and if dear Eliza would like the small copy and you keep that I will remit Miss Crews the money. I fear you will think this a hurried scrawl but the last day always brings plenty to do. I wish you could take a sail out to the Breakwater to see your face once more. God Bless you My Dearest Margaret - my love and affection all round. Blessings on you all. Your affectionate John Loudon.

3 July, Princess Charlotte off the Wight
We got under weigh at 3 o'clock this morning and are now at the back of the Isle of Wight when I little thought to be when we had one trip there four years ago. We are all exceedingly pleased with the Ship, with the men and with one another, the water is as smooth as glass and all the Young Ladies full of glee over my head on the poop quite enjoying it. Poor Mrs Fanshawe is left behind at Portsmouth but if she sets out to day which I believe she will by land she will be at Plymouth before us. I am sorry to say it is only a distant look at you we can have as we only shew ourselves to the Wolverine in the Sound and go off together. It is very sad for us all to be so tantalized but yet I cannot resist clinging to it as a last lingering look perhaps seeing my own house but not near enough for a sight of the dear inmates. My cabin is now most comfortable and I have nothing now to distract me but the sad thought of parting. Palmer goes on exceedingly well and makes me very comfortable - a more placid kind hearted man than Sir Robert I scarcely ever saw and all the Ladies seem to take a leaf out of his book. They come all to Breakfast at 8 o'clock - we have Biscuit and wine and water on the table at 12 and dine at 4, Tea at 8 and in Bed at 10 and this is one day. I very much fear poor Jeffrey will scarcely hold out as his sores and boils are coming back upon him - poor creature if he breaks down I know not what will become of him. Sir Gordon Bresner dined with us yesterday - he seemed displeased at Emma marrying without his consent in the hasty way she did but I told him as he approved of the attachment he should not feel offended and it is now all right.

1837

Tues 4th.

We have most beautiful weather but scarcely any wind - more and more am I delighted with Sir Robert he has been sitting with me in my cabin for an hour and we perfectly understand one another. Lady Stopford is all kindness and I could not venture to hope she would have been so perfectly pleasing and attentive in her manners having at first a Fanshawe appearance of reserve she is indeed a most Lady like woman and improves wonderfully upon a closer acquaintance. Capt Fanshawe is full of fun and humour, the Girls are all agreeable and Arthur the son as fine a youth as ever I beheld. You will say my Geese are all Swans and perhaps I speak too soon but those are my present feelings and certainly I am more sanguine than ever of all possible comfort, while the station lasts, but something whispers me it will be broken up precipitately, as he is certainly the first for Governor of Greenwich Hospital should any thing happen to Sir Thomas, and who knows but the chances may throw me with him? I am rather anxious to know how you like my picture. If you do Miss Crew will copy it on a small scale like Mrs Fanshawe's picture of Capt.F for 2 guineas and if you do not like it Eliza must be content with it as it is. I know Charlotte could copy it but hers are like those of all bad artists - made striking by deep lines and the deepest wrinkles of old age and sickness. I think my cheeks are not quite so lanky as Miss Crews has made them. 10 o'clock fine night off the Start within 40 miles of dear Plymouth I shall be there in the morning - good night.

July 5th.

Wednesday morning 7 o'clock we are now off the breakwater but such a haze that I fear we shall neither see nor be seen. The weather is heavenly and I have not given up hopes yet of seeing the dear girls in the Tender. God Bless you and them is the prayer of your affectionate husband John Loudon.. I am obliged to cut short for many official dispatches.

6 July, Princess Charlotte, The Channel

Perhaps tis as well our dear girls did not come out yesterday morning, as it could only have been tantalizing to us all - and the wind being fair though little of it we were soon at a distance from dear Plymouth and all I hold dear on earth. The sea is like glass and there is little wind still we jog on.

My Dearest Margaret...

7th. July, Friday
Still fine. The Ladies enjoy it and I have a dance after dinner on the quarter deck with the Young Midshipmen while Papa and Mamma walk the poop like Adam and Eve enjoying the young peoples happiness. The Admiral comes every forenoon into my cabin, seats himself in my chair (which by the by came back in the best order) and chats for an hour on all our matters and I see little more of him till dinner time.

8th. July, Saturday
Today we have some sea in the Bay of Biscay and the Ladies make a bad muster to dinner - 3 missing - we are 45 miles from Corunna and the wind is against us and I expect a long passage. Lady Stopford paid my cabin a visit and admired it much. Capt Fanshawe is always out and in as I am in his and nothing can be more comfortable.

9th. July Sunday
This has been a warm close day, a swell of the sea but no wind which at dinner gave the Admiral an opportunity of saying a good thing 'why is love like the Bay of Biscay?" "Because the course of true love never runs smooth". The first glass of wine after dinner Lady Stopford addressed herself to me and said "Mr Loudon let us drink all our absent friends" . I thought it very nice of her she did it with so much kindness of manner. We had an excellent sermon, and all we want is a little breeze to keep us cool and send us on our way - these two days have been lost to us - two of our ladies still sick.

10th. July, Monday
Torrents of rain over my head in the night - the air much refreshed this morning - cloudy and a light breeze - seen several ships but no land yet. Ladies all better - dance on the quarter deck in the evening. Our days shorten in fast, dark at 8, fine moon. Admiral paid me his daily visit - glad I had my comfortable chair for him. Jeffrey well again and Inch a most excellent clerk and young Couch coming on well. Palmer is as attentive as ever - plays the violin for the Young Ladies dance on the quarter deck. Captain Fanshawe really an excellent fellow - just come down from a long

10

1837

walk on the Poop with Willoughby Lake - McGennys comes up to me every day - in fact all are most attentive. I am now going to bed 10 o'clock. Prayers in the morning on 2nd deck first time.

11th July
Waked at 5 - Holystoning[18] and washing decks over my head - put me to sleep and did not wake till half past 7 - had to wash and dress smartly as we Breakfast at half past. Read my Chapter 16th Genesis from Lizzies Bible and then to breakfast - hard rain - cleared up which gave me a walk on the Poop - saw Cape Finistere 30 miles off, little wind. Usual visits from Adml, Capt Fanshawe and a chat with Lady Stopford through my skylight. No work yet but only of preparation. You are just going to Prayers (10 o'clock) and bless you.

12th. July Wednesday
The homeward Packet is just joining and we have no time. We are nearly off Lisbon with a fine breeze. God Bless you all. Your affectionate husband John Loudon.

14 July Princess Charlotte off Cadiz
Another chance has occurred for writing a very few lines by the return of the Malta Packet which has arrived sooner than I could have wished, but as I may not have another when I wish it I cannot let this slip however unprepared. We had a most delightful view of the Portuguese Coast yesterday and were saluted by Sir Wm Gage off Lisbon which we returned and a fine affair it was. This morning we entered in Station which gives dear Sir Robert £3 a day extra and the Play is commissioned. I am quite sure we shall do!. Capt Fanshawe is as we always thought him a most excellent fellow. I am as familiar to his cabin and all in it as my own - he is the most playful good tempered fellow I ever knew and I really had no conception of his worth till we have got close together. He threatens opening a correspondence with you and lugs me out for exercise and amusement without ceremony - I cannot tell you half of his beauties. But after all Home! Sweet Home! How I long to hear of it. I please myself thinking what you are about every hour

---

18 ~~Hailstones~~ Deck scrubbing

My Dearest Margaret...

of the day and at 10 particularly I know you are at prayers and I fall on my knees at my poor little bedside and pray, religiously pray for you all. Dear Liz can I help thinking of her quick turn to Mamma before the answer is out of her lips to help her up. God Bless you all - but the Packet approaches. God Bless you again and again your ever affectionate John Loudon.

16 Jul. Princess Charlotte off the East of Gibraltar
I did expect when I sent off my last letter of the 14th off Cadiz that we should have been at Gibraltar before now but the wind has come against and we are all working up with the shores of Europe in one side and of Africa on the other quite close to us with beautiful weather and all our Party in full admiration of the scenery round us. I know you are now sitting alone in the back parlour with the Newspaper and am glad to have five minutes chat with you, being myself alone in my neat little cabin. This will be my 3rd letter thus far commenced upon but when ended I cannot yet say. (We have just had prayers and a very good sermon). My health and appetite are excellent and Captain Fanshawe has just been complimenting me on looking so much better than when I came up to Portsmouth. Palmer goes on well and keeps everything in order and Jeffrey is again nearly well. Dear Hornby is a sweet little fellow and I think growing he has had a bad toe but that too is almost well - poor fellow he had written on Friday but his letter fell overboard in giving it to the Boat and of course was spoilt.

18 July, Gibraltar. Tuesday
We had a delightful day on Sunday having the wind against us blowing out of the East which obliging us to go firm side to side gave us a splendid view of the two shores of Africa and Europe. In the evening we got in and anchored and yesterday we went on shore dined with Sir Alexander Woodford and the Governor and returned at 9 - very glad with all our pomp and state to breathe the cool and fresh air of the ship. The Admiral, Capt Fanshawe, Arthur the son and myself - Captain Sheriff and Capt Newell - in all 20 and a sumptuous dinner we had - to which every thing being iced in no small way contributed. This is the first time they have had ice here, which has been imported by an American and they are likely to have many more cargoes for it is the greatest luxury such

a <u>panting</u> place can have - we shall gladly leave it tomorrow. They have got the cholera at Malta, but Sir Joshua Rowley is outside with the Squadron at sea and there we shall relieve him when we have been at Barcelona, which will keep us back a fortnight at least. We shall not go in to Malta till all this cholera ceases and I think myself we may visit Syracuse or Corfu first. I met with a cousin of the Pagets at the Generals a son of Sir Arthur - a fine handsome young man a Captain in the 52nd - but like many of the young officers - married, which I wondered at being quite boyish in appearance and manners.

19th July
A gala day on board - the Governor, and Heads of Departments a second Breakfast in style. I keep on board as the shore is so very hot and can feel very uncomfortable.

20th July
We are now weighing for proceeding along the coast as far as Barcelona though the wind is against us. I must now close. Remember me most kindly to all the Collins, Davies's Creykes great and small, I would give a great deal for a letter but must just have patience.

God Bless you Dearest Margaret and my ever dear Liz Charl and Fan - I have written Will and hope all will be right. Your affectionate husband John Loudon.

23 July, Princess Charlotte in passage from Gibraltar to Minorca
We left the Rock on Friday with a contrary wind which it still continues to be and a very unpleasant damp air it is. The Medea met us on Friday evening, with a letter from Sir Josias Rowley who was going with the Squadron to Mahon, the cholera being very bad at present at Malta. He is very anxious for our arrival and as he is so near we are now to relieve him and then go to the Coast of Spain. It is an anxious time for Capt Fanshawe but of course when the Packet comes out Mrs Fanshawe will join us at Minorca without going in to Malta unless the cholera's gone, which I hope will be by that time. It was a great relief to me to receive a little note from dear Eliza though dated 30 June. Today we dine in the Wardroom for the first time. Capt Fanshawe quite a boy always at play but I dare say a little fidget which I tell him.

My Dearest Margaret...

26 July Wednesday.

Dearest girl - we are now near Mahon but the wind is again rather against us so we do not expect to meet the Fleet till Friday. The weather is however much more pleasant since we have got rid of the Levantic, our very hot wind. You may easily suppose that having no outward objects to attract us I have the enjoyment of my Books but you were nothing to that teazing Capt Fanshawe - he is quite a torment, comes in and steals my book out of my hand and rouses me about most provokingly. He is indeed a most worthy fellow and tis hard to say whether he is oftener in my cabin or I in his. My dear good Admiral has had all the carpenters at work giving me a current of air from the quarter deck and comes in to enjoy it as if mine were his own cabin - we must go on well because all is sincere good feeling on all sides, and as for Lady Stopford she is a perfect angel. She says she hardly knows how I shall make it out in our house on shore at Malta, having my cabin so very nice and comfortable on board. We were certainly mistaken in Sam Knill - a more steady right forward and righthearted fellow cannot be. We have generally a walk from 6 to 7 o'clock every morning for they are so fresh and beautiful that I get up regularly at half past 5 read a chapter in my dear Eliza's Bible and then walk till 8 while Palmer puts my cabin in order, we have public prayers on the quarter deck and then to Breakfast at half past 8, I left my pen wiper behind. Lady S has just given me one and I am promised more.

29 July Off Minorca

And can I forget the day[19]. Perhaps I felt it the more being absent, as I have been many, but I do feel more than ever the return of that eventful day which if it threw much sadness over us has proved a blessing to me at least in having you and the dear girls and our dear Willy to cheer and comfort us in our downhill journey. May the Almighty bless you and them and a happy meeting to us all is my sincerest prayer. We are at last in sight of the Fleet and I fancy about Monday or Tuesday Sir Jos. Rowley will be turning the Caledonia's head to England. Lady Stopford has had a slight stomach complaint but is again better - the weather warm certainly

---

19 A wedding anniversary – they were married in July 1807.

but we get better accustomed to it and as for my part my health was never better. Jeffrey's leg is still in a bad way and I do not think I shall be able to keep him. He is now in bed when I want him most. Your health at dinner today.

30 July
This has indeed been a day of bustle and business - we have not only relieved Sir Jos. Rowley but forwarded orders to Athens, Alexandria and Tunis. In the afternoon we all went on shore to the Governors and I had a fine opportunity of rubbing up my Spanish. This goes by Caledonia but I expect the next one will arrive before it as I shall write by the Packet. We are going now to the East Coast of Spain with the Vanguard Rodney and Asia and to keep out of the way of this sad disease at Malta. God Bless you all and believe me ever Dearest Margaret Your affectionate Husband John Loudon.

My friend Austen of the Medea is to go to Gibraltar to meet the Packet and will bring Mrs Fanshawe here - poor Capt is very uneasy about her.

2 August, Princess Charlotte Mahon's Harbour.
It is rather provoking that I shall be obliged to write you again a short letter. Jeffrey is laid up with his leg and though Inch fags like a horse and young Couch gets on exceedingly well yet my time is much taken up with one thing or another when any move is likely. We are now going on Board the Medea to muster and inspect her when she starts immediately for Gibraltar to meet the English Packet and bring our letters, and at the same time he meets the homeward bound one and takes ours to her. We go off to day ourselves for Barcelona and there we shall get your letters. We are all quite healthy and I hope shall keep so as no cholera has made its appearance in this part - but at any rate it is clearly proved not contagious and nothing brings it on sooner than fear and I have none nor do I feel so incommoded by the heat of the weather as at first altho' it is equally warm. By this time Willoughby will be thinking of his return to school and I hope he has profited by Mr Beatson. The busy time is beginning as to him poor fellow and I only hope he will not break down in health in which case I shall be content whether he wins or loses the Exhibition. Poor

My Dearest Margaret...

Errington too I am naturally anxious on that score and long to hear all particulars from Lizzy or yourself, bearing as we must with whatever turns up and trusting in the all even outcome of events for his blessing on the event whatever it may be. How is my dear Fanny and Charlie and Lizzie and dear Mamma herself - poor Lady Stopford feels the heat much but she would not like it to be said perhaps to the Bedfords and indeed she is getting over it partly - certainly very weak - the girls dont mind it. I dance every evening on the quarter deck. I never thought Mahon so good looking a place as we now find it and the Admiral is quite in raptures with its fine harbour wishing his Head Quarters were here in place of Malta. We had a gay party off yesterday - the Governor and staff in great form and the Consuls in the evening to Tea and a dance which they enjoyed much. Now I must hear from you soon -

God send it may be good and with love and kind and affectionate regards around you I am Dearest Margaret Your affectionate Husband John Loudon. I have just succeeded in getting young Maddocks discharged into the Medea Steamer for Gibraltar thence to go home either by the Caledonian or the Packet - the latter certainly the quickest and best. Sir Robert was very kind on the business and Austen[20] is a first rate fellow. He is now starting and I must bid adieu we are off immediately ourselves. I trust all goes on well and that Jack has shown no more pranks, once more God Bless you.

1 Sept, Princess Charlotte off Genoa

My last was to dear Eliza of the 18th and although I wrote you the day before I rather think she might get hers first as it was by the Medea Steamer to Gibraltar and yours was by the Nautilus a sailing vessel. We have been at anchor off Barcelona ever since the 29th when we sailed with the Vanguard and Rapid Brig to join the Rodney off Nice where the Admiral had kindly sent her a week before that Capt Parker might see his wife who is there on a visit to Mrs Duckworth - all our Ladies were delighted with the prospect of meeting at Nice and being a fine cool day the forenoon was occupied in admiring the sublime beauties of the Alps covered at the tops with snow - a refreshing sight to us who had been parched

---

20   Charles Austen, Jane Austen's brother

in the hot oven at Barcelona, and the smaller heights as they descended gradually to the sea covered with dark green woods with villas and villages peeping out between - to those who have seen Torquay though on a small scale this picture will be understood - but alas! How fleeting are the pleasures of this world. We had been long straining our eyes for Villa Franca and Nice, every town as we passed must be it, but no Rodney was seen and at last just as we were going to Dinner we discovered that we had long past it before we got near the land and we could not return because the wind was strong and against us and all the party had long faces - not a word was said but I was pleased with Lady Stopford who said tho' it is a disappointment I am more sorry for poor Mr Elson than any body as I am sure he must be much hurt by it. This was the master who had been up all night and was very anxious but such things will happen.

We had a rough night but the Ladies are now good sailors and do not mind it. They surely are very lucky to have had such a view of Europe, Africa, Spain, France and Italy without expense and trouble and they make the ship very delightful[21]. We are anchored off the town but shall have no close communication as the cholera is not yet quite subdued though very nearly so and in two days we are off on our way to Malta where we have reason to think it has ceased. I shall not finish this till we are going so that you may know we are clear off.

But how many anxieties press upon me as to that dear girl and Willoughby too occupies no small share of my thoughts - but things must just go on and let us hope for the best. You have only to explain your wants in money matters and I know they must be many - to Mr Pridham and he will keep all right for you - so I hear tis all off with Capt Pennell and Miss Curry which I am sorry for. Our weather has been most oppressive but is now agreeable and many of us are wearing blue trousers. The temperature is 75 in place of 80 in my cabin at Barcelona. 10 p.m. We are anchored in the Mole but have no communication with the people though the cholera is almost gone and we are off to morrow morning for

---

21 Clowes (The Royal Navy, Vol.6, p.218) gives several examples of wives and families on board, despite an Admiralty order that no captain or officer should take his wife to sea without special permission. From these letters we gather that Stopford left the ladies in Malta or elsewhere on land when any naval action was threatened.

My Dearest Margaret...

Malta. Who do you think came alongside to see the Admiral but Woodley Losack who has been living here these six months - odd how we meet where we lest expect. Captain Fanshawe and I go on just as usual but he begins to get a little fidgetty about his wife and would be glad if she had been here to see this picturesque country. However she will soon now be on her way. How is dear Charlotte and Fanny. I hope however both are strong in health and the dear Ridgeway girls and them keep old Jack and their 'set out' going. The town and country trips will do them all good. Tell dear Harry I saw a portrait of Napoleon taken in the year 1799 and given by himself to a Spanish General her very image and he was then a fine looking young man - the nose, mouth and chin exact.

2 Sept

Beautiful day. Genoa with all hills, woods and palaces all around us and yet no communication. We shall be off today. Capt Mends[22] tells me he saw Sir George Eyre's death in the Papers. You must call upon Mrs Mends. He is very well and we are always most friendly. Therm in my cabin 70 - at 6 in the morning. God bless you dear, Your affectionate Husband John Loudon.

Shall send this through the Minister's Bag.

6 Sept, Princess Charlotte between Corsica and Italy

I wrote you on the second from Genoa and sent my letter by our Interpreter to Turin with a note to our Embassador there to forward it in his Bag which I hope he did. This interpreter was turned over to us from the Caledonia, a Genoese and of course spoke his own language Italian and French, but no Spanish and the Admiral finding no use for him discharged him in Genoa by which the Government saves £100 a year. He was otherwise a very gentlemanly man and many here were sorry to part with him. We left Genoa on Monday the 4th having been tantalized for four days inside the Mole in a Basin as it were in the centre of the town without going on shore, the ship surrounded with boats and visitors but not touching and nothing to eat or drink from the shore. The ladies were sadly provoked but Lady Stopford as usual put the right construction upon it "for after all what would our

---

22   Later to be Admiral William Bowen Mends.

1837

gratification signify, if only one man should be taken ill and die we should never forgive ourselves" and I liked her for the thought which is so much like Ldy Stopford. The fact is - it is not infectious, but something in the air which will affect those predisposed for any complaint in the stomach and bowels whether they are near others or not. We left Genoa in excellent health and the Wolverine meeting us at the harbours mouth from Malta gave me the delightful treat of my dear Lizzy, Charlotte and Fan's letters which quite set me up - thank ye dearest girls over and over for your precious contributions. We had a very stormy night after we left Genoa, and as my cabin does not well admit of a lot I was several times nearly rolled out of my bed in the night and very few had much sleep. In the morning it moderated and we found ourselves in sight of Leghorn, Elba - poor Bonaparte's island, Corsica and Italy.

Today it rains and being pleasantly cool reminds me of an Autumn day in Plymouth. We are all in Blues[23] and have been since Sunday, but I fear we shall soon return to whites. We are going very slowly on, however and shall not be at Malta for a week. Our last accounts are that the cholera is gone and if such be the case we shall go in, if not we shall be off to Athens. It is impossible things can go on better than they do on board - the Admiral the kindest best hearted man alive and all the family most agreeable. Captain Fanshawe full of fun and playfulness, the officers every thing and the midshipmen a most gentlemanly set and really, I believe, I am the spoilt child of the whole so do not you be calling my swans geese but believe me it is a true Bill all I say. I am much pleased with dear Will's epistle and only hope, though I must not expect, he will gain his £60[24] a year - it is now coming to the scratch and will probably be decided ere you receive this - I shall write him and Errington by this conveyance, I hope for some good. He will I suppose pay you a visit before going back, if so remember me kindly to him. I am so glad the picture pleases and I hope the miniature copy will be equally happy[25]. I think if Miss Crews were to set up in Plymouth for a few months she would make it answer - she is clever and talented in every way and the best Italian I have

---

23 Blue uniforms for Winter, white for Summer.
24 A scholarship Willoughy hoped for.
25 Loudon's portrait painted by Miss Crews

My Dearest Margaret...

met with for a long time and what is still more of an excellent character.

7th, Thursday
Unsettled weather - heavy rain and squalls of wind at times. Admiral wrote a beautiful letter to the Admiralty saying I had proved myself fit to be interpreter, that he had so appointed me and he hoped their Lordships would approve of it - which I know they will not. Still it is very pretty of him. The Duty is not at all hard - make yourselves easy about my sitting too much at my desk. I have four clerks and do very little but form the letters and see that all is right - and you may rely on my taking early steps if I find any thing the matter with my stomach - I never was better than at present.

8th, Friday
Close to the West end of Sicily and to the high Rock called Maritime where the Sicilian Government confine their State prisoners - several other islands around us and the High land of Sicily with its towers, towns and promontories so famous in former times looming high in the haze on the East. The sun is just going down, Lady Stopford is sitting on her chair on the front of the Poop, Sir Robert is standing by her with his spy glass under his arm looking all primitive good nature, the girls are passing backwards and forwards with their young Beaux and all are enraptured with the setting sun and the western sky a beautiful red, tinting the wide expanse of deep blue sea under it with purple. He is set - Good Night! Up starts the moon veiled in a dark cloud which she soon draws aside and my spy glass with many others are pointed at her silver bow while we are lost in admiration of her quiet magnificent march poised as it were in the regions of space more bright from being only half visible with our dark earth covering one half and a black cloud around her. We can almost hear the breaking of the surf at the foot of the rocks, but indeed we were all lost in such a scene of beauties and so went down to tea.

9th, Saturday
We are now off Grigente the celebrated Agrigentum but particularly infamous for the Brazen Bull of Phalaris which may

be a Fable after all. The finest remains of Antiquities in Sicily are here - it once contained 200,000 inhabitants and now appears from the sea a considerable town falling down upon the sea and in former times must have been very strong. I cannot describe my feelings on seeing the Remains of a place so celebrated laying in still and solemn state by almost a deserted shore with the sun's setting rays giving it an unearthly glare little in concert with its mouldering ruins, more like the churchyard of a town that once was, than one inhabited by beings of the present hour.

10th, Sunday
Up at half past 5 according to custom - 16th Chapter of Exodus. Off Malta beautiful morning - running along shore - passing St Paul's Bay - see Rodney and two Line of Battle Ships off the Harbour - the Buildings of Valetta - now telegraphing with the town of the Palace "Hoping the sickness is abated" answer "Sickness finished" and well it may after nearly Five thousand victims since I saw you last - almost all Maltese - very few English - a poor man Mr Sammert a Surgeon in our Navy on coming out in the Ariadne the other day was not aware of the cholera till his arrival in Malta when the first tidings he received were that he had lost two grown up daughters by it. He fell like a stone, as you may suppose, in anticipating the happiness of rushing into their arms. He was paid off in the Jaseur and I was introduced to him at our Reading Room by Captain Cammillieri. We are now off the Port and nothing but saluting in all directions.

12 o'clock
Now we are in the harbour, nothing but firing and saluting we pass a Turkish Frigate with Captain Pasha, or their High Admiral on Board and an Austrian one with the Archduke Frederic the Son of the celebrated Archduke Charles, the Rear Admiral Sir Thomas Briggs, and the Governor General Sir Henry Frederic Bouverie come on Board, and we all dine with the Governor to morrow - quite a day of bustle, Sunday though it be, plenty of work but I get through it. The Admiral and Lady Stopford have seen the house and like it - they say my apartments are very nice but I shall see them tomorrow and judge better. The cholera has quite disappeared here, but I believe some cases occur in the neighbouring island of

My Dearest Margaret...

Gozo. Mr Collings is just come off looking in high health and good spirits, Lou has had a nice note he says from Fanny. He is coming off again at 8 o'clock in the morning when I shall hear more news from him. The only part of our Squadron here at present are the Rodney, Bellerophon and Rapid - we shall have no letters from you till the 19th - a very tiresome time to wait. It is now 10 pm and I am all alone in my snug little cabin and shall be glad of a larger room on shore. I threw off my blues yesterday and find it hot enough. Thermometer 83 where I am sitting but a beautiful night. I am going to take a walk. Goodnight.

12 Sept., Malta Harbour

Yesterday we all dined in great state with the Governor to meet the Archduke Frederic a very fine boy of 16 bringing up to the sea. I sat by his naval instructor a Captain and the Commodore of the Ship both Venetians and with Col Cardew and Sir John Stoddart the Chief Judge on my left felt quite at home. We went from the Barge in carriages and great was the concourse of people looking at us, but what most took my fancy was the cool dress of the 92nd Highland Regiment ranged on each side of our broad stairs with their kilts and naked knees. I thought myself at home - people dont sit here after dinner and away we set at 6 to meet the Ladies at Capt Fanshaws house - the prettiest I have seen in Malta surrounded by a garden and most delightful parterres - and then on Board to tea. Today we have had the Archduke and Staff on board and a vast fuss it makes. We then dined with Sir Thomas Briggs with all the Ladies and a most pleasant party it has been. The Admiral and the Ladies sleep in the House to night and I go in the morning with every thing packed up and Palmer with me, but we shall go to Athens, and be away a month, before we settle for the Winter.

14 Sept., Wednesday

Just come in shore and taken possession of my rooms - a nice large lofty Bedroom, the coolest in the House, having a door from the Lobby and another into my office and a window besides, the doors being partly glass answer for windows, the office has three large windows to the street and still larger than my room so that

1837

I am cool and comfortable. The House has Pillars at the Door - a large Porch - splendid lobby and staircase all stone and marble dividing off in two easy ascents to a beautiful suite of apartments lofty airy and light in every way magnificent. It was a palace of one of the Knights of Malta and gives one a good idea how those fellows knew to live - but we re going to sea again on the 26th to take a round by Athens and perhaps Smyrna and then take over quarters up here for the Winter. The Admiral is yet undecided whether he will take the Ladies or not - they wish to go I think. We are looking out for letters from you every day - only think six weeks since your last but we shall get letters oftener now. I have a nice letter from William Eyre now in Zante and may see him. The cholera has taken its leave here but is still very bad in Sicily.

15 Sept., Thursday

Today we went out in carriages and saw Capt Fanshawe's new house which looks most cheerful and is surrounded with gardens with a fine view of the Country. We then went a cross the water in a fine covered Gondola of Sir Thomas Briggs's to Lady Briggs's Evening Party where all the fashionables of the place were congregated and there I saw dear little Lou, very pretty but delicate. The Archduke Frederic was there and a very good shew of foreigners - the thing ended with Rockets and Blue Lights and we got home at 1 o'clock. Lady Stopford rather poorly this morning - the heat does not agree with her but she does not complain nor like to have it noticed. It is certainly very hot but this is the last warm month and we are off to Athens as soon as the Packet arrives which we expect in a day or two. By the by I see Georgie's marriage in Galignani's Messenger[26] and I see Errington's promotion in the United Service Journal. I suppose too dear Willoughby is with you at this time and have no doubt you are in a bustling way.

18th, Sunday

The Packet will be here soon - Lady Stopford better but very delicate - the poor Admiral was rather complaining last night the worst is we have none of our doctors on shore and he sent for Doctor Sankey - he is now well. Capt Fanshawe and I dined three

---

26 A daily newspaper published in Paris and a reference point for the English-speaking community on the Continent.

My Dearest Margaret...

miles in the country with Mr and Mrs Christian, to whom I had letters from Capt Falcon. We returned at 9 and enjoyed it very much.

19th

Just imagine the nervous state I am in - the Packet is reported from the tower of the Governor's Palace - it is now 10 and she will be here at 12 God send me good accounts. The poor Admiral has exposed himself too much in the day and has been obliged to be bled this morning since which he is much better, He is full and has too good a colour, so that the blood easily mounts to the head. I am not troubled that way and never felt better in my life - excellent appetite and good digestion - you may rely upon it.

20th

Oh such a heat this morning - all the letters came yesterday but none from you. Mrs Fanshawe was kept in quarantine till this morning when all my delightful Budget came on shore and though pressed with a mountain of Public Despatches today I absolutely devoured them - but I shall not be able to write particularly till next Packet as our mail goes at 10 o'clock in the morning and I have work till the last minute. I am always up at 6 and yesterday I was going with 4 clerks all day except my breakfast dinner and tea till 10 not writing but conducting- this occurs from the mail returning so soon upon the arrival of the one from England - now I shall have quiet for a fortnight. I have written Mr Parven and sent my dear Fans letters as an additional amusement to them - As to dear Will I made orders with Mr Predham to answer his calls upon Sir John Lubrik for £200 a year and upon his calling or yours he will tell you it is all right and do it. I have a very satisfactory letter from Errington which I shall answer if I can by this mail - if not I shall by the next. Tell my dear Willy I am exceedingly content with him and not to think of the Exhibition so long as he has laid in a good stock of knowledge. Mr Beatson speaks of him in the higher manner particularly in Mathematics where he says he cannot be touched. I shall write him by next Packet - Mr Prudham will tell him all about his money and perhaps order him a few blank checks which he must be very careful in filling up. Love to you all - dear girls when the nasty Packet is gone I shall have a treat in reperusing your dear dear letters. God Bless you is the prayer of my heart. John Loudon.

18 Oct., Admiralty House, Malta.
We left Salamis Bay on the 11th and took a lingering look at Athens and the Acropolis which seemed to keep us company behind the intervening heights till it consigned to our view the remains of the Temple of Jupiter Olympus about 17 splendid pillars 60 feet high like the broken portal to a magnificent city. The numerous Islands and Mountain Cliffs all as it were passing in review as we sailed along were too much for my powers of description, the next time I see them, perhaps I shall collect my ideas better. Our passage was very fair and we were all eyes as we passed around the south end of the Pirates Country - Capes S'Angelo and Matapan. We had some thunder and lightning and arrived here on Monday morning the 16th. At 2 we moved on shore for the Winter - Lady Stopford and the Ladies of course glad to see us. Malta is now very different to what it was when we were here last - no cholera - and cool - plenty of thunder and lightning and last night torrents of rain and hail. I am just come from the Lazaretto where I have had a most agreeable chat with Mrs Wylie - she is obliged to perform quarantine for ten days so we spoke with a space of 6 feet between us and two huge Railings. She gives a poor account of the Court of Greece which is all intrigue and anti-English. She found herself ill treated by the Courtiers and unsupported by the Queen and found it high time to come away. She asked very kindly after Willoughby and you all - she has met with a severe loss since we saw her by the failure of her Banker. Mrs Fanshawe is looking very well but fears they will be sadly tormented with mosquitos in their new house. I like her better than ever and as for him he is as full of tricks as a monkey.

19th, Thursday
The mail bag is just closing and a pretty tight morning we have had - what keeps the one from England we do not know. It ought to have been here on Tuesday - Lady Duckworth and Annie and Mrs Parker are just arrived by the French Steamer from Marseilles. I have not yet seen them. Only think of our cooling our wine yesterday with congealed hail that fell the night before

My Dearest Margaret...

in a thunderstorm. We have had quick promotions among the midshipmen. The Admiral's son Lord Mark Kerr and Mr Oliver are made Lieutenants - the last in the room of poor Derrick who died on the 4th on Board the Asia. Another poor fellow on Board the Portland blew his brains out. Lt. Newman one of our additional Lieuts in a bad state of health took poison, as did a Surgeon's Assistant on the Confrance - sad accounts of the Squadron. God Bless you - in the hope of good accounts. I am your affectionate husband J. Loudon. Love to all.

29th, Oct., Sunday, Admiralty House, Malta

I take this quiet hour while they are all at Church and I know you are talking to me to sit down and have a cosey chat with you. The Rhadamanthus arrived on the 24th and brought me a glorious packet which quite set me up and delighted me. Poor dear Willie you cannot think how I felt for him, dear fellow - it was as he says hard after all his fag to be defeated, but his letters on the occasion show a degree of good sense and proper feeling towards his competitor that raises him more in my estimation than if he had succeeded. Besides he reaps the solid advantage of all his studies which will be more serviceable to him perhaps through this defeat than if he had carried off the palm and fancied he had nothing else to do - in money matters too I am quite sure he will be more careful when he knows it all comes from his own family than if he had had his £60 a year to play with[27]. I am very much pleased with the waggish girls account of your outfit and the sage counsels you were instilling into him as to his domestic economy with his sage attention to your advice, drinking it up with both ears, but I am sure it will not be thrown away upon every young hero and you will both understand matters better when he comes back. I can easily understand your cares about money matters now it comes upon your shoulders. I used to think it flew yet in looking into our Expenses Book I never could perceive much extravagance.

Mr and Mrs and Annie Duckworth are here and this appears to promise a gay Winter. Jealousies I expect to see however as elsewhere. In fact I believe each has a looking glass for itself and another for her neighbours. Poor Lou Collings is far from strong -

---

27 Willoughby apparently had failed in his application for an Exhibition, worth £60 per year at Cambridge.

the dearest sweetest most interesting creature possible and it wrings ones heart to see her pining and drooping as it were into an early grave. The weather is now delightful and we are all wonderfully set up in health - like a September day in England. We had a fall of hail a fortnight ago which kept for a day or two and we cooled our wine with it. We have always iced wine and nice fresh iced butter for breakfast having two cows. Mrs Fanshawe is quite well but a sad sufferer from the mosquitos - bit over the face and nose and all over - I like her more and more. Young Hornby is quite well, I think growing fast - very quiet and attentive to his duty and really a clever fine promising youth. I do not say this by way of puffing him off to his fond Mamma but it is really the truth. Cholera gone. I suppose Capt Errington is by this time with you, and indeed if the thing is to be done I think the sooner you get it over the sooner we shall all be reconciled to our fate and in the event of its taking place before I hear again you have my leave to put a check for £100 in her hands on the day of the wedding as your own present if you like. Poor dear Girl my heart quite misgives when I think of parting with her but something yet whispers "all's well". She will give her hand to a worthy man who I am sure will cherish and protect the charge of which he must be conscious of the value.

I had a very nice letter from Mrs Andrews about dear Will's good behaviour there, and it was well after all he went to her, where he will always have a warm welcome in the vacations from his College. Jeffrey still goes on very well - and I assure you honor bright I have no fag - for by giving to each clerk his own duty we go on well without any fuss at all excepting on the sailing of a Packet - we expect one on Tuesday the 31st, I shall send one on Thursday the 2nd Nov which will take this. Now though I am delighted to have letters from each of my dear girls and all are most amusing and entertaining to me they must not expect to have letters from me at the same time as I should not be able to diversify my epistles as theirs naturally are having something new or in their own way in each. They must all drink at the same fountain and continue to write me as before which is indeed a most glorious treat to me. Charlotte must keep up her household news Jack and Jones and Hannah and Mary, I think her plants and all other particulars so well and so graphically told - births, marriages and deaths. Dear Fan! As soon as she has recovered her red eyes must tell me all

My Dearest Margaret...

about her equippean expeditions upon Jack which I hope she continues to the amelioration of her health - and dear Liz as maid of all work upon whatever comes uppermost to her - and your own dear natural epistles must not be shortened; indeed you are all very good and I have now all your dispatched before me like the Ducks, coming to Dr.Syntax each saying draw <u>me</u> first. I hear no more of the veranda but strongly suspect Mr Dash was the cause being always a common disturber - at all events I shall have no longer any scruple as to building a Library and Boudoir if we think it would be an improvement. I am sorry for Lizzie's watch and hope it can be mended. I shall write Will by this conveyance and I hope Mr Beatson - I correspond with Capt Mends and often see his son William who is here in the Rodney

5 Nov., Malta

I dispatched my last on the 3rd and should not perhaps have begun again so soon but for Dear Willoughby's Birthday when I know you will all be drinking his health in Durnford Street as I shall be here with Capt and Mrs Fanshawe with whom I dine today. I have now an easy time of it between the Packets - but I must tell you I have sent Jeffrey to the Hospital where he must be invalided and sent home. I cannot depend upon him and am obliged to be hard hearted and resist all his entreaties to try him longer. This will give young Couch a step up by and by, who deserves it, for a steadier youth I never saw, nor one more ready to learn and make himself useful. Jeffrey is the only black sheep amongst them and now he is gone we have plenty to do the work. So here goes health and success to Willoughby.

9 Nov.

Fine times still - nothing but dining out or having company at home. I met Mrs Nugent at a Dinner Party last week and by her playing and singing I found she was a daughter of Sir George Whitmores - you may be sure I was most gratified to meet her. Mr Nugent is treasurer of Malta and a man fond to a degree of music, a great Patron of the Opera.

12 Nov., Sunday.

A little more chat Dear Margaret - I dined with Captain Price of the Portland last Thursday who gave a handsome Dinner to 16 of

1837

his friends at the Club, his ship being in the hands of the Caulkiers. He is soon going to England and will readily take anything I have to send. He is sure to call upon you and I hope you will be as hospitable to him as you can for I shall be sorry to miss him. The Pembroke has just joined and I think we have a very nice man you may tell Captain Woliege in Captain Morisby - he is now going to Athens. The weather is delightful and thermometer 64 - in most houses there are fires - we have them occasionally of an evening when the nights are raw but we shall have nothing like the cold you have in Winter. On Wednesday night a Grand Ball to be get up for Sir Thomas and Lady Briggs[28] who are great favourites here and been very hospitable - it is given entirely by the Officers of the Squadron and at least 5 or 600 people are expected.

15 Nov. Wednesday - 10 pm.

My Dearest Margaret I am just going to the Ball but somehow I dont feel in spirits - "My heart is not there" we shall have 700 people and I shall see the elite of Malta which are never seen on any other occasion for the Maltese and English do not mix and they never entertain themselves though they go wherever they are asked. There is to be a gay Champagne Supper but I shall not stay for it as I have to be up at 6 in the morning to dispatch this Packet. The Ball could not have been given at a more inconvenient time but that was not thought of. Yesterday the Admiral, Flag Lt and I dined at the 92nd Mess and on the 29 the Governor gives a Grand Ball. My relish is gone for such things, still I must make my appearance and I only wish you and the dear girls were here to give me some satisfaction in going. You must really think of it next Winter if we are all spared - the place is cool enough to be agreeable. You have plenty of time to look out for a tenant for 2 years and I will find you a house that will please you here. My plan would be through France with Will.

16 Nov Thursday morning 7 o'clock

The Ball was a brilliant affair - all the world of fashion - at least 500 and not crowded. Rooms lofty and long and large and in suites - moderately decorated with a light valance of wreaths and

---

28 Sir Thomas Briggs was made Rear Admiral and Superintendent of Malta Dockyard in 1832.

My Dearest Margaret...

the Supper Room with Flags - all seemed happy. Mrs Wylly like a Queen - by far the finest woman in the Room. The Admiral came home at 1 - I came at 2 as I did not like to slip off without asking Lady Stopford if I could be of any use. The rest came I think at 4 - adieu Ball. I am dreaming of poor Liz and shall write her, Lotty and Fan, by the next Packet - and the one from England due two days ago has not yet arrived. I suppose Errington is with you and long for particulars - make my kindest regards to him. He shall likewise hear from me. Yesterday I was not out till 10 but soon I shall have little to do and my health is excellent. Young May is well and dines with us on Monday - tell his Mamma, with my regards. God Bless You, your affectionate husband John Loudon.

22 Nov., Malta[29]

The joy I received by your dear letters of the 20 Oct was sadly changed to the deepest sorrow on the unexpected blow coming upon me of dear Barbara's[30] death. Well may we say "in the midst of life we are in death" but in place of all your kind and endearing anxieties looking towards this quarter, how little you must all have been prepared for hearing that the dreadful and mysterious visitation was coming from the North. My Journal tells me on looking to what I was doing at the time - that on Saturday the 21st Oct we were "Mustering and Inspecting the Portland - Capt Price dined with us - Evening pleasant" Sunday 22nd morning before "Breakfast - took a walk by the works and saw Sir Ralph Abercromby's Monument and Sir Alexander Balls, the first killed 21 March 1801 aged 68, the second died at 52, a Rear Admiral" thus I was among the dead of byegone days giving way to useful and mournful contemplation but little thinking that nearly that very hour deprived me of a dear sister, which I ever considered Barbara - poor thing she had well done her duty and had but a dull career, for all which she is no doubt amply rewarded and it must have softened her last sufferings to have had Robert by her bedside. I give dear Fanny great credit for her presence of mind in keeping the sad event from you at a time that it would have been most imprudent to have communicated it, but I think how much the poor girl herself must have felt in the midst of all your mirth

---

29   On self-made mourning paper
30   The wife of John's brother Robert.

and conviviality in the too sad conviction of what she was soon to reveal.

I never saw a nicer letter than Mr Beatsons to Willoughby and I think we may consider him quite safe in such hands, but I long to hear what commencement he has made. The dear girls crack their nuts at you and Will preparing for his campaign and it is a most amusing thing to me to run over their facetious accounts of his outfit and maternal instructions received with due filial gravity on his part - but I only hope he will attend to such good advice and that they may copy it when they have a son going to Cambridge, for in such things is a wife a real helpmate and infinitely more worth than another who may bring Ten Thousand Pound fortune. I only know they like and admire it, indeed they say so, and I admire their waggish account of it which all tells in favour of dear Mamma. I hope he has written you, for it must be an anxious time for you till you hear how he is getting on. They must not always expect me to write to each for this letter you know is for all - and dear girls I wish I could kiss them all round. I have a very nice letter from Errington. We have Mrs Duckworth and Annie here and I am much pleased with both. Mrs Duckworth is the nicest and most agreeable person I have seen for a long time - much of poor Duffs still and quiet mild softness of manner. I had an opportunity of doing a good turn to Mrs Wylly the other day - she permitted her maid to marry one of the Suite at Athens on condition of her accompanying her to France or England, but the man either has or pretends to have broken his leg and wanted her back which would have cost Mrs Wylly at least £10 and money I believe is in greater value with her than formerly, so I got Capt Moresby to give her a passage in the Pembroke. I am happy too, to have given a move for young Couch from the List of Admirals Domestics where he had £22 a year, to be Secretary's Clerk at £60 and 1/6 a day or £27 a year for his Provisions while on shore in the room of Jeffrey, who was yesterday Invalided at the Hospital. I have not had a months work of him since he joined and my friend Allen was the man who advised me to take him. He is no loss in any way.

My Dearest Margaret…

23 Nov Thursday.

Fine cold morning therm. 65 in my room. I take a walk from 8 to 9 upon our Lines which present the picturesque beauty of Land and Water you can fancy. The Island has a hard and stony look in Summer but now all is green and fresh, and on the rising knolls (for we have no Mountains or Rivers) are groups of villages and churches, indeed the whole Island is studded with white Buildings and looks like a Beehive. The population being excessive 125,000 in so small a space - but there is much poverty in the Country and almost every third person you meet, though not a beggar by profession, will yet hold out his or her hand for Carità - they are an odd people for they have no Fathers or Mothers nor anything to eat - nix Padre, nix Madre, nix Mangeire, Carità Signori Carità! - but there is no such misery here as the poor suffer in England from the rigour of the Seasons. Here they are all barefooted and bare legged without any inconvenience. All the world are studying Italian. Mrs Fanshawe has a Master as have our young Ladies, a Roman and Mrs Fanshawe is beginning Maltese - a bastard Arabic just to comprehend a little of what they say around her, though the greater part speak Italian and English. We have the Prince of Capua here and his wife Penelope Smith that was and her sister. An application has been made to the Admiral for a Passage for them in our Steam Packet Hermes to Marseilles as they are poor and he cannot receive his rents, they are therefore going to live upon the rents of her estates in Ireland. They are not acknowledged by their own court of here - but I cannot think it will be always so, she is in the family way. Young Hornby is quite well from toe to toe - his Mamma will know the meaning of this. he is most attentive to his duty and keeps his ground in the good opinion of every body. Willoughby Lake the same happy fellow as ever - in fact she is a very happy ship. I have long letters from Jessip - poor Mrs Jessip has fallen back upon her old bilious complaint and I fear there is something radically wrong in her constitution. Errington does not seem a sighing dying lover and proposes next May which gives latitude enough for all Lizzie's preparations and prolongs the evil day of separation - a great respite to us all. - but I must go and have another treat at my letters - they are a source of perfect enjoyment to me and I go to bed contented every night to sleep and dream upon them. The dear girls write in such a varied style and each

1837

delightful in its way that I cannot describe to you the treat they give me all together and I shall always be woefully disappointed if in addition to your own (of course first prized) letter they do not continue each and all to write me long or short as they can.

I am to take a long walk with Lou Collings and her Papa and dine with them at 6 this evening. We had 20 to Dinner yesterday with the Governor Sir Henry Bouverie, who is, I believe, very nearly related to Mrs May. He is the first man here and very much liked. On Monday we entertain the Duke of Saxe Weimar and his son - near relations to our Queen Dowager. In fact there is no end to these entertainments but they become no more than my common Dinner at home and I never found my health better than under them. I have not dined a day without Soup and Fish since we left England and I find a good appetite for the substantials afterwards. Our dinner hour is generally half past 6 - and by the time Coffee and Tea are over and a short evening in the Drawing Room it is the hour of bedtime half past 10 and I am up and dressed by 7, which is our daylight at present. This morning going on my usual walk I heard the strains of music in a small Chapel which is usually shut up. I went in and found the centre filled with people kneeling, 6 or 7 Priests at the Altar and an Orchestra over the Door with the most beautiful vocal and instrumental music - it is the Feast of St. Catherine - the Chapel is an Octagon with a beautiful cupola painted in fresco, and rows of lighted tapers before every altar of which there were 4 besides the main one with one dazzling mass of light half way up the grand Painting of the tutelar Saint rising over the main Altar. I should have no objection to this show were it not that the people fancy that by going there, saying a Certain number of prayers and counting their beads, they fulfil all their duties. It is certainly very imposing but comes very much towards the ridiculous and I wonder the Priests can meet one another without laughing. On Thursday I dined with Captain Dunn, who is very attentive and anything but mad - Captains Jackson, Corry and Copeland, Mr Blount, young Hayes just made Lieutenant and Mr Kitson our Clergyman made the party. Tell Sir Wm Elliot I saw his table and that it is going home in the Hermes or perhaps the Portland as the Hermes is ordered.

My Dearest Margaret...

26 Nov.

Sunday morning. Yesterday Collings and dear Lou called upon me at 3 we walked out attended Vespers in the grand Church of St John, again the most beautiful music - a fine organ and still finer voices - quite Canterbury Cathedral and this every night at Vespers. We then took a walk through the Public Gardens and the more private Botanic Garden. Collings being an enthusiast in flowers. We had to cross the Harbour to his house where we dined and I passed a most pleasant evening. Mrs Collings is far advanced but seems to be terribly out in her reckoning and is quite a martyr to nervous headaches. I am glad to say Lou is now quite healthy and looking the most beautiful girl in Malta. You are now writing me I know and it is pleasant to think we are conversing together though so far apart. You are by a good fire - I dont want one - never was there a more beautiful climate than this in Winter - fine clear day therm 60. What do you think of my proposal for next Winter if all spared? Dear Will must at all events learn French before he travels and if he gives his mind to it he will soon conquer it. Palmer gives me the most perfect satisfaction - steady and most scrupulously honest and attentive. Mrs Fanshawe improved in every way - health, openness and spirits and he the same kind playful boy as ever, like a monkey - upsetting my papers, putting the end of the sealing wax in the inkstand - so that I know who has been there in my absence. I dine with them on Tuesday - Tomorrow we have Duke Saxe Weimar and 20 people.

28 Nov Tuesday

Dearest Margaret I must now seal up. The Hermes starts - yesterday we had the Duke of Saxe Weimar and his son to Dinner. He was the Dutch Commander who beat the Belgians so much till the French came to their help when we were at Deal - a fat fair moustached man of about 45 who married Queen Adelaide's sister. The Admiral to give him a passage to Sicily. The poor Prince of Capua had his carriages arrested last night in the act of embarking from some claims for deterioration of furniture in his house but all is settled and he is now embarked. He is an excellent man and says he will cheerfully undergo every privation for the woman of his heart who he doats upon. His brother the King has behaved shamefully. The Tolls are certainly a drawback but two ponies cut

1837

such a dash - How is old Jack? and your Household - the household tales amuse me much Charlotte's way - and how is Nancy? I hope going on well - in short every little piece of history is interesting to me. I am particularly anxious about dear Willoughby, who must be exposed particularly to much expense with setting off. God Bless you - The Hermes now goes to Woolwich direct and will not even be able to take the table - ever my dearest Mammy and girls yours affectionately John Loudon. 12 o'clock.

My Dearest Margaret…

1838

Eliza's wedding - a picnic - a drowning - planning Willoughby's tour - visit to Vesuvius and Herculaneum - Coronation Ball - Toulon - Willoughby's letter - meeting with Willoughby - Carthage and Troy - with the Turkish Fleet - Queen Dowager's arrival - Christmas

My Dearest Margaret   *1 Jan., Malta*

A Happy happy Year to my dearest wife and children God bless them with the fullest desire of my heart. Your circle I can easily conceive - dear Will and Errington adding to its conviviality - yet there is something sad in the notice one is obliged to take of the progress of time constantly stealing over our heads and almost imperceptible except upon such occasions. Here all is gaiety among strangers as Malta is a place of strangers altogether. Both Christmas Day and this our people dine altogether, myself the only stranger but made one of the family. Mrs and Dear Annie Duckworth, Captain and Mrs Fanshawe making up our circle. He is the same good humoured playful fellow as ever and she is quite a different person to what she was in Durnford Street, though she says her health is not near so good - her digestion bad and she thinks upon the whole the air does not agree with her. I had the greatest treat in the dear girls budgets of the 25th and 27th Nov which I received on the 30th Dec (Saturday) but there was no letter from "La Madre" and that was a blank though I cannot complain as you had written me on the 25th which I received ten days before. Wm Mends is married - Capt Mends quite disappointed - not a penny between them and he is very angry with Dr Stilon[31] her

---

31   Dr. Stilon a former medical officer in the French army, then the English Navy, had settled in Malta where he had a private medical practice.

My Dearest Margaret...

father. Mr Godfrey and Lt Eyre brought all your budgets carefully. Wm Eyre's Regiment is ordered home from Zante and the 11th from Corfu by the Russell and Bellerophon. The Tribune which takes this may put in to Plymouth - if so pay every attention to Captain Tomkinson who has been very attentive to me as have Sir Wm Dillon and Capt Jackson. In short they are all nice fellows here. I suppose Errington is gone back to his wife the 57th. I agree with him and every body that the station is the best military one going, but it is far and poor Lizzy a bad sailor - the absence is heavy, but all is in good hands and we must now hope the best - he is certainly a very reasonable lover at least and as far as he is concerned he deserves the prize. I long to hear of dear Will who is now with you as this is a most interesting period of his life - Thursday week the 11th will I hope bring me good accounts. God Bless you My Dearest Margaret and believe me ever Your affectionate Husband JL.

4 Jan

I send a small Frail of Smyrna figs as I know you like them and they are good for you.

11 Jan., Malta

We have most delightful weather and are all enjoying it much. My health and appetite keep up and if I only had you out here very little would be wanting to my thorough contentment but I fear that cannot be from the disjointed state of things at present. I am more than commonly anxious to know about Willoughby and how Errington's visit ended. I expect you now having a little quiet and enjoying your Winter evenings as we did last year - mine are generally occupied with our Company at home, as we do not sit down to dinner till near 7 and break up at 10 or half past. I generally take a walk before Breakfast which gives me a famous appetite and at 10 we begin our work being then very busy till 2 or 3 when I visit or take a walk - every body riding but the Admiral and myself. We hear of the disturbance in Lower Canada and suppose it is for that two 74s the Bellerophon and Russell are now going home with two Regiments from Corfu and Zante the 11th and 73 - which I suppose will delight Wm Eyre, whose health in this Country has not been good. I see nothing

1838

like wars or rumours of wars here. I did not fail to drink many happy returns of the day to dear Lotty on friday the 5th - God Bless her dear girl - and the same to my dear Liz on the 5th of next month - Monday. May they both enjoy years of happiness, both giving and receiving blessings wherever their lot may be cast. I dined on Sunday with Collings and dear Louisa, whose health is now much stronger and could she be a few months with you she would be quite stout - I never saw a greater change than in her, and she raves about our dear Fan - but that cannot be as the passage is now so difficult, Lady Stopford is at home tomorrow evening as she is once a fortnight on Friday evenings when we sit down 20 to dinner and about 100 altogether for quadrilles and walzes. There is another Grand Ball at the Palace on the 17th - a sort of Omnium gatherum English and Maltese to the tune of 5 or 600. I hope you have good accounts from Robert - poor Mrs P was afraid to wean her child and feared her consumptive tendency would take her off so says Peter. God bless you all and the dear Davies's. I shall give you a longer letter when I get yours and ever am My Dearest Margaret Your affectionate Husband J Loudon.

21 Jan. Malta

Your dear letters of the 10th so full of tenderness and anxiety almost unmanned me on the perusal of them - and I believe those who saw me thought I had received bad news from my watery eyes and broken voice which I could not control. I assure you I almost blamed myself for being away at such a trying time, but the short experience you have had since I have left the finance in your hands will convince you that it is my duty for the childrens sakes to do the best I can for them and I think still I should have regretted throwing away such an offer as was made to me without my own seeking certainly. I believe I should have been the greatest child of the Party on giving away dear Liz who had so engrafted herself into my heart's core and been a blessing to us all - but I hope it is for her good and that it will all end well.[32] Something may yet turn up to keep them at home, tho after all, for his prospects, abroad is the ground and no doubt he would soon be a Major - he is a fine noble fellow and I am sure will make her happy wherever their lot

---

32 Eldest daughter Eliza married Arnold Charles Errington - later Lt.General Errington.

may be. I trust the ceremony is by this time over as, with it I think, will go half your troubles and anxieties and by degrees we shall all come in to the same way of thinking with others whose daughters marry soldiers. I make myself quite sure of seeing her before she leaved England if she even should in the end do it, which I hope may not be the case. How delightful too are dear Lotty and Fan's letters on the occasion and I look much to them for supporting you and Lizzy through it, for otherwise I am sure she would break down at Church. I want to know how you liked his Brother and all about the family you know.

Yesterday we had a grand Revies and sham fight and I really never saw anything so brilliant as appearance and movements as the 92nd which totally eclipsed the others. It was given in honor of the Admiral and I never saw (except George the 3rd Reviewing the Troops in Hyde Park) anything so noble as my fine venerable Admiral's appearance raising his Hat from his fine snow white head in returning their passing salutes. I cannot say dear Will's letter was so satisfactory as I expected from a young student at Cambridge and could wish he would be a little more particular in even dating his letters. It has always been a besetting sin with Willoughby to be thoughtless in these small points and I am sure it has told much against him as the reverse has told in favour of boys of less merit. I hope he is now with you to keep you alive as I fear you will have much need of his high spirits and cheerful amusing manner.

25th.

The Packet has arrived and all your letters of the 26 Dec with her. How to express myself I know not on such a treat as your dear letters have given me. I am only sorry and sad dearest Margaret at the excess of excitement you are under and regret deeply I am not with you to keep your spirits upon the occasion though your own good sense must dictate to you that she is given to a man in all respects worthy of the treasure we give him and who of all the others the man who will supply our places to her. I am delighted she is to return to you and I fancy in a week or ten days more she will be in her old place the centre of your coterie which will always be her right while she choose to use it. Your next letters will tell me all about it, and the troubles and anxieties being over I trust I shall have from you, dearest, more cheering accounts for this letter

1838

makes me quite melancholy. How pleasing that dear Will was with you - his presence always brings sunshine - I am much pleased with his letter to me - He was of course hurried, but his weak point is heedlessness of the ornamental part of literary correspondence. His thoughts are bold and original and often astonish as well as please me but he seems to go on like Mazeppa's Wild Horse through bog and mire without regard to break or brush but still shewing the high mettled steed regardless of all obstruction. I am confident he has a good stout heart and real genuine abilities. I must say I have a strong idea of his yet becoming a <u>great</u> <u>man</u>. Dear Fan - I understand is your Factotum - and right glad am I to hear so because it must save you a great deal of trouble and is of great use to her in the House Keeping way. What an influx of kind friends you must have had - at such a time it would I hope break in upon your brooding thoughts as to dear Eliza and keep your spirits up on so trying an occasion - What an interesting letter your next will be! but I have yet a fortnight to wait for it which is very tantalizing. I am delighted with Errington's letter - so noble so feeling - so like himself. I am sure they are made for one another. As for myself - the Dinners, Balls etc do not disagree with me because the former are every day things and as I dont dance the latter do not tire me.

God bless you dearest Margaret - say every thing kind for me all round. I live upon you asleep or awake. Seldom I lay long awake you know but of late I have tossed and tossed till 3 o'clock. I know not why. All here are very kind - Lady Stopford drank to you all today and I find from their kind enquiries they are not ignorant of what is going on. We shall talk the Malta matter over when things are a little better arranged - living certainly cheaper but travelling is dear and fatiguing - Ever Dearest Margaret Yr affectionate Husband John Loudon.

19 Feb. Malta

Your delightful Budget of the 11th the day after the marriage almost overpowered me - so glad you must have been to have it all over and a quiet house for a little after your bustle. I only fear that after so much excitement you may have had some of your attacks of headache and I dreaded that part of the business about the time your courage was called up. I am glad however to find that both

My Dearest Margaret...

you and dear Lizzie behaved nobly - not doubting we owe much of that to dear Charlotte and Fanny as well as our kind and dear friends the Davies's, always cheering and encouraging. I was much pleased with your account of Mr J Errington and hope he may take a liking to the West for by all accounts he is a first rate man and seems attached to his brother. You did quite right in presenting the Young couple with the little Purse - and by last Packet I sent Errington the first years allowance of £50 knowing that at first setting it is an expensive concern. I am in hopes however they will both be prudent and with that their small income will do very well. The letters of dear Charlotte and Fanny are perfectly beautiful and I am so proud of them that I let Mrs Fanshawe and little Lou see them and both are quite enraptured with them. Will's ever the most descriptive and characteristic picture of Jack and his dress and appearance I ever read - I fancied I saw him before me and even what he thought and felt - Will had him so to the life with the embroidered hem of his white pocket handkerchief sticking out and so forth - tight fitting trowsers - Willy is a great wag. On Wednesday I hope for more letters after Eliza's return.

We have nothing lately but a round of gaieties - and this whole week continues them - a regatta to day and upwards of 100 people have a Dejeuner with Captain Fanshawe on Board Princess Charlotte - a Regatta tomorrow and a Public breakfast with Capt Parker - Rodney, a Regatta Wednesday, the same Entertainment on board Vanguard with Sir Thomas Fellowes and I am invited to the 77th Mess to meet Sir Thomas Briggs and the American Commodore, but that I have refused as a Champagne Breakfast, Champagne Dinner and a Regatta Ball in the evening is rather too much. In a couple of months more we shall be off to sea. The Admiral or rather Lady Stopford gave a Ball last Wednesday which cost £30 - in England it would have cost £60 and they have Lady S at Home once a week - cost about £7. I send you by this 2 boxes of our best Egg oranges, a Box of fresh Maccheroni and another of Vermicielli from Naples and a small Box of best Mocca Coffee 10lbs - with a jar of Honey. You will of course have to pay Duties - I think them heavy - but they are all useful and if Eliza goes to Chatham she will find Maccheroni of such a superior kind no bad article of House Keeping. Mr and Mrs Bergman a sister of Mr Godfreys of the Dockyard go by this conveyance, the Volcano

1838

Steamer and by them I think of sending a Gold Chain for Lizzy as Papa's Wedding Present and a pair of Earrings by Commission for Lady Elliot - the cost of which is 22 Dollars or £4.11.8 which Sir Wm can pay you and I pay the jeweller here, or in whatever way he arranges, only it will be necessary for me to know. Tell me what you think of them - I shall have another opportunity of writing you soon and I hope your letters will come in time to answer by the Packet. God Bless You dearest Margaret is the prayer of Your Affectionate Husband John Loudon.

I suppose dear Will is back to College. You must not fret about expenses. It is an expensive time - I should like Will to keep a separate account of his.

8 March. Malta

The Wasp has brought me all your valuable Budget and the Bride cake into the bargain which I gave Lady Stopford who kept one half to herself and divided the other into seven sections which she made up and addressed herself according to my directions - Capt and Mrs Fanshawe, Mr and Mrs Duckworth, Lou Collings, Mr and Mrs Cardew, Mr and Mrs Christian. Captain Falcon's nieces, Miss Thornton, Sir Edward's niece and a nice agreeable person. The Wasp had bad weather and the Box unfortunately got wet which did not add to the richness of the cake but they were all much pleased with the compliment and Lady Stopford had it handed round the Table at a large Party with the health of the Bride and bridegroom. She really is very nice and good-hearted. The sad accounts of dear Eliza's wedding trip really wring my heart. I hope it was only the reaction of all her sustained feelings during the trying operations of the day and not any repentance for the step she had taken - at any rate I can fancy what poor Arnold must have felt, and as I see by her letter from Sidmouth she is in better spirits. I hope all is right, it was well she had such a true friend as poor Sarah with her at such a time. Much have I thought my dearest Margaret on all this weighty concern falling on your shoulders, but I weighed matters more perhaps than you thought when I decided on accepting the offer made me by Sir Robert Stopford - I know a most expensive time was impending, what between Lizzy and Willy and I am always unwilling to break in upon what will be their share when you and I shall no more want

My Dearest Margaret...

it, but you must not make yourself uneasy at your late outgoings - I know you must have had almost an open house and it is well we have a good stock of wine for that would have added much to your troubles. I admire Charlotte and Fannys resolutions - I cannot afford to marry them till Will comes from College - indeed one must remain single to take care of Mamma and as Fan is so notable an accountant I think the lot must be hers - What do you say, Fan? - You will be a little fortune to us. Then again there would be the loss of our musical Evenings - I believe we must keep both.

We go on as usual here. Lady Stopford Queen of the place - but the Admiral will not take much money home with him - keeping open house as he does and giving magnificent Entertainments in the evenings - one thing he has no second table to keep - all his expenses are here and we are Ten besides myself and Mrs and Miss Duckworth who live at a Hotel but dine here almost every day. You must know I am a great admirer of Mrs Duckworth - she is the most placid kind hearted pleasing person I have almost ever met with and is beloved by every body as is dear Annie a most thorough favourite of mine. I had a very nice letter from Wm Eyre who is now at Gibraltar on his way to Canada and much disappointed at our not meeting. They have had dreadful weather at Gibraltar and the Bellerophon was all but lost at her anchors - our poor little Tender the kind I was very anxious about but I find she has got into Plymouth safe tho with the loss of her masts. Here we have had nothing but fine weather excepting yesterday and the day before when it rained a few hours and then cleared up with a brilliant sun. In about a months time we shall be thinking of our Summer cruise and as we shall always be making descents upon the various shores of Italy and Greece, perhaps Turkey, I anticipate a pleasing Summer. I have adhered rigidly to my promise not to mount a horse, but I assure you it is much against the grain where every person almost lives on horseback, however, I take a good walk almost every day for an hour before Breakfast and another before Dinner and I find every thing agrees with me. Only a slight cold attacked me lately which a good rattling dose threw off and I was as well in two days as ever. Capt and Mrs Fanshawe are invaluable - when in this cold - he became Mrs Loudon, ordered me the Doctor, shut people out, ordered my servant and myself with all the authority and consequence of my own wife, so much

1838

to the life that I think he must have taken a leaf out of your book. With all this he is most teazing and annoying and whenever he sees me fidgeting about anything and gets a snappish answer he begins rubbing me down the back like a cat or dog saying dear Johnny be good now - be good - till I am obliged to laugh at his monkey tricks - however they annoy me at times.

My dearest Lizzie welcome back to your happy home which will ever be to you lass what may. I trust Arnold is not too sanguine about staying behind but the dye is now cast and we must submit to our fate. God bless you all I look for letters tomorrow. Ever truly and affectionately your poor Husband and Father John Loudon.

16 April. Malta

Again the Packet time approaches and I sit down with pleasure to have a chat. The weather is just the temperature I wish it - neither cold nor hot though I am glad to wear my worsted socks and blues. I had a delightful trip last week with the Admiral's family at a Fete Champetre given by Mrs Parker about 10 miles in the Country at a pretty Place called Boschetta. We were about 20 in all, Capt and Mrs Fanshawe and I went in one carriage - I should say Mrs Duckworth for Mrs Fanshawe was not very well. Imagine a barren looking country hedged in by stone walls and all at once falling upon a deep winding valley of the richest verdure and covered with orange and other trees - laid out with walks and all kinds of picturesque beauty. We sauntered about as we were disposed, picking oranges and strawberries for our dessert and then sat down to a repast in which the demolition of cold Pies, Turkeys, Ham, Gellees, Ices, Champagne and I know not what, all went on at a brisk pace after which we had rural fiddles and a guitar and the Morris Dance performed by some ragged little urchins in really very beautiful style. It reminded me of some very old scenes up the Tamar and St Germans and being the first day I had spent in the Country since I left England I enjoyed it much. Mrs Parker a most excellent little woman and has been most kind in her attentions to me. I am disposed to cultivate the acquaintance of the respectable people in the country, who all speak Italian and had another trip to one of their country homes about 6 miles off - the day fine and a very pleasant Excursion! This family is the Baron Testaferrata but you must not consider titles here at all coming near our English

My Dearest Margaret...

nobility. We had then a Review of the Marines and two of the Miss Stopfords and Annie Duckworth and I walked to and from the Ground abut 3 miles, and enjoyed it much. The Admiral with his fine tall manly figure and grey locks made them a pretty complimentary speech and the Governor and other military men said they went through their manoeuvres exceedingly well and they mustered 450 - many of the ships being away.

On Saturday I dined with Sir John and Lady Stoddart who gave us a Haggis of her own making and a most excellent one - it was only to poor Lady Stoddart's horror the English Cook had not pricked it enough and the poor Haggis burst its coat - perhaps all the better for it is not very sightly for an English eye and it came up in a nice silver tureen. Every body, Ladies and Gentlemen, were helped twice and extolled it to the skies. She is a daughter of Sir Harry Moncrief the Moderator at the General Assembly in my day, a regular Scotch wife, Sir John is the Chief Judge and was a great friend of Sir Walter Scott, upon whose first work he wrote the Critique in the Edinburgh Review. Their daughter or son is married to one of the Whitmores - talking of that I see a most delightful person she is just like all that family, who were much respected at Malta - poor thing she is thin and her health delicate, she has quite the faculty of the family in languages and music - to all these gaieties we have the Opera thrice a week but seldom get there till 10 and it is over at 11. Tomorrow we go to a Play on Board Capt Parker's ship the Rodney and we had an amateur one by our Midshipmen with some of the Military at the Opera House 10 days ago,

22 April. Malta

I am determined to begin on time and not to be so hurried as I was last Packet, when the one from England arrived in the morning which kept us hard at it till the other left us at 3 - I know too you are now employed writing to me and it is pleasant to think we have our thoughts with one another at the same time. You will see a great favourite of mine, Mrs Nugent, a daughter of Sir George Whitmore who all at once took advantage of Captain Dunn's escort to go home in the Packet in which I think she was wise but I never was so astonished as when the Admiral told me. He was looking at the packet from the ramparts before her house and saw

1838

the white handkerchief waving between her and her servants, who were all in tears for she was the kindest Mistress and the very best hearted woman in Malta by every bodies account, but I was much disappointed I did not know of her sudden resolution tho I was so busy that I could only have wished her a hasty goodbye. Two of my widows as I call them are now gone Mrs Wyllie and her - we have yet six or seven widows bewitched which Malta is quite the place for. Lady Hamilton Chichester, Mrs Duckworth poor woman a real one - Mrs Waugh, Copeland, Calvert, Ward, Thorne, Brock occasional Mr Brock away surveying. She is a very nice person and brought him money. He has become very stout - in fact we have very little English Society. Our weather is yet cold but the sun too is strong. How sorry I was to see the death of poor Mr Mitford in the papers - I met him often at the Admirals and thought him and his wife very superior people. He had just got possession of his living - such a tenure is life. We have just heard of our first disaster - the poor little Rapid a 10 Gun Brig is on shore at Cape Bon on the coast of Africa but the people all saved. We have not yet got the particulars but have dispatched the Carysfort to give all the assistance possible towards saving the wreck.

26th Thursday
Still fine weather - dined at Capt Fanshawes who gives excellent dinners and a very pleasant Party - Mrs F always most agreeable and so would he be if he were not always surprising me by a slap on the back or a significant look to keep my head up. On Tuesday forenoon I escorted the Family of the Testaferratas to see the Ship on landing from which at 1 o'clock, I put myself in a Calese[33]. I joined Lady Stopford's picknick at the Inquisitor's Palace a magnificent spot 8 miles in the Country. The road was most picturesque but very abrupt and uphill in some parts - the driver bounds barefooted by the horses side at a hard trot and never tires. I feared I should be too late for the lunch but was soon relieved by seeing the party all wandering and sauntering about in groups in the pleasure grounds almost under my feet as I wound round a fearful terrace road having as abrupt precipice on one side bounding a steep Ravine with a rushing stream running down the centre hid

---
33 One horse chaise

My Dearest Margaret...

at intervals by the trees and thickets among which I should have had a precious topsy turvy if the horse had shied or the carriage wheel touched a stone or gone against the wall of oak which bounded the right side of the road. Before the House it was like a Fair with Carriages and Horses and the mottly groups of Servants and Peasantry - 6 or 8 Boys dancing with great glee the Morris dance to the 3 scraping fiddlers and guitar we had at Boschetta. Lady Stopford was pleased at my coming and I could not promise getting clear of my visitors in time. We then all clambered to the top of the rising ground and right enough it was with fragments of rock, stones and stone walls without mortar so that in getting over them the Ladies gowns made a sad sweep and gap fit to let a Horse and Cart pass. The Admiral was foremost in climbing over and all the Ladies, even Mrs Duckworth, performed miracles in that way, which nothing but the enlivening nature of the thing could have enabled them to do but we were all well repaid when we got to the top and the beautiful open sea burst upon us on the opposite side of the Island, where the land falls abruptly down and I never saw anything so like the back of the Isle of Wight (you may judge of my association) - beautiful Country Houses and Gardens laid out and at a little distance a Romantic rock rising out of the water about four times the size of the Mewstone[34] - then came a very welcome sight to our stomachs a Table spread out in the Palace with Ham and Turkey and cold Pies and all other tempting things which were set to upon with all the freedom of Picnics in general. The younger folks taking their repast in the Garden scented by innumerable flowers - the Geraniums growing wild all round us. I can hardly tell you how we enjoyed it. At 5 we set out on our return and at half past 7 sat down to our Dinner with what appetites we might - no great things in that way. At 10 I went to the Opera (Torquato Tasso[35]) and then I think I made a tolerable day. Last night the Governor gave the Navy a Ball and a very nice one it was tho not so crowded as ours were - I got home at half past 1 - pretty well considering all our Balls here have a Supper.

---

34 Mountain-shaped rock off Plymouth
35 Opera by Donizetti

1838

27th Friday.
I must now change to a more solemn tune - the Honorable Lieut.Kinnaird Commanded the Rapid a most excellent and promising young man from the Corse of Gowry about 27 years of age - always cheerful and constantly at this House when in Port - four days after the wreck he wrote us an account of it and four days after he was a corpse. He went off in a small Boat with two boys to adjust the Buoys which he feared would be washed away by the surf. A heavy sea was running, and one terrible wave struck the Boat and turned over upon them, the two boys were saved by swimming but poor Kinnaird, not being a swimmer though he had often tried to learn and being besides entangled with his coat, sunk to rise no more. His body was washed ashore and a friend two days afterwards stripped naked and on its face, no doubt plundered by the Arabs. It has been brought here with part of the Crew in a Merchant Ship and I am just returned from the funeral.

29th Sunday.
This is your day again and I think I hear you telling them to leave you a good pen as they are going to Church. I am beginning again to look out for my busy time. I have just seen the death of my poor friend John Pridham - which is another proof of the uncertainty of this life. Admiral Haye's death is more in the course of nature though he was looking very well when I saw him last June at Portsmouth - these things cannot fail to sadden us, yet I see no good in brooding over the fickle state of Being the Almighty has been pleased to place us in our own time coming fast enough of itself and a cheerful preparation must be much the best. Many of my friends are leaving this for England - a very nice family Mr and Mrs Christian our first merchant and Banker he is a Brother of Mrs Falcon of London, young Falcon's mother and was the first here to invite me to Dinner with Captain Fanshawe at his Country House. He wants a furnished house in your neighbourhood for the Summer and I told him you would look out for him. Something like Capt Footes would do as it is rather a large family and you and the girls must pay them what attention you can. You will like Mr and Mrs Christian - the last much admired here. Mrs Phillips is Mrs Christian's sister and she and her Husband all going at the same time - very nice people - indeed we have altogether a good society - and very cheerful.

My Dearest Margaret...

3 May
Thus the Summer wears on and we are likely to remain here three weeks longer at least to receive your letters on the 17th. The mail which ought to have arrived yesterday most provokingly is not yet come and I am kept in suspense as to the budget from you. I am interrupted every minute with notes from my friends to post these letters in the Admirals Bag. We are leading the same gay life we have done all Winter - on Sunday I dined with Capt. Moresby and a large Party on Board the Pembroke, yesterday with Sir Thomas Fellowes on Board the Vanguard - today with the Governor and tomorrow we have a grand Party here on Friday - I must now be thinking on Willoughby's trip and give the necessary orders for his supplies. I find he could go on to Florence by land as cheap as coming here by sea and if he had a good travelling companion much cheaper, a Friend of mine Capt Erskine who has himself travelled it is to give me a route. I expect we shall be at Naples to pick him up but next Packet will decide all this - I only long for good accounts - God Bless you my ever dearest Margaret believe me Your affectionate Husband John Loudon.

17 May Malta [To Willoughby Loudon addressed to Corpus Christi, Cambridge]
Dear Willoughby
Altho I have not heard *from* you since the 30th of March I have heard *of* you and am glad you are enjoying yourself as well - in Town, at Chatham, Sheerness and Canterbury and I am far from finding fault with your improving your experience by seeing every thing worth seeing which I am sure you will lay up in store for a future day when you will have only your own merit to depend upon. It is on that account I am willing to depend upon. It is on that account I am willing to encourage your trip to see me and the more I reflect upon it in a pecuniary view to myself and a profitable one for you the more I consider your trip by land from London to Florence as embracing both as preferable to coming direct to Marseilles and Embarking in a Steamer when you lay in a plentiful stock of sea sickness and lay out a plentiful sum of money (Ten Guineas) without profiting by the travel. You may chuse your route - I should prefer the Simplon, Milan, and Lakes Maggiore and Como but you will consult Robert and buy Mrs

1838

Starkes Guide - from Florence you will write to me at Naples and I shall if possible meet you at Rome. At Florence you will of course call upon your cousin Dr James Playfair and if he shows you any hospitality you will of course accept it, if not you can do as others do and no thanks.

I have written my Bankers to furnish you with what are called travelling cheques which you can get money for at any Town you pass through and as you only sign them when you get the money they are safer than carrying a sum with you - they are for £40 and you can take £10 in your Pocket which will carry you on I hope some way with management before you begin upon your cheques. I am so well convinced of your good judgement in travelling that I leave your route whether by Paris or Ostend and the Netherlands, the Rhine etc entirely to yourself, consulting of course your Maps, Robert or any other experienced friend and if you fall in with a congenial friend of good character and talent you may profit by all. Now this My dear Boy is a trial for you and I am sure I shall not repent it. One thing you must first keep a regular account of all the money you receive and all you pay away. I have always done so - and then you must keep as exact Diary of your travels - what you see, all that is worth observing in the Character of the Country and the people, Churches, Museums etc for historical Recollections - and every occasion while fresh in your memory, otherwise you travel to no purpose and your money is only thrown away - but I hope and pray this may not be the case. Two will travel cheaper than one but be careful how you trust a stranger - I remember when I thought myself a capital fellow at ways and means but I think now you beat me. Avoid meanness - that I need not tell you - but the difference between that and liberality is generally not more than 6d. Your vacation should not commence till July I think. You must consider your studies the first thing if you wish to succeed. If you go by land you must consult Errington about going by Geneva and Switzerland - but it has just come to my knowledge that the Bellerophon, a fine 80 Gun ship is coming out to us from Portsmouth and will sail in June - now that would be a famous chance to save my pocket and give you a sight of Portugal, Spain and Gibraltar and then either going home you will have your travels by land or come out again next year when your French and Italian will make you fitter to travel with profit.

My Dearest Margaret...

Mr Thorne the Purser is a particular friend of mine and I shall write Sir Wm Parker one of the Lords of the Admiralty to give his sanction to you having a passage, sending my message to Peter to give you that you may deliver it yourself as I introduce you to him - that is if every thing suits as to time and inclination. You would be an honorary member of the Wardroom or Gunroom Mess, paying a stipulated sum a day and you would much improve your mathematical studies and even add Navigation to them - both theory and practice - but all this I leave to you - only write me as soon as you can and name the day your vacation commences. I fear however the Bellerophon will have sailed and you will therefore have recourse to Errington for your route.

God Bless you dearest Willy. Kind regards to Mr Beatson. If you find Bellerophon sailed you need not call on Sir Wm Parker unless Peter tells you there is another going. I directed my Bankers to answer your demands for £250 but I hear there are some fears about the City of Londonderry Packet - it went on the 10 April last but I have again written to day. Ever Yr affectionate Father John Loudon.

17 June Princess Charlotte going from Naples towards Leghorn

My Dearest Margaret

I will not tell how many years I am old but this is my Birthday. We left Naples yesterday and met the Confrance with our letters - Yours of the 15th were indeed a treat to me. I had previously received your Dispatches by Bellerophon and altogether I am quite made up. It was very natural for you my dear Margaret to grieve for the parting with dear Liz. I know what a comfort she has always been to you but you must consider she is still at your door and what would it have been had she gone to Van Diemans Land? You have yet every comfort about you in dear Charlotte and Fan and blessed you ought to think yourself in such good and affectionate props. Indeed we ought to bless God for such dear children, Willy too promises well - God send he may realize our hopes for his own sake. I am delighted at the idea of his coming in the Talbot and give you great credit for your judgement in so managing it. You may think me vain, Margaret, but I am told right and left the Station never was so happy and comfortable and I believe there is not one who would not be happy to do me a service, as it is my disposition to do good to all.

We are now on our way to Toulon where we mean to honor the Coronation by a Royal Salute and to have the French Admiral and Captains to dine with us - very different from blowing our fingers Winter after Winter in time of War and playing at longshot whenever they put their noses outside. I have been at the depths of Herculaneum - where many Houses have been excavated since I was there 38 years ago - very much resembling Pompeii but buried 42 feet under lava and ashes mixed. The paintings are as vivid as ever on the plaister walls - generally birds and figures and many valuable articles have been found but what strikes me most is the Prison having a Dungeon for criminals and the Iron bars being still on the windows for Debtors. The Stocks very like our own in Country Towns. The same day the 15th I climbed up Vesuvius very much to the wonder and disappointment of the Porters who are always ready with Ropes to assist those they think ought to want them. Pride made me persevere but I had a very severe pull and slipt often knee deep in dust and ashes to look down on the fine bay of Naples below. We were a party of 4 - Lt. Wellesley, a nephew of the Dukes, a very fine young man, a son of Sir Thomas Aclands now travelling for his health, and my dear little boy Guy Campbell, our friend Fred's nephew - a young man of 14. Wellesley's sisters had very thoughtfully made a Basket for us - we paid a poor man a Dollar for bringing it up with us and we eat a jovial Dinner in the great Crater of Mount Vesuvius - burning the boots nearly off our feet, and roasting our eggs in any little crevice as hot as an oven, with a thousand little chimneys sending out volumes of smoke around us. Nothing can look so desolate. In the centre of this yawning cavern is a cone of about 100 feet high like a Glass House which we ascended and were nearly suffocated in - approaching the mouths of two deep openings quite level under us with the walls hanging over all round on fearfully reaching our necks forward and looking down a vivid flame was seen bursting out from one corner like a furnace and a hundred Blacksmiths Bellows blowing with a confused noise like a Steamer and while we were fearfully looking down upon it a horrid rolling noise and flame and smoke burst forth which made the guide himself fear the Mountain was to be naughty. I confess I was startled and the cone

My Dearest Margaret...

coming in to a small point we had not much room to move. The Mouth is oval and presents two great orifices the easternmost I have named and another vomiting out volumes of smoke and very often stones and Lava with which all the waste of the great Crater is filled - black cinders and burnt masses of stone with the Cliffs around of a greenish yellow, like a Spring Greece which Acland who is a Draftsman thinks beautiful. So it was in the setting sun. I tremble yet to think of thoughtless Campbell on the very brink of the Precipice where all was loose cinders and overhanging the deep abyss throwing stones at the place the fire was bellowing from, where had he fallen he would have been swallowed up in an instant. I was obliged to speak very severely to him for his foolhardiness and he was very ready like Wellesley and myself to lay down full length and look over the cliffs to the smoking and most outrageous volcano divided by a thin partition from the other. It is a thing to see once. We came down fast enough and remounted our Donkeys - mine was a dear sure footed Creature coming at its own pace down a horrid path of lumps of lava in the dark and never made a false step. Wellesley mounted a Young Horse like my old pony which threw him 3 times in this rough road and kicked him but providentially he got off with a few scratches. Dr Wellesley his Father is here a Brother of the Dukes and a very nice man. His sister is here Lady Chelsea, the prettiest woman I thought I saw at Court excepting a young Lady I admired very much who they told me was a Princess, the Mother of 10 children but in this country they marry quite children themselves. I have paid all the attention time would allow to Mrs Thorne and her sister. She brought him Ten Thousand Pounds and her sister is talked of to marry the young Marquess Burbari - of an old noble Family but Titles are nothing here in our eye though they're everything in theirs.

18 June, Monday, Waterloo
Fine sea - the islands Ischea and Pinza and Mt Vesuvius almost calm.

20 June off Rome
The wind has been battling these few days and we are now only off Ostra which we see clearly and even the Dome of St Peters from which we are about 28 miles. The weather delightful - what a fine rich Country Italy looks from the sea.

1838

23 June Saturday.
Anchored last night in Piombino By, it being a calm - this morning we get under weigh - and I rose at 5 to admire the beauty of the Country. We are now close to Elba - Buonaparte's Empire - an Island which looks very picturesque but derives its exceptional wealth from its mines of iron. We seem surrounded by beautiful green shores and some rocks rising to a great height in the middle of the sea.

3 July
What a treat my dearest Margaret, Lottie and Fan are your letters of the 26 May which have just been brought me from Malta and how ready they make me to fall down on my knees and thank God for such blessings as you all are to me and that every thing goes well with you. Dear Lizzie's Letter too was such a treat and I had one from Arnold expressive of every thing I could wish - He duly appreciates the treasure he now possesses and I am in hopes they will do exceedingly well - the reception given by his sisters is truly gratifying and it is no small comfort that dear Lizzie's nervous feelings on a first introduction are over. She may be a little sad at first but she will soon be surrounded with as many friends as she wants and I am well aware she will never lose one worth keeping after she is known to them. He says his relations have been liberal in the furniture way - and if you approve of a small Piano you can make her a Present of it and let me know the amount and I will send a Cheque. I wrote you a few days ago and sent my letter on Sunday the 1st. I suppose you would receive it on Saturday the 7th just as we are going to a Grand Ball to be given by the French officers to us in honor of the coronation[36], for which purpose they are now covering in an immense Square. Yesterday the Admiral had a Dinner given him by the French Admiral attended by all the Captains and Commanders and the French Officers in all 36 and a most brilliant thing it was. The Band about 50 played in the Square - and all the Population were on the Promenade looking on. It was curious to hear a French Band play a God Save the King in Toulon where many a widow's tear had flown for our former deeds, but all seemed now friendship and good feeling. It is a poor place to

---

36   Queen Victoria was crowned on June 28 1838

My Dearest Margaret...

get anything at there being no trade, whereas Marseilles about 40 miles off is all bustle and life. I am disappointed at Willoughby's want of thought in not writing either you or me - I hope he is now on his way in the Talbot. I have a letter from Peter of the 9 June - he was looking out for him on his way from Cambridge. I see there were some Boat races about that time which may have taken his attention up - but he must mind his manners as to writing. I am always so delighted with your graphic descriptions of the House and Garden, Jack, Jones, etc, not forgetting dear Mamma and Don Ricardo with their Menials enveloped in the glorious Majesty of Dust. I must say I agree with you at present as to moving and a fine line heartily comes into your proposal as to Paris. We have now been one year Embarked but time counts from Hoisting the Flag - 7th April. Do tell Lizzie to write in darker ink and I could wish Arnold to make his hand less crabbed, though I begin to get over it pretty well. Her acrostics on his inverted Stilts look to me like the Blind leading the Lame. - or rather a parcel of Pothooks and fishhooks mixed. I am glad to observe Errington has got a hoist though Capt Mainwaring becoming Major and I think him a rising man.

7 July Saturday morning

This might be a busy day closing our official despatches and all my Letters - Dinner on Shore, a Ball in the evening and as the Confrance Steamer starts at day light in the morning I must close all today - Oh what a delicious dream I awoke from this morning fancying I was with you and we were so happy. I saw Charlotte too but not Fanny who was coming in as Palmer awoke me at 6 o'clock to say all was ready for my getting up and it is to close this letter - I have written dear Liz thro France which will surprize her and I think I hear the dear Girls extasies on receiving a Letter from Papa in 5 days which I think she will do at Chatham. The Bellerophon now at Athens - and think the Squadron will be much drawn to the Eastward by the intended Rumpus between the Pasha of Egypt and the Sultan, the former being determined upon asserting his independence[37]. - Captain Fanshawe is now sitting in his free friendly and waggish way on my Bed and teazing me as usual so

---

37   This is the first mention of the conflict which keeps the Fleet in the area until May 1841.

that I scarcely know what I am saying. He begs his kindest regards and says you know not how much you are obliged to him or you would take him round the neck and kiss him - again God Bless you dearest Margaret Your affectionate Husband John Loudon.

28 June, Toulon Harbour

I was fully occupied the 3 weeks we were at Naples in seeing all the Lions of which your friend Pompeii was not the least. I was introduced at the Kings Levee, dined with our Embassador Lord Palmerston's brother and we had His Majesty and Court on Board. We left Naples on the 16th and have been 12 days coasting along here. How often I had seen the outside of Toulon Harbour in chase of the French Ships when they ventured out a little, but never thought to be at anchor inside the Battery Buonaparte gained his first laurels at is before. It is a place full of associations. We have been saluting the coronation and the French have kept us company all dressed in flags - a government steamer is now come out playing 'God Save the King' which we return by the Parisienne and the Marche de Marseillies. The harbour covered with Boats. All the Captains dine with us and the French prefect and Authorities tomorrow so you see what a let off we are making. This is really a picturesque country - the Town and Arsenal in our front and every height crowned with a fortification the country gently undulating and ring clothed with cottages, vineyards and trees of all sorts well up the hills which rise to a stupendous height till scathed by the storm they present the bare rock - a grand but desolate contrast to the lush scenery which they shelter. We only remain this Tuesday by which time we expect the Corisanne with our letters from Malta and I hope dear Willoughby if he came out in the Talbot which I hope he was lucky enough to do. I was quite made up by your Despatches up to the 17th May - I enter into all your feelings in losing poor Eliza, but yet you are blessed in two such good substitutes formed in her school and not unworthy to take her place considering too that you are so soon to see her again. Poor girl she must be happy and give happiness wherever she goes. I see by the French papers the Talbot had not sailed on the 18th but was about to do so – if Willy comes by her I must not look for him for a fortnight to come - the worst of our ships is you cannot trust to them - this time is going on. I am in hopes travel

My Dearest Margaret...

will do him good and if he comes out by sea I shall send him home by land - only think 3 days would take me to Paris and 3 more to Plymouth. We have your news up to the 20th but on the 3rd of July are all about ship for another excursion.

29th June

Many happy returns of the day to my dear Fan and that she may never taste greater unhappiness than she has done in old Durnford Street. I hope she will think a very fair Father's wish but dear girl she deserves it with her happy laughing face which can pout a little at times and what face does not - not mine I'm sure - many many thanks to Lotty and her for their most welcome and clever Epistles. Never forget the Household Live Lumber Jack and Jones and the 'Grate Polisher'. I mean to bring home some Neopolitan tiles like the Dutch for the Bath - they are like the Dutch in some measure - very pretty. Kindest regards to Sir Wm and Lady Elliot who are so very kind and to Capt Wollege and Immanney now I suppose is an Admiral. So Sir David Dunn has picked up a woman of fortune I hear. I wonder he condescended to marry a Plebeyan. Toulon is clean and well built but I think its people coarse and plain. The French Admiral and other authorities are coming off to dine with us - 21 to dinner. I long to hear how the nice married couple are getting on in the furnishing way and I want to hear from you before offering Lizzie a present of a small piano which you may make your present if you like it. I will send a cheque for the amount. Poor girl I would set her up. God Bless You Dearest Margaret and my dearest Lotty and Fan and believe me always most tenderly your affectionate Husband and father. John Loudon..

1st July

I do not expect Willoughby as the Talbot only left about a fortnight ago. The Admiral and Captains with his suite dine with the French and on Saturday the officers give their Grand Ball to the English Navy in honor of the Coronation - after which we shall move off and perhaps pay a visit to Mahon. But our motions are as yet unsettled. I believe I shall let this go as it is. Good bye God bless you.

1838

14 July Princess Charlotte, Mahon
 I wrote you on leaving Toulon - or rather the day before - on the 7th - that evening the grand Ball took place. The Admiral and Staff went to the French Commandants at 8 o'clock, met the Ladies and were ushered into a Fairy Scene of Lights-Music-Mirrors and Hangings, English and French Flags mixed - God Save the Queen struck up. Escutcheons all round the Hangings with an English and a French celebrated man out together in each - the English first. The Picture of old Thames and the Seine watering a tree of Union, Peace, Agriculture and Commerce. The immense Saloon was lined with Ladies three deep one row rising over another and the centre filled with Officers and Diplomats covered with Orders and rich uniforms but my Admiral towered above them all the very emblem of calm majestic bearing and so cheerful and winning in his manner that all admired - the Ladies loved him. Two side rooms were filled with refreshments and at one a neat Supper was laid out like magic on a line of small tables along both sides of the Room and across - holding 8 each and abundance of room for attendance. I cannot say much for the beauty of the Toulonese Ladies - among about 200 I think there might be ten rather pretty and twenty very well - the mass were rather plain and certainly I never saw less grace and worse dancing - but all were affable and good natured and as another instance of French Politeness it was given to understand that the Ladies were to refuse every Frenchman till the English had all Partners who wished. The prettiest woman in the Room I heard tell a French Officer who asked her that she had danced all night with the English, but if she was not asked when a Dance was called she would give him the chance with which he appeared very well satisfied. We came away at half past 2 but it was kept up till 5. There might be about a thousand - 1400 Tickets were given - the Expense must have been serious for they kept plying our people with all sorts of Refreshments, Ices, Jellies, Creams, Confectionary and Champagne, of which I am told 60 Dozen was drank. It was a subscription Ball among the French Officers to ours and their attentions to all and each were beyond all possibility of expression.
 Next morning we sailed - a fine breeze and a beautiful display our Squadron made - the Princess Charlotte firing a farewell salute and a great many Boats in the Bay seeing us out. A fine refreshing breeze brought us here on Monday evening. Mahon is

My Dearest Margaret...

a favourite place with us all but we cannot stay long at one place and this morning we are now all underweigh leaving it. I am now (10 o'clock) in the open sea on our way to Palermo where we may remain two or three days at most and then away for Malta where I hope to meet Willoughby.

20 July
Just arrived at Malta - no Talbot but your dear Letter and Lottys give me the most satisfactory Accounts - and we hear from Captain Mends that Talbot is calling at Mahon on her way here so I expect to see Will before I send off this. It is very hot and I must say I should dread your feeling what I do while I write this.

25 July Wednesday
No Will yet but we hear satisfactory accounts of him. The Talbot was at Barcelona where the Castor left it and had to call at Mahon - so that Willoughby will have seen a great deal on his cruise out. You could not have done better my dear Margaret and I rejoice you did not receive my letter sooner so as to alter his trip which would have been so much more expensive without profit from his imperfect knowledge of French. I only hope he will be here before Saturday when we start for Tunis - if not I should not wonder if he go up to Smyrna in the Talbot and join us at Athens where I think we shall go after Tunis. I have had a most busy time since our arrival here but the Packets will all be despatched tomorrow and Friday and then I shall have I hope a little quiet. The nights are terrible here at present and my perspirations are beyond conception still I eat and drink well and keep up the system though thin as usual. Your letters of the 11th June are a great treat to me dear Charlottes and Fannys full of rare good things never failing to make me laugh heartily.

26 July
No Will yet and I must send this away. I have received Harrises account - a precious morceau but I must say nothing about that at present. It has been necessarily a most expensive time for you and we cannot help it - I see £154 of it is for Will but I would get his explanation about all that - I wish I saw him poor fellow. We are off for Tunis on Saturday but you will hear from me by the next

Packet. I shall be much more quiet to morrow but still I have a mail to make up for Egypt and on Saturday another for Naples. To day I pack off one to England, one to Gibraltar, one to Corfu and one to Athens and the weather is very hot. Tonight at 8 I dine with the Rt Honorable Mr Frere who was our Minister at Madrid and the innocent cause of Sir John Moore's disaster. Now the advantage of weather is greatly on your side. Lou Collings is quite well. The Small Pox has been much about and in some cases fatal even after vaccination. Mrs Waugh has had them but I believe they have left no marks. I have written Errington and long much to hear from them - Charlottes account of their Housekeeping and the Dog and Bone - to the life - I hope she will be soon able to give a better account of all their goings on as I am very glad she is to pay them a visit and hope she is already there. The Ladies Stopford and Mrs Duckworth are still at Naples a very expensive concern I believe - Mrs Fanshawe here - as well as usual - the place she resides at has a nice current of air - and she is less troubled with mosquitos - we have none - on board. I feel a load off my back as I write this while my clerks are closing in the Mail. God Bless you dearest Margaret thank ye Charlie & Fan for your nice notes so full of amusement but dear mammas always first - How I long to peep in upon you though from your dear Letters I all but see you - Again Heaven bless you - Your ever affectionate Husband & Father John Loudon. My dear Mrs Duckworth had a fall from her Donkey but she is better again.

16 July, Talbot, Gibraltar
Letter from Willoughby in Gibraltar to his mother.

My Dear Mamma

I suppose you will have been looking out for a letter from me, but I thought I would get a little more on my journey after the numerous visits to the sound, we got off at last I dare say to your great surprise. The weather was extremely fine the first day I therefore suffered very little, but not so the next day, the sea began to stir a little and so did my stomach. I kept continually going to the gangway. The following day though rough was better - we had now entered the Bay of Biscay and the following day from blowing hard all day it came quite a gale in the Evening and though rather an awful night, it was a very splendid one, the Talbot with only

My Dearest Margaret...

her gib flying going down, as it were, into a bottomless abyss & then rising in proud magnificence to the top again. I was not at all sick and in fact enjoyed it. The next day was fine & a fair wind & we rattled on then but soon to our annoyance it changed again & we speeded but very slowly. In fact I thought we never should get over the bay. At last we got a view of Gallian the extreme point of Spain. The next day we weathered Cape Fisterra & with a fair wind passed inside the Berling to the Tagus & anchored opposite the Town. A new object now came to my view Lisbon stretching out in every direction with palm, orange & lemon trees in every direction. I found it excessively hot - thermometer at 93 in the shade. I was delighted with the appearance of the houses - five or six houses with windows down to the ground and balconies to each. The streets are dirty with very little pavements. I went to the Opera in the Evening much delighted with the house which was only inferior to London though not well lit. It is kept up a great deal by government the orchestra is very strong and fine, the stage is larger than at London & the scenery & drapes are exceedingly good. The Opera was Parasina[38] exceedingly pretty, many of the singers would have done great honour to the Opera in Town. After it was over Acland & I went off in a hasty sixteen miles off on horseback & went full gallop all the way. I never experienced such hard riding in my life. The road is paved all the way in a terrible manner & it is astonishing.. the horses go down the steepest hills. We arrived there at two o'clock & had rest then we met some more of our ships mates & they all went off to Mafra except Creech & myself who went to bed & next morning went to the Rock Convent two thousand feet above the level of the sea, the highest & was the strictest convent in the world, much delighted with it - the Gothic Cloisters were exceedingly fine & the altar of cut marble perfectly beautiful, several peasants with clean white stockings & a white handkerchief over their heads. After that we went to the cork convent through the most beautiful scenery, this convent is scooped out of the rock and lined with cork, the cells are just large enough to admit the body of a man and to allow him to lay down his body when in. Outside are stone table & seats & shady trees where the monks sat and took their

---

38 Opera by Donizetti,

1838

evening draught & a little further on in Heonanica's Cave formed by three rocks tumbling down and falling so as to leave a little irregular opening in the middle, this half man is said to have lived there sixteen years, on our way up were wooden crosses, we went through orange and lemons groves with waterfalls and fountains in every direction. If we looked down we saw the curling smoke from the peasants cottages and looking out different fruit trees and flowers of every description. On the top were the remains of the Moorish fortifications which seemed to frown with splendour & a little distance the pretty little town of Chalaris to which we were going added a beautiful object to the view of Mafra the largest palace in the world.. as we approached down to Chalaris, now and then we met a peasant on a donkey - she though not pretty had always a smile on her face. Before coming into the town we went into a pretty little shop and had a bottle of chalant wine & it was exceedingly welcome & good. Our guide who was a dark picturesque looking fellow with a red cap, no jacket, a waistcoat, but blue trousers with a red handkerchief to keep them up, led us on to more beautiful scenery and brought us to the home of an Englishman of the name of Beckford, most beautifully situated, we then went thence to our hotel which is very prettily situated affording a view of thirty miles around. The garden below very much resembled Thankling so you may imagine how splendid the views must have been from the Piena convent - we could see a fifty miles around Lisbon and the Tagus.

The next day we went to see the Queen at High Mass (this is generally at Curia during the Summer). It was a St day called San Pedro all the peasants far and near came to a kind of fair dressed in their best clothes & on donkies generally with a gold chain, as is a custom with them always to buy a chain directly they have any money & they pride themselves on it. Some were lucky enough to see the King & Queen, the latter, being in the family way, looked particularly fat, the former was dressed and looked quite like a dashing Englishman. It was crowded with the peasants who looked very picturesque. We went off to Lisbon & saw the aqueduct which was very magnificent & went to the Opera in the Evening and we sailed that night. I left Lisbon with a great deal of regret, it is a dirty town but I was so delighted with it that I cannot help thinking well of it. The third day we arrived at Cadiz.

My Dearest Margaret...

I went on shore with Creyke as soon as possible & on our way as soon as possible to the English hotel and found that all the inhabitants were at a Bull Fight - we tried to get in but found it so full that it was impossible. Cadiz is a well built and beautiful town, clean and in every way delightful. I went to see the Cathedral which has been a hundred years building & is not finished yet it is exceedingly fine built entirely of marble. The architecture is extremely good. It is in the shape of St Pauls but not as large. I went afterwards to the Armieda which was full of the people, the Ladies are exceedingly pretty & the mantilla which they wear is of the richest work possible. The next day saw G. Lovel of the Tylla who took us all over the town which is built at angles, the streets are narrow and high being built so owing to the heat of the sun. I bought some gloves which are excellent, the chocolates also here are very agreeable to the palate. I left the place with great regret. We sailed that day & arrived at Gibraltar the next day went on shore & proceeded with Creyke to the barracks to see Surtees of the 52nd & brothers of a friend of mine at College. The rock is very wonderful and capable of withstanding any force. The excavations in the rocks are extraordinary. It seems as if it were impossible to be taken. The town is not large but straggling. It is filled with Jews and Moors who are exceedingly picturesque, they are very fine dark men with large beards they wear a turban over their head, high trousers which come down to their knees and show a fine calf, morocco slippers with the heel turned down cover their feet. Over their body they wear a loose kind of jerkin which is variable in colour.

The next day I rode off to St Rock a town about five miles from the rock and I went over the streets which from this side went up quite spectacularly. St Rock is pretty, situated in high ground with very few persons on the street except a few little ragged spaniards, the spaniard peasant dress is exceedingly picturesque, they wore blue breeches with worked leather gaiters kept up by the red handkerchief, some wore light jackets & others not. Donkeys are in great use, they are rather larger than ours. I dine that day with the 52nd and the next day we sailed, 22 of August, when we arrived here I found that my letter which I had left unfinished in order that you might know I was quite well & to be sent immediately, I found it had not gone. I am sorry I can not finish it but you will

1838

see my journal hereafter, it does not much signify. After leaving Gibraltar we sailed to Almeria and thence to Barcelona & from there again to Minorca & then going round the beautiful island of Sicily, came through the straits of Messina here I found Papa in the midst of work but looking very well. We sailed the day after to Tunis. I enjoyed wandering over the ruins of old Carthage - was much delighted with the appearance of a Turkish town - to the Bay and took a three days journey into the interior with Acland. I would give you a description of it but from the great exertion it caused a swelling & though otherwise quite well I am obliged to lay in a horizontal position till it goes down, which it does then very rapidly. I have written all my remarks in my journal so you will see everything when I come home. Ever your affectionate son Willoughby. Affectionate love to your only inmate Fan and the others when you write.

4 Aug Princess Charlotte Tunis Bay
My Dearest Margaret

The Packet had just gone when in popped the Talbot with Willoughby on Board as large as life and in prime state and condition. He had been most fortunate in seeing Lisbon Cadiz and Gibraltar and its environs in Spain, Barcelona, Mahon, Palermo, the Straits of Messina and Mount Etna - and I was glad to find he kept a Journal and made very good remarks. We had only a day to ramble over Malta when we sailed for this place where we arrived on the 1st and are now lying about 3 miles off the celebrated Carthage - what a thing for him - On Thursday my good friend Capt Moresby of the Pembroke sent a boat for him at 6 in the morning to go and breakfast and then took him on shore with himself and Mr Acland a fine young man travelling for his health - a son of Sir Thomas Acland to the Town of Tunis about 12 miles from the ship and I leave him to give an account of his proceedings.

The Admiral, Capt Fanshawe, the two sons and myself went on shore at 2 and landing at what is called the Goletta or Neck - being the Sea Port. We found carriages waiting for us which took us 8 miles over a dusty plain part of which was Carthage and by the side of a large Salt Lake to the Consul's Country House where we had the most hospitable reception, every accommodation and a splendid dinner prepared for us. The Consul made us up five beds

65

My Dearest Margaret...

and next morning we rode into the town where I saw Willoughby full of enthusiasm and already well informed of everything from the acquaintances he had made and particularly a Missionary where they drank tea the first day and dined the next. Today we all went in carriages to the Beys Country Palace where Will was introduced with a number of the Officers and all the Captains - nothing makes so much the Old Testament times - but he will enlarge on this as he is well calculated to do. We then adjourned to General Consadines to a splendid Dejeuner a la fourchette in a most beautiful house lent him by the Bey and from this we came off - glad am I to be on Board for the dust and mosquitoes are not endurable on shore. The day we left Malta, the 29th, was an eventful one and I did not fail to drink the health of those far away - with the pleasing reflection that I had Will with me and that the rest come all well. Willoughby is in great feather having made another friend of Capt Fisher of the Asia who takes him on Board the French Ships this forenoon so that I fear he will not be in time for the Pacquet. He is pulling up French and Art and Acland is to teach him Sketching. This trip will be of the greatest advantage to him. I received your cheering letters by Volcano of the 12th - I am glad Lotty is gone to Liz tho a hard pull upon us at this time - we must settle down by and by. This is said to be a most healthy place but it is warm at present and dusty - and a ditch with a most horrible stench almost surrounds the town which they say is salubrious. I am going after Church to look at the now desolate Carthage of which there are only a few broken columns and some mosaic pavements remaining but the very ground it stood upon is linked with many sad recollections - To day we dine with the French Admiral Lalande and on Tuesday he dines with us. Willoughby is still on his excursions with friends with a moderate share of perseverance on his part to make the most of them. You would have laughed to see the firm step with which he strutted up when it was his turn to be introduced to the Bey on his Divan in the midst of two rows of Mahomedan Scribes and a host of Moors standing round and staring with all the eyes in their head - his journal will be curious. But I must conclude - God Bless You - Ever your affectionate Husband J. Loudon.

1838

To daughter Fan
Dearest Fan.   *Monday 6 August*
   It would be very ungracious in me not to give you a line now you are a good girl and alone with dear Mamma in return to your nice little contributions to my happiness here which mainly consists in your dear accounts from home. Will is in his glory and learnt a great deal in the Talbot. He is now ranging about with the Captains in the Squadron and sees everything - already well versed in the different Castes of Mahomedans, Jews and bad Christians but you will have his own account next Pacquet. I am obliged to conclude as I am full of business and lost 3 days on shore. Willy and I are going to explore the Ruins of old Carthage, the Hill over the Ships lying where many a Romans Galley lay threatening the destruction which has long since overtaken her. God Bless you Dearest Fan. Your Aff. Pa J. Loudon

My Dearest Margaret   *11 August, Princess Charlotte Tunis Bay*
   When I wrote you a few days ago Willoughby was on an exercise up the Country with Mr Acland and one or two more from whence he returned on the 9th much gratified as well he might be with his trip. He was 3 days away or rather four but the first they were exploring old Carthage and I shall leave him to give you his own account. I have been twice among the Tombs of that once celebrated City and am quite astonished at its stupendous Ruins even at this day - for Miles and Miles a chain of Hills present images of Ruined Fortresses, Amphitheatres and areas that both surprize and puzzle the beholder. The whole ground is perforated so that one is apt to fall down through Holes covered with weeds and grass. It is a melancholy thing to walk through a Churchyard but a buried Churchyard and a Dead City, one containing 700,000 Inhabitants rivalling Rome itself - so rich and so powerful is beyond description, solemn and impressive. Many fine specimens of Art having been taken away it has lost some of its attractions but still enough remains to make Carthage an object of great interest to a mind of the least reflection and a spark of an imagination.

                                                       13 Aug
   We sailed yesterday and are on our way to Tripoli whence we return to Malta for our Letters by next Packet on the 21st. I have

My Dearest Margaret...

one from Sir Wm Burnett of the 17th who saw Charlotte in Town. Will has been rather poorly from the heat and fatigue but is getting round again, he is of rather a feverish or inflammatory habit and would not do to go to Timbuctoo. We are showing him the lions in great style and this is a chance he is not likely to have again for there is every probability of his visiting Asia and Greece and then returning by Italy and France in time for his term at Cambridge.

17 Aug. Off Tripoli
We have just seen the sandy coast of Tripoli with the Town and extensive Forts - we see vast woods of the Palm Tree growing out of the sand and that is enough for us turning tail for Malta, leaving the Barham at anchor to bring us the Consul's Letters. Willoughby is again quite well and making the best of his time.

20 Aug. Monday
We are again at anchor in Malta but we are in quarantine coming from Tunis which is very unfortunate for poor Will. Our future motions must be guided by our news from the Admiralty. The Minden is now joining us but I expect no more news by her. Mrs Sharpe arrived by the Packet. I should indeed have been disappointed if Charlotte had come out without you altogether as I have no establishment of my own and it would have looked odd in the eyes of our little busy world here. I trust however the change of air of London and Chatham will do her good, as I am beginning to be very uneasy about her delicate state of health which seems to continue. I shall be very anxious to hear about this and shall write her and Lizzie by this Paquet. The heat does not suit Willoughby who seems to partake a little of mamma in that respect and I almost fear to let him loose in Greece at this season. You cannot fancy how pleased Lady Stopford and Mrs Fanshawe were with their Bags but indeed I shall inclose Lady Stopford's Note. I wish Fan or Charlotte would make a nice little Bag for Mrs Duckworth with the sober colours I sent Lady Stopford - she is a prime favourite of mine - all the cleverness of the Fanshawes with great softness and mildness of character.

23 Aug
What a glorious budget My Dear Meg - all your letters up to the 5th of this month and all good and satisfactory as well as from

1838

Arney and dear Eliza - How precious! Will is laid up a little with a slight glandular swelling on the thigh from a strain but it is nearly gone and he is otherwise in excellent health and spirits. We shall take him with us to visit the Plains of Troy where we are now going and I shall send him back through Greece in time for his Term. He will have seen a great deal and keeps a regular Journal.

30 Aug Princess Charlotte Malta
We are now (4 o'clock in the morning) getting under weigh for the neighbourhood of Smyrna to have a month or six weeks cruise - but as we unfortunately do not touch Athens, or indeed go on shore at any other place to keep clear of quarantine when we come back and Willoughby was most anxious to see Athens and our friend Captain Mends was going there and offered him a passage it was too tempting to refuse and he sailed yesterday morning. Captain Mends has given him the side apartment of his after cabin with the water closet and every other convenience - the Chaplain Mr Payne is an excellent man to have as a mentor. The surgeon is a clever worthy man for Willoughby is delicate and the heat at Tunis was against him and altogether they are all very fine young men. Captain Mends has two sons on Board and has been most kind in promising to give him good advice and treat him as his own son - Willoughby is rather costive[39] and I impart it to his having left of segars[40] which are not encouraged on Board ship, and to which I fear he had accustomed himself. He is very sensitive and rather impatient of advice but he has many fine points about him and I hope and trust will turn out well. My only fear is for his health for I can see he is not strong nor do I think a warm climate good for him but he is going into a colder and will have good sea air. My plans are that he should take 10 days to see Athens and its vicinity - then cross from Corinth to Patmoss and Zante where he will meet the Malta Packet the Commander of which has promised to give him a lift here where we shall meet and about the middle of October I hope to send him by the Marseilles Packet so that he may arrive in Cambridge in time to save term 11 Nov. The Rhadamanthus went before to the Mouth of the Dardanelles and Mr Acland went in her to cross the Country to Constantinople. Willoughby wished to

---
39 Constipated
40 Cigars

My Dearest Margaret...

go but this sympathetic swelling which is common here not being quite down I would not let him go. Everybody here is most kind about him and if he arrives before me he will not want a home. I am still anxious about poor dear Charlotte and long to hear she is again strong. Mrs Blount and a little sister now Mrs Clavell are come out in the Hermes & were rejoiced to see me. The Stopfords return early in October and then we shall begin to sail. I trust all goes well with dear Eliza and that she had got the piano. As for dear Fran she is worth her weight in gold. I can fancy her watching dear Mamma like a cat and hope Mamma is an obedient mouse. We have had nothing but feasting this last week - Turtle soup and Iced Champagne every day and I am glad we are going to sea. If I can I will steal a march to Athens of all events I shall hear by the Belleraphon which ship Talavera relieves. Give my love to dear George and the dear girls. Remember me kindly to Mrs and Miss Christian as well as to Mr Christian. Best regards to Sir Wm and Lady Elliot and hoping to send you satisfactory accounts of our young traveller, I am, Dearest Margaret, Your Ever Affectionate Husband John Loudon.

7 Sept Princess Charlotte

Here I am My Dearest Margaret looking over the Plains of Troy close off Tenedos on the West and seeing Mount Ida losing its far famed Head among the clouds over a range of Hills in the East. But most provokingly we cannot go on shore as we should have in that case to perform quarantine for 20 days on our return to Malta. We left it on the 30th and having a fair wind through the islands anchored here on the 5th so we got to the Mouth of the Dardanelles in 6 days - As we passed Athens we saw the Talavera going in - And at 5 oclock before I knew it on Sunday the 2nd the Admiral had ordered the signal to be hoisted 'How is Passenger' but they were too far in and could not make it out - it was very kind of him. Willy would be there that afternoon & I hope is able to see its interesting remains. He said it was his principal object in coming out and I know he would have been very impatient here.

10 Sept. Voulca Bay near Smyrna

We are just anchored here and are now all together - we are to cruise with the Turkish Squadron by way of keeping them separate

1838

from the Egyptians it being our interest to prevent their going to loggerheads & I think there is no fear. This is the most picturesque place I have seen yet - we are surrounded by Islands and the Hills peer o'er hills till they lose themselves in the clouds - well cultivated and several villages on the declination of the Mountains.

12 Sept
I fear Willoughby will miss his Term at Cambridge as he must perform a fortnight quarantine on his return to Malta. He is only two days sail from us & yet I cannot get at him on account of this provoking quarantine - the plague of the Meditn. This goes upon short notice I shall soon have a more satisfactory letter for you but half a loaf is better than no Bread. Will has swellings of the glands - very common in this country - his was small and getting well but they are in general tedious. The weather delightful - I hope to be in Malta by the middle of next month. My affectionate Love to dear Fanny and the children of the East. Ever Dearest Margaret Your Affectionate Husbd John Loudon.

15 Sept Princess Charlotte off Smyrna
In all my wanderings I feel a kind of Home in sitting down to write you. I went to Smyrna the day before yesterday with Sir Thomas Fellowes of the Vanguard - Breakfasted with him on board & set off in his Barge 19 miles at 9 o'clock & arrived at 2 - the town being on the side of a Hill falling down to the waterside presented a beautiful appearance with abundance of shipping in the Harbour & a Romantic castle at the top but the moment you get in it, you find it tries to conceal itself in narrow winding streets forming a labyrinth we could not get out of. We arrived at 2 & Englishmen like ordered dinner at 6 before we went round to see the place. The Bazaars on 'Radfords Street' were endless but we wished rather to look round us than to buy & I believe we left many rather disappointed. I found great discomfort in the place & was kept awake the first part of the night by the Dogs & in the morning before Daylight by jingling Bells on the Camels - this being a busy time with them carrying the Grapes from the country & lines of them following one another along the narrow streets - so that there was no passing them but by stooping under their loads which are hanging suspended from each side - they are the most

My Dearest Margaret...

patient tractable creatures possible but very provoking to one in a hurry.

We got up at 6 and I was pleased with many handsome places of worship. There is a Jesuits College School of 150 boys, Two handsome Roman Catholic Churches - a Greek and Armenian Church all in beautiful Squares - a Mosque - & I enjoyed to see the Turks washing their feet legs and hands at a Fountain for their ablutions before entering the Mosque to say their prayers. Smyrna has many things worth seeing but time is necessary as a stranger sees only miserable narrow winding filthy streets & is jostled or splashed every moment from the main in the middle by man and beast slipping into it when walking along. Our beds were very well but the Man had no idea of soap Towel & a certain article till I told him if he expected English he must have them all. I got on very well - yesterday I was asked to take my passage back & dine in the Talbot about to sail two hours after our Boat but I preferred sticking by Sir Thomas Fellowes tho' in an open boat and as the wind was at first battling & I was scorched by the sun & then we got aground & then got into squalls & a heavy sea which required a good look out for 6 hours I regretted I had not accepted the Talbots kind offer but I found myself right after all when I heard one of the squalls we were in, in an open boat, had taken the Talbot & carried away her two topmasts & jib boom & then congratulated myself I was safe on board. The Talbot is now all to rights & we are enjoying the refreshing breeze at Sea just joining the Turkish Squadron. How delighted I am with dear Fan's care of you & I am much pleased with her very nice Epistles which give me a very picture of you all. I fancy I see all she writes. I have likewise an excellent Letter from Lottie & am in hopes she will improve under Lizzie's good guiding for she is quite a rake herself & would certainly commit suicide if left to her own overflowing spirits. She went down very seedy as tis called that is jaded with too much excitement & fatigue but was under their care recovering fast. I do not know what to say to this jaunting about in Colchester but of course I shall be satisfied with what you have done & as poor Aunty is away Charlotte has no help for it & I suppose will accompany them.

1838

16th Sept Sunday
I can now fancy we are speaking to one another as I know Sunday forenoon is your writing day & I am staying from our Church to write you. Our air is delightful & my health never was better - the Turkish ships are now in sight lying between Scio[41] & the Main at a place called Tzisnie or Chisme which Fanny will shew you on the map & it is a fine sight to see our noble ships standing for them in a beautiful line 7 of the finest men of war in England with the Barham Talbot Wolverine & Rhadamanthus Steamer - the Capt Pasha who commands is the same as our Lord High Admiral & the second man in the Empire. We have just saluted him with 19 guns - 1 oclock we are just anchored close into the prettiest spot you can fancy - the Town of Scio - pretty looking Houses among Groves of Trees in the bosom of a Steep Mountain with fine rock scenery all long the sea shore but alas! coming to look closer all this fair outside is a Charnel House within - the roofs are all off - the walls partly burnt & partly down.

9 Oct Princess Charlotte, Smyrna, Voucla Bay
Yesterday in the middle of a heavy squall & a deluge of rain arrived the Rhadamanthus from Malta and brought us two huge leather Bags the produce of two mails - and (to me the most interesting) your nice dispatches worth ten times all the other put together, up to the 11th of last month. Thank God all good and gratifying in every way. Dear Fanny is a jewel and her nice little Notes are pretty pieces of Embroidery about yours - full of all the goings on in what I am so much interested but a sad piece of intelligence is whispered about which I hope is not true that poor Sir Wm Elliot is no more. Still I am fearful from hearing of his infirm health. Poor Lady Elliot how grieved I should be on her account but we have no freehold in this world. I have not heard from Will for an age. He is not thoughtful in that respect but Sir Edmund Lyons our Minister at Athens mentioned in a hasty note on the 29th Sept that he had had the pleasure of making his acquaintance - I have written Beatson having little doubt he will now lose his Term which cannot be helped - this nuisance quarantine keeps everything back. I am in hopes of seeing Willoughby here as the

---
41 Chios

My Dearest Margaret...

Talavera is ordered to join us. If so I shall be right glad as I have seen but little of him. The Admiral's son is now on his travels with Willoughby's old friend Acland, seeing Ephesus and the other Seven churches. I was much gratified with the Plains of old Troy & the splendid Rivers of Alexanders Generals & much Embellished by that wonderful People the Romans who have left stupendous monuments of their greatness all over the Country. We are on the best terms with our companions the Turks - their Pasha or Lord High Admiral has only been two years at sea but is a remarkably fine clever fellow of about 40 & calls my Admiral his Father. This instant I have received a Letter from Willoughby & although I find his complaint not entirely removed I am rejoiced to find it is nearly so & that he is in his accustomed good spirits. I send you his letter which though rashly & carelessly written us yet to me very satisfactory & now that he must miss his Term I shall be very glad he stays at Athens for a month or six weeks longer but from my last letter I expect him here with the Talavera. Captain Mends writes me a very nice letter about him & I have no doubt he will find his way. He has written Mr Beatson & Mr Calltrop of his College, very properly explaining the cause of his absence which I shall send through the Admiralty with letters from myself. The only loss is £2 for his rooms - there will be no loss of time for he is improving every hour and sees more & more the necessity of improvement. You seem to think I am overworked - I assure you my duty is mere play to me as I have three excellent Clerks and everything goes like clockwork. Between the Packets I am quite an idle man. Captain Sharpe I see often as well as Capt Knox. Poor Mrs Sharpe has had the fever at Malta & was bled severely but is getting better & the Misses Austens[42] have had the fever at Athens - in fact, when are we free from sickness? I have most delightful packets from Chatham from the happy trio. The Hero & Heroine & Charlotte crowing over them, one would think from her lively style is in the most robust health & I do hope all this bustle & visiting will do her good as it keeps her active & romantic mind alive. You tell me to burn your letters as well may you tell me to put my hand in the fire - they are my great resource & comfort many a half hour before I go to bed & I would not part with them

---

42 The daughters of Admiral Charles Austen (one of Jane Austen's brothers).

1838

for the world[43]. We are now anchored in a most beautiful Bay with the Turkish Fleet making together about 15 sail all in high order and great beauty - the Capt Pasha with Sir Robert, Capt Fanshawe & myself are going to Smyrna about 20 miles off in the Rhadamanthus Steamer in great style - I shall return in a day or two & before this goes I hope I will be able to tell you Willoughby is with me. If he should not prefer staying at Athens.

14 Oct Sunday morning
Your day My Dearest Margaret. I received last night another Billet from Willoughby with a most kind one from Captain Mends which I send you. He is not yet sound but I trust a few days more will set him up. His general health is good but those glandular swellings incident to this climate are most tedious. I have just been visiting Clazomenae a small island close by where the Ionian inhabitants of this beautiful country fled from the Persians and a memorial of Alexanders great mind - a connecting causeway between it and the land 40 feet broad & about a quarter of a mile long - which is yet so perfect that you may walk along it - many foundations are still clearly marked out by the lines of the walls and a strong position it must have been - but in fact all this country betrays symptoms of former greatness over which the ant crawls and the grasshopper leaps with not a Human Being excepting a straggler here and there to be seen. The richest finest and most picturesque Country in the World - laid out for Gentlemens Seats only plant the House and you have the Parks & Grounds with their Trees Copses and Lawns ready laid out by nature - this is all over the Country. I doubt if the Davieses could sell their home without a great sacrifice not can they get good interest for their money. I should think their best way would be to sell off the furniture & let it unfurnished when they may give a lease for 7 years and the Tenant pay the Rates and Taxes - they could not get more than £1000 for it and the interest on that would not exceed £30. But if they could get £1200 they might then save themselves much trouble by putting the money in the Funds. You do not say how your neighbours on the right behave now, so I hope you are easy in that respect but Dash[44] must be a sad annoyance to <u>them</u>.

---
43   Sadly, the letters must have been lost or destroyed.
44   Dash the family dog

My Dearest Margaret...

21 Oct Sunday
The Talavera has at last come from Athens and Will in famous spirits but poor fellow not yet recovered of his swelling which keeps him confined from walking but as little as possible it seems they are the most tedious things possible & nothing could have been more unfortunate at this time of all others he should have been able to go about. He had however been twice at Athens, dined with the Ambassador & seen the Acropolis & the greater part of the other Curiosities but only enough to awaken his desire for seeing more. He will be allowed this Term upon sending a sick certificate from the Surgeon & he has gained much more than he would at College notwithstanding his ailment about which I am now easy as he is with me & nearly well but I was very far from comfortable when he was absent. Capt Mends has acted like a Father to him & shewn the very kindest attention - having him in his own cabin & lecturing him when there was occasion - which was generally about his want of care of himself just as he would his own son - indeed his friendship has been unbounded. We are going into Malta but Willoughby is so eager to make the most of his time now he is here & feels himself comfortable that I think of letting him remain with Capt Mends that he may have another peer at Greece & return to Malta by the Ionian Islands as first proposed. So you need not make yourself uneasy - his health is excellent. God Bless You & all round the fireside is the prayer of your affectionate Husband John Loudon.

9 Nov Princess Charlotte, Malta
We left Smyrna on the 27th October & after a rather tedious passage arrived here safe and sound on the 7th. I left Willoughby in most excellent health in Talavera to pursue his Travels which he would be able to begin in a few days, and finding he was quite up to the work I have given him a carte blanche so long as he is Home by the next term. He is in most excellent spirits but has suffered much from the plaguy tumor which was sluggish & difficult to heal - his general health is excellent & Capt Mends is in hopes of accompanying him on these further travels. He is just returned from the Seven Churches with Arthur Stopford. He is a most valuable companion - correct in principle and economical - free from the vices of smoking & drinking & particularly clever in sketching in

1838

fact well equipt for a traveller & Sir Thomas may well be proud of such a son. I have now a piece of sad news for you - poor Mrs Sharpe is no more - she was buried last Sunday week having died while they were looking out for a nurse for her though she was sometime ill. Capt Sharpe of course was dreadfully affected on his arrival but not altogether unprepared. Poor woman she was alone in a lodging in a strange place - a sad finale. She was the last person I took leave of at Malta & I never saw one in better spirits - though I hear she told Capt Sharpe he would never see her again such was her presentiment. I much fear the news of poor Best's death is too true - what will become of them - for the poor woman will only have the Pension & the children under 21 I think may have £8 or £10 a year each by proper applications. Speaking of the ornaments sent by Mr Foote I had only one Box - in which were 2 vases & I think 2 basin stands for flowers or any other ornamental thing you choose - I sent you some Honey too. All the Ladies are on Board - 9 in family besides Capt Fanshawe & myself - Mrs Fanshawe is delicate in health & must wait poor woman with patience on shore till our quarantine is out - a sad drawback for both while the Admirals family are enjoying themselves together. The Miss Fanshawes are expected next week from Naples. Mr & Mrs Duckworth are at their old Lodgings on shore - both well and always kind to me. The Queen Dowager[45] arrived at Naples on the 31st & leaves it on the 15th for Palermo on her way here, the Admiral has sent the Carysfort to meet her & take Her Majesty's Commands. Her health has much improved. She intends returning in March next. I shall be very satisfied with £50 for Lizzie's Piano but she should have it on as small a scale as possible for a soldier's wife moving about - next month I shall send them a cheque for £100 and by paying ready money for the Piano a very great dedication is always made. I would have written them now but this quarantine is a great cheque as every letter we send is opened smoked and cut. God Bless you dear Mamma and Fan and believe me ever Your most Affectionate Husband John Loudon.

---

45 The Queen Dowager is Adelaide, Princess of Saxe-Meiningen, the consort of William IV and Aunt of the new Queen. Widowed in 1837 aged 45, she spent much of the remaining 12 years of her life in poor health travelling in the Mediterranean region in search of a favourable climate.

My Dearest Margaret...

10 Dec Malta

As I hope to send this through France I write upon new paper. We have had great doings with the arrival of the Queen Dowager. The Hastings appeared off the Port on the 30th and as the wind was foul we sent Wakefield in the Rhadamanthus to tow her in. The Ramparts were soon covered with people, salutes fired from the Batteries - and our own Squadron - the Yards Manned & three hearty cheers. It was the most striking thing I ever saw. Her Majesty was on the Poop surrounded by her suite Lord Howe, Lord & Lady Denbigh, Lord & Lady Sheffield & the two maids of Honor Miss Hudson & Miss Mitchell. On the 1st inst. Her Majesty landed under salutes from the shipping & all Malta out or looking from the Balconies & proceeded in the Admirals open Barouche to the Palace to look at it & returning in one hour afterwards I was in the Admirals Barge which escorted her & in hopes she would have gone direct on board but Her Dowagership gave us a pull round all the squadron & all the creeks & corners of the Harbour, Capt Worth in full uniform steering. On Sunday she came on Board the Princess Charlotte when we were all Introduced & on Tuesday she landed for good amidst an amazing concourse of people cheering and showering flowers upon her from the Balconies as she went along in the Admirals carriage. In the Evening the Town was brilliantly illuminated the Streets crowded in every way. Her Majesty had a most enthusiastic reception but as I find I cannot well send this thro' France I shall enclose a full & particular account of it in Italian - for the Girls to translate it to you. Mrs Blount has got a little Girl - I dined with them on Thursday & went to the Opera - and on Friday she was confined. Yesterday I dined with Mr Collings - dear Lou quite well. There is no force I believe for her marrying Mr Leonard a very respectable Merchant here & Banker for the Queen Dowager who is a great patient admirer but like our lasses at home she is so surrounded with empty Butterflies that she looks down upon a plain coat. I find again I may send this and hasten to tell you that Willoughby is at Constantinople from his last letters when he was about to set out from the Talavera at the mouth of the Dardanelles. He would then go to Smyrna & back to Athens in the Talavera when I should expect him here about the end of the month. He will then go across to Marseilles & be in time to save his term - with a fresh stock of health & knowledge.

1838

13th.

I am glad to tell you Willoughby is arrived in the Pembroke perfectly well & his usual high spirits but he must wait for 23 days more in quarantine at the end of which I hope to get him a passage to Marseilles in one of our steamers with the India Mail when he may be in London in six days - but he may take ten or a fortnight passing a week in Paris. He will be in time at Cambridge on the 1st. February. I shall see him for an hour or two every day but we must not touch. You will see he is a good hand at description but abominably careless and slovenly in writing & spelling - which as you justly observe he has not patience to be spoken to about or to correct & this is most provoking - but I shall get him out of it if I can. Yesterday I was at the Queen Dowagers Levée & in the Evening at the Governors Ball a gay affair & very full. The Misses Fanshawes have arrived. I suppose your two stray Daughters will be with you by the time you get this and the letter with the description of the Queen Dowagers arrival must serve you all at present for in spite of better resolutions I am always pushed at last My benediction to all your Christmas fireside. I shall heartily drink your health on the 25 as I am sure you will mine. God Bless you all your affectionate Husband J. Loudon.

23 Dec Admiralty House Malta

We are close upon Christmas & I am writing this on Sunday forenoon - both solemn occasions. All here are at Church and the house is quiet - how can I employ it better than in having a little chat with you who I fancy all now chattering with me. Would that it were together again for I am really weary of this absence & shall hail with great joy the day which puts an end to it - not but that every thing goes on well & I am happy as I well can be away from my own Fireside. Lady Stopford has bespoke the Fanshawes & it will be a family Party of about 20 myself included. The expressed great disappointment that Willoughby's Quarantine will not be out but he will be as happy and merry as a cricket with his Friends on the Pembroke where, as everywhere else, he has the knack of being perfectly at home. He is now as stout & healthy as ever & in a day or two after his quarantine expires (4 Jany) I am in hopes to have a chance of sending him to Marseilles with a friend of mine who takes the Indian Mail, who will readily give him a seat in his

My Dearest Margaret...

carriage but as he travels night and day for six days to London I propose Willy being set down at Meurices in Paris where he will have a few days to rest & see the place prior to resuming his studies at Cambridge. I think you will next see him improved. The weather is as cold as I felt it at this time in England & we find fire not only comfortable by necessary.

The Queen is the greatest lioness - a nice tame one she is. Everybody is delighted with her agreeable manner & she seems much pleased with everybody. To the officers of the Hastings she is like a fond Parent. We are obliged to send that ship upon a short service and Her Majesty would go on Board & bid them Goodbye. She had Capt.s Lock and Worth to dinner & was almost shedding tears & could scarcely speak when they kissed her hand & took leave. No doubt a great deal is owing to Worth's good tact and management to have made everything so agreeable & there is no question of his further promotion as soon as his time is served as a Commander. He is a first rate officer and a most excellent fellow. He was over with Will yesterday. Perhaps you don't understand a Pailatorio? It is a large room or three with two railing the whole length & a space of about 4 or 5 feet between so that you can lean on each railing, converse together but not touch. He comes from the Ship generally about 3 o'clock & I go across the water to meet him. We may stop all day as we like & there is some amusement in it for the officers all go to chat with their friends & it is just like a Fair. All the difference with me is that lately I was on the outside of the railing & now Will is, & I am on the in. I have just got a card as large as a pane of glass to the Dowager's Evening Party on New Years Day.

25 Dec

A merry Christmas to you all but what am I to think whether you have completed your plan of being together - I fear not. Will is here as happy as a cricket. Dear Eliza I fear will not leave her Husband or rather I almost hope he may yet accompany her, & Charlotte I suppose is at her Aunts in Town. I should not wonder then if dear Fan & you have the house to yourselves except the dear Girls from Ridgeway who I suppose will be with you. Here we are one family of 20 people to dinner and 24 tomorrow - in fact we never dine under 16 or 17 hardly & I don't think the Admiral will return much heavier in pocket than he came out - but he had all his family with him & that is a comfort. As to Charlottes coming out here alone, if you knew the place & there people you would say it is perfect madness & those of delicate constitutions leave it as fast as they can.

26 Dec

Everybody was very kind yesterday particularly Lady Stopford - but I must confess I felt a loneliness & sighed for my <u>own</u> dear little circle. I could not get my spirits up at all not withstanding Capt Fanshawes slaps on the back to keep me up. Mrs Fanshawe could not help remarking that she and I were the only two out of the family of 18 present. Dear Will was very hearty on Board the Pembroke & is in prime spirits. Our friend Wakefield is likely to give him a lift to Marseilles next week if out of Quarantine in time which I think likely.

27 Dec

What a treat my dear Margaret I have received all your Budgets up to the 7th of this month including dear Eliza and Arneys delightful effusions from Sheerness & now all but him poor fellow you are at home. You will see how Will passed Christmas by the enclosed Letter from Capt Moresby by the Captain of the Pembroke - & my only other fear is that he shines in that way more than in his studies at Cambridge, but as you justly observe he is very impatient in hearing advice than thankful in receiving it. Happy New Year to you all I wish I were with you - I should prefer it to being with the Queen Dowager at night or the Governors Levée in the morning. God Bless you all, your affectionate Husband J. Loudon.

I have heard nothing of Nancy, Jack nor Jones nor Hannah Moore lately - what are you about Fan? Knox says Charlotte's house is a regular Rookery at the foot of the Garden. This is very last scratch before closing the Mail - again God Bless You , you know I cannot always write to each & dear Liz is still & ever will be one of the family as will Arney who gains upon me more & more by his attachment to <u>his</u> Liz.

My Dearest Margaret…

1839

Fancy Dress Ball - Regatta - departure of the Queen Dowager - two weddings - Gozo - Palermo - set sail for Syria - political affairs - family expenditure - Constantinople - Turkish affairs - Basika Bay - court martial - St. Andrews Day - more courts martial - last Christmas away from home?

                                                            21 Jan Malta

My Dearest Margaret

    Another fortnight is running on since I last wrote you. Willoughby left me on Wedy night the 9th on the Rhadamanthus but he would poor fellow have a rough passage as a strong gale of wind came on the next day right in their teeth. He was to stop a few days in Paris to recruit from his fatigues so as to be at Cambridge by the end of the month. We have had coarse weather here but very seasonable. The Small Pox has carried away about 800 this last year. Poor Bacon is now at the Hospital and will be sadly marked he was in great danger but is now getting well which I am sure will delight our dear Ridgeways. 2 o'clock I have this instant received your most welcome budgets by the Megaria - Capt Fanshawe is charmed with his Purse & full of thanks & all kinds of pretty sayings to dear Eliza - as is Mrs Duckworth for Charlotte's Magnificent Reticule[46]. Mrs Duckworth is indeed an excellent creature and dear Annie much liked but this is not a marrying place however gay. Mrs Fanshawe is very delicate but she has a great acquisition in the two Miss Fanshawes who are very agreeable nice people. Young Arthur Stopford goes home in the Barham & should she put in at Plymouth I hope you will be kind to him - Captain Corry too is one of my prime favourites - a most Gentlemanly man whom I am very sorry to lose.

---

46 A small drawstring handbag.

My Dearest Margaret...

We just hear poor Sir Thomas Hardy is very ill & in that case I think you will see me sooner than you expected as it is thought here Sir Robert will succeed him. We are certainly kept alive here but yet not very gay. I am out of late I think four days of the seven to dinner & the other three we have company at home - tomorrow the Governor gives a grand Ball - I see little of the Queen who has had a slight cold but was out yesterday on the water. Jamie Stopford steers her & threatens to stick her in the mud if she does not ask him to dinner - we all continue very pleasant & I certainly like Lady Stopford & the Young Ladies more & more. I think you will see Commander Stopford in his Brig Zebra on his way out. It is a pretty compliment to the Admiral giving his son a command so soon but if he goes to Greenwich he will lose his patronage in that respect and he has many yet to provide for. I fear I must agree with you about College being a bad place for a Young Man and I am not without my fears that Willoughby's conduct will depend much upon the hands he falls into. He is in many respects heedless thoughtless & careless but has promised to be more correct in money matters about which I was not well satisfied with him but his eyes seemed opened when I laid down the Law to him in a way he did not at first relish, that he at last came in with an apparent good feeling. This trip has done him much good & excited his observation to objects he never knew or cared about before. I sent a Bill for £89 for his last 2 quarters at College and £30 to Mr Wallace for his last half quarter at Canterbury which had never before been sent me & he says he found it among his things - another instance of his care in money matters. I likewise sent the £50 to Errington & shall be ready with another £50 when they choose the Piano.

24 Jan.

I find I must now conclude as the Packet starts in two hours more & I must mind my public duty. I came home early from the Governors Ball last night (12 o'clock) on purpose & it is now 8 in the morning but the sun does not get to you till an hour later. I have seen John Foote who gives me very pleasant accounts of you all and Commander Hutton to whom I feel very much obliged for his attentions in calling. Palmer is overwhelmed with thanks for some assistance you gave his mother in a time of great distress and he is to pay me out of his wages. Such acts of kindness to the distrest you know must always meet my approbation. He is quite a treasure to me and what is more will not leave me to better himself. I told Will to write you from Paris but he is so full of the present time that he has no great relish for breaking in upon it by communicating with his friends on paper - never sitting down to write & be the last minute when all is hurry and bustle. The Barham trails in on Saturday for Portsmouth and I hope to have some Honey and Figs sent by her, but Portsmouth is very inconvenient an account of the Customs and then sending round on the steamer - I must only keep back other things till a direct opportunity appears. Tell Mr David I have sent his Wine but the Captain says the Barham is a full as an egg & I must await a better chance. Mrs Sheddon his niece is here in good health I met her last night at the Ball looking very well - a first class dancer - danced a Highland Reel before Her Majesty at the Ball with two Officers. Love to all & believe me my own dear Margaret Your Affectionate Husband John Loudon.

10 Feb Malta

My last was a very short Letter to you but as Elizas was long I am in hopes you would excuse it as I gave her an account of all our goings on which would serve for all. If the Barham touches at Plymouth you have a most particular friend of mine in Captain Corry and I will thank you to pay Young Arthur Stopford all the attention you can. Commander Robert Stopford will very probably put into Plymouth on his way in the Zebra. He is an excellent fellow & I need not say any attention to him will not be thrown away. Our Carnival just begun three days folly but no riot or disturbances, all good humor and cheerfulness, fond of going in carriages and masques through the Streets. Tomorrow night the Governor gives a Fancy Dress Ball which will be very full and amusing - there were between 7 and 800 at ours. The gaieties will then be over in Lent. Today I dine with Collings. Louisa quite well & much admired but no bids except poor Mr Leonard who has a warm home like a Palace to put her into but the Blue bottles and Lobsters keep the poor merchant in the background and they won't and indeed can't come forward for they have only their poor £40 a year from their friends and no home but a friends to put their Heads into - alas poor Lou!

My Dearest Margaret...

17th Feb

Another week gone and very pleasantly passed. On Monday was the Governors Fancy Ball where there were about 700 people & many male and female well chosen characters. I was quite at a loss to discover a Lady with a Masque & dressed in the costume of the time of our Elizabeth who put her arm on mine and cut all kind of antics. I thought it was a boy till Mrs Duckworth hinted to me it was the Marchesa Testaferrata the mother of I think 10 or 12 children, one of her Daughters about to be married to an English Officer. Mrs Shelden was in an Albanian dress & the youngest in manner in the room. One of our Mates came in as a Nurse with a young scape goat of a Middie 15 years of age as her Baby to the amusement of everybody - very small but very heavy so he soon tired his Nurse. We had French Swiss German & Spaniards, Jews, Turks, Greeks in Capital costumes and well kept up till 4 in the morning with an excellent Supper but not such wines as we gave. Everybody was pleased & I never witnessed a livelier scene.

We are now in Lent & I expect no more Balls so much the better. Yesterday the Governor, Lord Denbigh and Lady Denbigh with the two Maids of Honor Miss Hudson & Miss Mitchell dined with us. The Queen I rather think will leave us in March & go direct to England. Her Majesty has been presented with some broken columns from Carthage which she is to have worked into an Altar Piece and Steps which I think a good thought as they have no distinctive character or beauty as antiques. Our weather is delightful neither hot nor cold & famous for walking & however much I wish <u>you</u> know I must not ride.

19th. Feb

Dearest Margaret you have quite made me up again with your nice new stock of letters to 31st last month. Willy was at Paris on the 28th & meant to start on the 31st for Cambridge. I send you his letter. Had he not received the £10 from Captain Walker it would have been a most expensive trip. I gave him £15 in his Pocket & a cheque for £4 which I only meant as a standby in case of need. However with the additional £10 making in all £29 he used it. His passage was free on the steamer & would have been very little with Mr Calvert a Kings Messenger to Paris which I had fortunately bespoke for him, but Captain Walker's object being time, he paid Willy the difference to take his place - I wrote Will a rather sharp letter upon his expenses altogether - particularly at College - where he seems to have run into all the idle expenses he can. I fear I was too harsh but it is time he should understand his position and must no longer think of turning places of Expensive Education into amusement and self-gratification - we have given him every advantage and if he throws it away he will himself be the loser. By this time you must have heard from him & I have no doubt his letters will be amusing for he has a happy knack at descriptions but is supremely careless in his writing.

21 Feb

This must now go - no new occurrence - all goes on well & my health excellent but as usual I am bustling in sending off the Packet - for I have one for Corfu one for Gibraltar & a vessel for Constantinople. I am indeed much relieved about dear Lottie's health but I hope you keep her under control & her wonderful flow of spirits down to her delicate frame. I am much pleased with her thought & feelings in buying you that comfortable cape which seems so suitable. Here we are all enjoying the finest weather I believe in the whole year & everybody is on Horseback but your poor old Johnny - never mind I am pleased in keeping my word to you. I cannot tell you how much Palmer contributes to my comfort. He is so very steady respectable & well principled I really never met with his equal. I am exceedingly pleased with the Miss Fanshawes who live with their Brother & I must say I like Lady Stopford & all the family more & more as I know them better. The Admiral - a trump - and Captain Fanshawe always the same playful friendly fellow as ever. In short I am as comfortable as I well can be from Home and two years of the time will be over on the 7th April. God Bless You my ever dearest Margaret. Your affectionate Husband John Loudon.

17 March Malta

I had no letters from Willoughby since his arrival in England so that I am kept in a teasing state of ignorance of all your proceedings. I am pretty sure however you all continue well and everything going on to your wishes. We have had fine cold weather making a fire very agreeable but more so a walk (what riding is I don't know) and every day it is becoming more so. I generally get up at 7 and take an hours walk till 9 when we have breakfast. Then to work till 3 when, if nothing particular comes in the way, I am a free man till half past 6 when we dine and in the Evening go to the Opera or to bed as it may happen. Our two young ladies have had falls and broken or disfigured faces but they are now well again and have not been frightened from mounting - they know nothing of riding having neither grace nor a good seat and the Horses are not always safe so many of them together. Yet everybody rides save your poor Lord (not Master) who religiously sticks to his promise - much against his will. My health continues excellent - no colds as yet.

19 March Tuesday

Dearest Margaret your Budget today up to the 16th of Febry was indeed a great feast to me. Eliza's and Charlotte's were delightful pictures of your fireside & a most kind one from Arney made me perfectly happy. I had likewise one from Will very satisfactory as to his studies & I hope he is putting on good resolutions against past errors. Mr. Beatson's letter to Lizzie is very amusing & if Will would only follow his advice he would give me more satisfaction. The Queen Dowager was to have laid the foundation stone of our new Protestant Chapel today but it has come on such a Gale of Wind, Hail Storms and Rain that it is put off till finer weather. No doubt the Catholics will consider it a judgement upon us Heretics. We would have had a Regatta on Thursday, Friday & Saturday & next week. Her Majesty returns in Hastings to England. She has much endeared herself to everybody & her departure will be much regretted. I am sadly grieved to hear that poor Sir George Eyre[47] is no more. I know not what there was about him that won my respect - I certainly never had so much for any other. Poor Lady Eyre & Daughters will feel it sadly & William too will be terribly shocked for I believe it was sudden and unexpected.

20 March Wednesday 3 o'clock

I am just come from the ceremony of the Queen Dowager's laying the foundation stone of our new Church where there was a

---

47 Sir George Eyre served for 57 years in the Navy, rising to the rank of Vice-Admiral of the Red. Loudon had acted as his Secretary in the South American station.

1. Admiral Sir Robert Stopford. Portrait by unknown artist, 1840. By permission of the National Portrait Gallery.

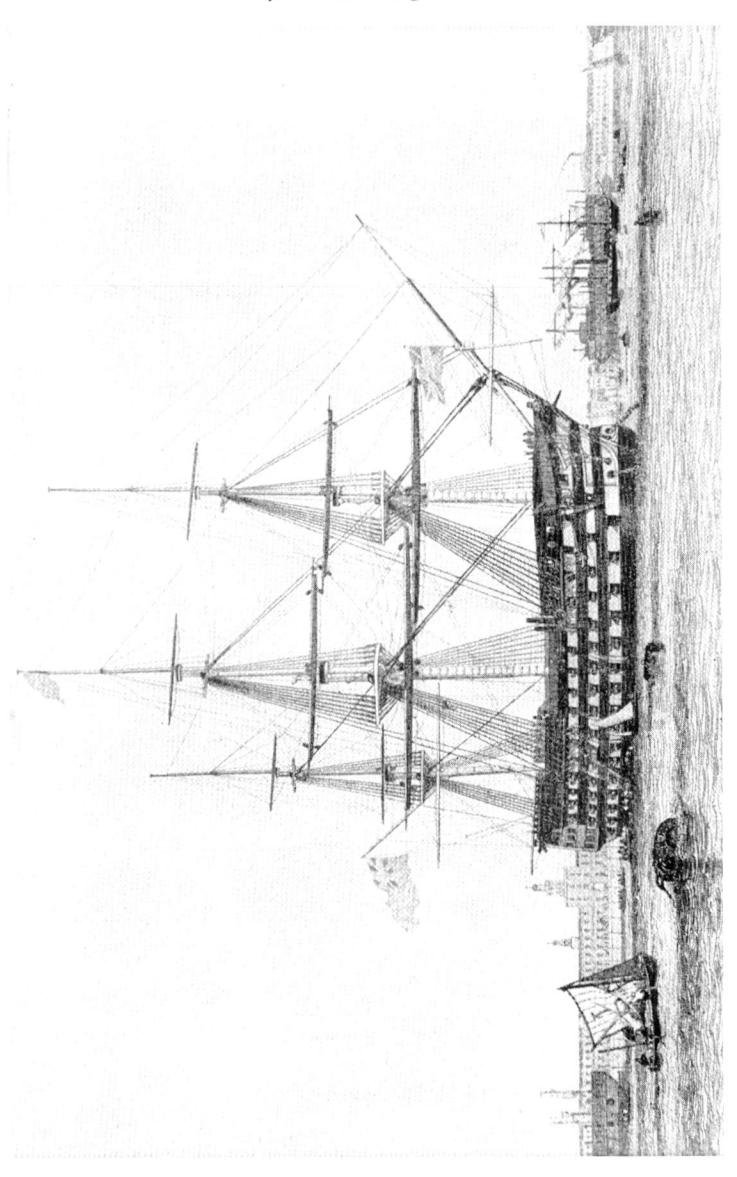

2. The Princess Charlotte. Engraving by permission of the National Maritime Museum, Greenwich.

3. Photograph postcard of Durnford Street, Plymouth, late 19th century. By permission of Derek Tait.

My Dearest Margaret…

4. Loudon's family house in 2013 (previously numbered 44). By permission of Sara McMahon, The Family History Company, Plymouth.

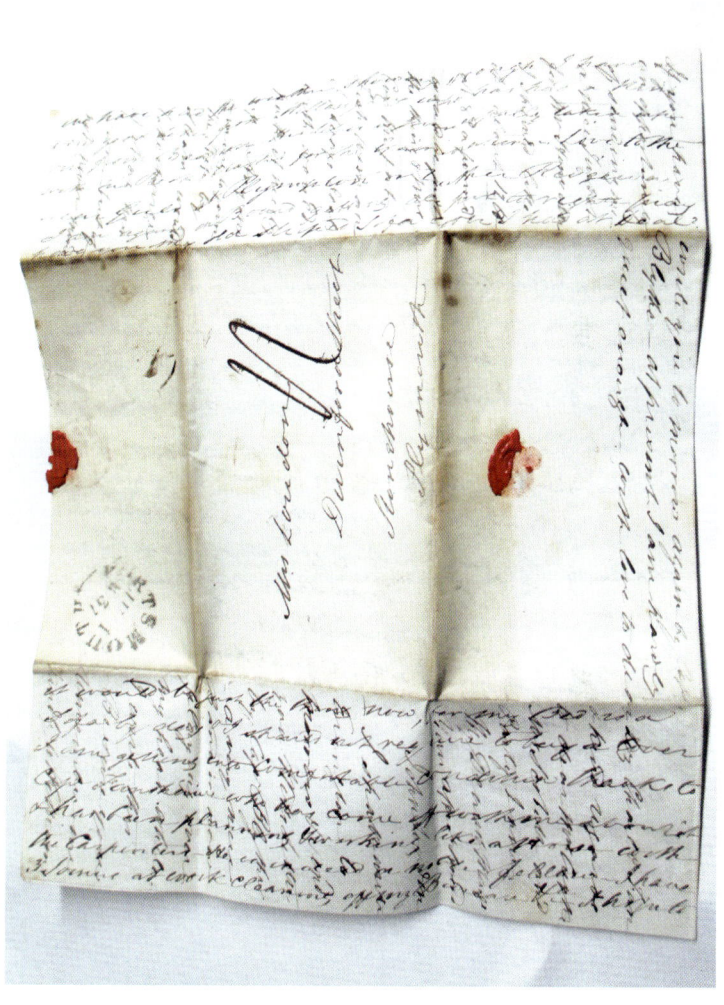

5. Letter from John Loudon to his wife in Plymouth, July 1837.

6. Letter from the Princess Charlotte off Palermo, June 1839.

Illustrations

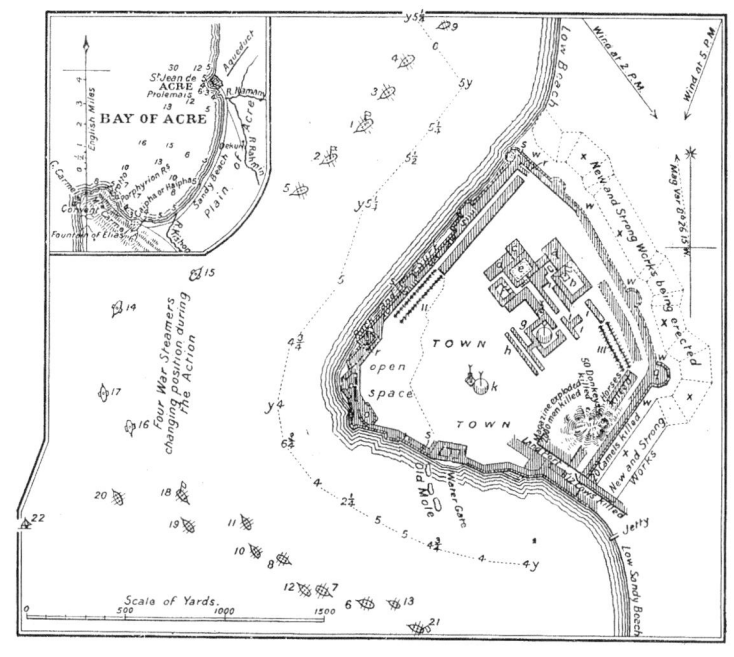

BOMBARDMENT OF ST. JEAN D'ACRE, NOVEMBER 3RD, 1840.

(*From the chart by Mr. J. C. Brettell, sometime Engineer-in-Chief to Mehemet Ali.*)

REFERENCES TO THE PLAN.

SHIPS.

1. *Princess Charlotte*.
2. *Powerful*.
3. *Thunderer*.
4. *Bellerophon*.
5. *Revenge*.
6. *Benbow*.
7. *Edinburgh*.
8. *Castor*.
9. *Pique*.
10. *Carysfort*.
11. *Talbot*.
12. *Hazard*.
13. *Wasp*.
14. *Gorgon*.
15. *Phœnix*.
16. *Stromboli*.
17. *Vesuvius*.
18. *Medea* (Aust.).
19. *Guerriera* (Aust.).
20. *Lipsia* (Aust.).
21. Turkish 84 (flag).
22. Turkish cutter.

a. Harem.
b. Castle.
c. Abdallah Pasha's harem.
d. Governor's divan.
e. Hospital.
f. Accountant-general's divan.
g. Mosque.
h. Bazaar.
iii. Stores.
k. Mosque.
l. Fortified khan.
m. 45 brass field-pieces.
n. 47 brass field-pieces.
o. Half-moon battery.
p. High battery.
q. Unfinished work.
rr. Observation towers.
ss. Mortar batteries.
tt. Traverses.
ww. Outer ditch.
xx. Glacis.
yy. Soundings.

7. Plan of the bombardment of Acre, November 1840: showing the ships and the town. From Clowes 'The Royal Navy' Volume 6, first published 1901.

My Dearest Margaret…

8. Attack of St. Jean d'Acre showing the ships *Pique, Bellerophon, Thunderer, Princess Charlotte, Powerfull, Revenge, Gorgon* and *Phoenix,* dedicated to the Admiral Sir Robert Stopford and officers of the Mediterranean Fleet. Lithograph by permission of the National Museum of the Royal Navy, Portsmouth.

1839

numerous assemblage - the streets in the vicinity lined with Troops and the windows & Houses tops crowded. The Stone was in a sunken area with steps down - after Prayer Her Majesty descended from her Pavilion - the Secretary of Governor presented a Silver Trowel on a velvet Cushion to the Governor who presented it on one knee to Her Majesty, the Architect then dipped it into a small portion of mortar & returned it to Her Majesty who spread it on the Stone as you would bread & butter. She then applied the Plummet & Rule to see that it was level & square. Some Parchments were then placed in a square cut for that purpose with some coins and a brass Plate with an Inscription covered this square. The Queen returned to the temporary Pavilion - a Royal Salute was fired, Prayers read & a Psalm sung - away went the Queen, the Band up God Save the Queen & thus ended the affair.

21 March

All bustle for the Packet after dispatching the Mails for England & Corfu & Athens I am going on Board the Princess Charlotte to witness the Regatta & have a dejeuner where the Queen is to make her Dinner & have nothing but Tea when she returns - the same tomorrow on Board the Rodney to which Capt Parker has been kind enough to invite me & again on Saturday on board the Asia where I am invited by Capt Fisher & all these days the Queen is to save her dinner at home - thus we go on you see Of course dear Liz & Fan have left you & I think them returning with Arney would be as well as you moving but just suit yourself in this & whatever you do I shall be satisfied. I hope Willoughby will really be careful & make up for much money he has cost me. I hardly ever knew what it was to have a son before but I trust he will soon qualify himself to support his own expenses & yet come out a blessing to his family - the £30 is some help & he assures me he will economise in every way he can. Capt Mends & his sons quite well - remember me kindly to Mrs Mends . Ever my Dearest your affectionate Husband John Loudon. I should like a good Atlas - but on second thoughts I can see the Admls when I like.

31 March Malta

With all our gay doings since I last wrote you I never for a moment forgot my dear Home & the offshoots from it. I can fancy

My Dearest Margaret…

you now sitting by yourself talking to me while the rest are praying for me in Church & it is quite a treat to me to have a quiet moment with you. The Queen Dowager has been very active - on the 21st, 22nd & 23rd she went on Board the Princess Charlotte, Rodney and Asia & witnessed our interesting Boat Races, after which she partook of a Dejeunez & witnessed the dancing on each Ships Quarter deck. On the 26 she went on Board the Hastings for good. She came here to a family Dejeuner on the 28th and Yesterday she went in a steamer to the neighbouring Island of Gozo returning in the Evening & tomorrow she starts on her return for England. She is a most active woman - a plain likeness of our Liz with a heart I am sure such another - she has quite Liz's manner & look & always reminded me of her. We are now in the enjoyment of most delightful weather & this winter I have escaped colds. I expect in a Month or six weeks more we shall be off again to the Archipelago and I rather think the family will move somewhere in that quarter but nothing is yet decided on - I suppose we shall again join the Turks & our object will be to prevent their eating one another & then let Russia devour them both - that we must prevent for if Russia gets a looking at Constantinople her Squadron in the Black Sea may give us a great deal of trouble and oblige us to thresh it at last. We fancy too they have an eye upon our Indian Possessions & it is necessary to prevent their obtaining too great a preponderance which we shall be obliged to clip with more difficulty hereafter. Still she is too wise to go to war & I do not expect it this Summer at least unless she shows a more hostile feeling than at present. On the 7th April our Flag will have been hoisted 2 years - one more and our time is out - How sincerely I wish for it! My heart sickening at this tremendous absence which strikes me more and more with sadness but there is no remedy circumstanced as we are with dear Liz and Willy.

3 April

The Packet goes in the Morning - Her Majesty left us on the 1st at 5 in the morning - I got up to see them off & a pretty sight it was - a most beautiful morning the Queen herself & her maids around her on the Poop waving her Handkerchief, and the Squadron & Batteries saluting - but it was not as on her arrival - not a creature up to look at her though the churches were crowded at their foolish mummeries - everything wears out. She is much regretted however by all. The Admiral very gallantly sent her an Escort as far as the West end of Sicily and 3 Line of Battle Ships & a Frigate under Capt Hyde Parker - we are now looking for them back, but I fear Her Majesty will have had bad weather for it is blowing a Gale right against her. The family here were much rejoiced at the arrival of Commander Robert Stopford in the Zebra - a very nice young man & always my favourite. Every thing continues to go on well I am only anxious to hear good accounts of Will who is very lazy but writes well when he begins - I agree with you it is now an anxious time with him. I dined on Board the Talavera yesterday and all spoke of him with great kindness. Poor Sir George - I cant help thinking of him. He had somehow got hold of my feelings, that I could scarcely account for it, but so it was I respected him more than any one I almost knew & yet he never shewed half the warmth Sir Willoughby Lake & others did - He was no doubt a most excellent man & I feel truly for his loss - I write Lady Eyre by this Packet. Poor William will feel it terribly - & Sir Charles Paget too & poor Dr Scott my ship mate for 3 years, a most worthy fellow. The days are lengthening here but you would hardly believe I am now sitting by a fire & glad of it. John Foote & all that party are returned here from Constantinople where they could have no command in the Turkish Service indeed no one thought they could as it is against the Turkish Law for any Mohometan to be commanded by an Infidel as they consider us. God Bless you My Dearest Margaret Your Affectionate Husband JL.

12 April Malta

I received all your cheering letters with dear Eliza's and Charlotte's up to the 4th March and all your former ones dated 5/10 January 27/31 Jany & 12/16 Feby - all giving me delightful accounts of your goings on & Errington being with you must have quite electrified you all - I sent him a Bill on my Bankers for £50 on the 10 Jany and another for the Piano by last Pacquet which must content them for some time. You must just choose for yourselves whether you go up or they come down in the Summer. As things turn out Fan will I hope not be disappointed of her French Trip. I am anxiously looking for letters from Will as I almost dread the success of his 'little go' from having lost so much time. I have

My Dearest Margaret...

written Sir David what I suspect will astonish him the news of his niece's marriage with a young man of about 30 a Lieutenant Watson of the 47th Regt. and there appears a great disparity on the wrong side it has made a great sensation among the Gossips of Malta of which Class it is pretty well stock'd - I knew nothing of it till calling at her Hotel on Saturday last I saw some Papers signing and Smelt a Rat. She then told me they were going off in the French Steamer for Rome in the morning & they found they could not so easily accomplish it there, they were trying to get it done here by Licence before setting out & then she asked me to give her away which I did the same night by Candle Light in the Royal Chapel at 9 o'clock there being only present the Clergyman, the Bride & Bridegroom Major Gordon of the Regiment & myself & next morning they were off in the Steamer. The Major gives him a high Character and she told me it was not her money that won him for she was to retain all power over it. She is I believe a charitable good hearted woman but a little eccentric in her dress & manner & lost friends last Carnival by her mode of dress in the Albanian Costume.

We have another marriage on the taps between a Lieutenant of the Vanguard & Miss Testaferrata, a Daughter of the Marquis - but you must not fancy these empty fillies any thing like ours & I dont think the Young Lady will have a penny. He is the son of an Admiral Newell long since dead & I believe has as little fortune as her but she is a very nice girl & I hope will make him a good wife. I am asked to give her away as her Father being a Catholic is too much under the dominion of His Holiness to do it at a Protestant Altar though the Pope has given his dispensation. Little Lou is to be the Brides Maid & it is to take place on Monday. I dine today at the Governors and shall be finely roasted about all this - we had two marriages a few weeks back the Clergyman himself Mr Clough & the Commander of the Beacon Surveying Vessel so that we fly off from one Amusement to another rapidly - but no great matches made. The Squadron are all in readiness for a start the moment the Orders come and we look for them by every Pacquet now. I shall be more cautious in selecting what I should send - what do you think of giving the Table to Liz, or Charle or Fan as a work Table? It only cost me £1 & shd not have paid so much duty. Do not my dearest make yourself the least uneasy about my health for I assure you I never enjoyed better, and except a passing cloud occasionally my spirits are excellent & I find myself perfectly comfortable in the family. The last year is at hand and once broken into it will soon wear out. I shall only regret my poor £400 going out with it when Willy must expect to be snibbed likewise so he must now make the best of his time & I trust he does. The Misses Fanshawes are going to Athens and Constantinople and then back to Torquay - they are great Favourites of mine of a certain age but clever & very nice women. You will be sorry to hear that you could scarcely know Henry Bacon he is so marked with the small pox. He was so ill that his loss was despaired of but he is now quite recovered and doing duty again & I am in hopes the marks will soon wear out and indeed they are begun to do. He still looks a fine manly fellow perhaps more so than with his fine smooth face though less dandyish. We had a very pleasant Party at the Generals last night. Sir Fredk Peregrine Maitland & Daughters & Sir John Mackenzie & Lady Mackenzie & Miss Johnson her Sister & other little folks, to the number of 20 including 5 of the Admirals family & staff. Young Elliot, Lord Minto's son and Mr Vance a son of the Doctors who though he will have forty thousand Pounds fortune very creditably seeks his own Bread and intends entering the Church - He is at present Tutor to the Governors boys but received with respect in the first Society.

13 April

The Firefly will not start till morning - I long for Rhadamanthus & letters from Will - today we have quite Plymouth weather - pitting.

14 April

One of the Passengers going home, poor Mr Barlow is in the night gone to his Long home - such is life - Lady Stopford was very kind to him. God bless you My ever dearest. Your last dear letter was quite balm to me - Ever your sincerely affectionate Husband John Loudon.

17 April Malta

How much I feel your anxiety My dear Margaret about my health and comfort - now do take my word for it I never was better

My Dearest Margaret...

in health in my life. My Dearest Admiral is on the footing of a personal Friend & I never could speak so freely to any other I have served with. There has been Sun shine & shade occasionally, but very little of the latter in the female line but really I ought not to say so for on all occasions I have met with the kindest attentions from them all & more especially from Lady S. herself who certainly has a little of the manner of Lady B - without any vanity or lackadaisicalness. Hers is only the family quickness of the Fanshawes with the kindest heart in the world. I have been within these few weeks very prominent in giving away two Brides - the first Mrs Shedden a rich widow having a son 20 years old to a Lieut.Watson of the 47th - about 34 - & the other yesterday the Daughter of the Marquis Testaferrata 18 to Lieut. Nowell a Son of Adml Nowell - on board the Vanguard - a long string of Ancestry from before the Guelphs and Ghibellines but very little cash - neither could speak to one another a twelve month ago but they made love by the eyes & he now speaks Italian so as to be understood - She too is a Catholic & they were married by dispensation by the Pope but none of her friends would come further than the vestry in <u>our</u> Church & her Father begged <u>me</u> to give her away - We had a splendid Second Breakfast & away the happy pair set to their House in the Country - but you cannot suppose how much his friends here were annoyed at his marrying a Catholic & without a fortune but all is right now as they could not break it off. I regret you had much duties to pay or I think I would not have sent so many things but all I sent was good though the <u>tea</u> was certainly as dear as if you had bought it at a shop - no more of that. I shall not forget a Table for Liz.

18 April

I wish I knew what to send but I really cannot think of any thing excepting 3 pairs of net gloves of this Countrys manufacture which are much worn here in Winter. I was glad to her the Traveller had arrived safe but I regret dear Liz is still so great a sufferer for sea sickness which seems incurable & that is a sad misfortune for a soldiers wife. Where our people go is yet undecided & I rather think they will remain where they are or at least in the Country where there are several good houses but enormously dear and that does not suit such a large family - not over heavy on pocket

1839

for the Admiral here if he keeps himself up is subject to many expenses. The place is full of strangers of distinction - the Duke of Devonshire is come back and dines with us on Sunday - God Bless you My dear Margaret & believe me ever Your Sincerely Affectionate Husband John Loudon.

To daughter Charlotte
18 April Malta

My dearest Lotty

You must be content with a very small return to your very nice Epistle by the Rhadamanthus which placed me quite at old 44 again. Lady Stopford was quite pleased with your note & begged me to thank you for it in her name. Willoughby was right in her manner but with an apparent stiffness & personality she is an excellent hearted woman and I assure you I am most comfortable with them all - when I do walk in the Country having them all around me and dear Annie Duckworth into the bargain. The youngest is Charlotte & as your pretty paper cutter was much admired at the breakfast table I thought you would consider it well bestowed in saying it was from her Namesake in Durnford Street which she begged I would return you her best thanks. She is a dear sprightly good natured girl as indeed they all are - though a little subdued in their manner from training by their Mamma - but no family can be more endearing & united. Here I know they are thought stiff & proud & young men keep rather aloof so that I expect they will all return in single blessedness as they came - but indeed I see nobody here fit for them. I have just written dear Liz and am quite delighted she is safe back at her quarters with dear Fan who I hear has grown tall - which I never expected. The Pacquet is just going & I have only time to say God bless you my dear Girl Your Affectionate Father John Loudon.

I am very much pleased with Willoughbys Letter. He is a fine clear sighted manly fellow. I hope he will profit by the Lawyers.

26 April Malta

My Dearest Margaret

I cannot tell how pleased I am at your great attention in writing me, for altho the Rhadamanthus arrived here before the Packet yet your letter of the 26th was a great treat to me and came like

My Dearest Margaret…

the Chronicles after the Kings in the Old Testament winding well up all that was said in your other Letters. I think Hamilton might have saved some of your expenses at the Custom House but what we lose in purse we gain in wisdom and I shall be wiser another time. I hope you liked the oranges for they cost me 1d a piece being very dear this Season. We go on here in our usual way plenty of gales & I regret the poor Queen Dowager after being tossed about 8 days in a fearful gale & very Seasick was obliged to seek shelter at Palermo whence I understand she sailed again on the 16th & I fear has not much better luck since. We have sent the Rodney, Bellerophon & Talavera with the Castor Frigate to Crucae among the Ionian Islands for 3 weeks about which time we shall all be thinking of sailing on our Summers Cruise - Where the Ladies go is not yet settled & I rather think they will remain where they are - as moving about drains hard upon the Pocket. I could now bear a fire but soon it will be scorching. We are all still in blues & not a bit too warm - tremendous thunder & lightning last night with a deluge of rain blowing a Gale. What a good for nothing fellow Palmers Father is! His poor Mother on going to Sheerness found he had again lost his place from drunkenness & such is the poor creatures reduced state that she has not a Chair or Table or a Bed & almost naked. I have never given him any thing for his attentive & faithful services & I really could not hear his wretched state without sending her a cheque for Five Pounds - we shall be none the poorer for it. He sends her his half pay and is now going to send her a Remittance from the rest. He is a most careful poor fellow and an excellent son - what I shall do with him I scarcely know - I offered him to be Steward of small frigates more than once & as he could not tell me all he thought I send you a Letter he left on my desk explaining his views - He is not one of my geese I assure you but I never yet have had his equal - he is the best violin here & plays at all Lady Stopfords Evenings at Home. What does Sir David think of his dear niece being married? It was a seven days wonder here - She is certainly a very odd woman - and did not much take here though I believe a good & charitable creature as ever lived.

1839

29 April

I send this through France as a special messenger with the India Mail gives me an opportunity. We have had rough weather - plenty of rain thunder & lightning but now clearing up. No appearance yet of our moving - we have not cast our blues which are very comfortable. Tell dear Charlotte with my love I shall write her on Thursday - meantime I hope she is making you comfortable and happy. May all thats good attend you both. My German has many breaches in it and comes on slowly - I am thankful to you for prohibiting my riding - many accidents happening to young men in that way. Again God bless you Your Affectionate Husband John Loudon.

To daughter Charlotte
1 May Malta

My Dearest Lotty

I had a nice long letter from you today dated the 10th last month - & by it I find other people have gaieties as well as I. Admiral Warrens must indeed have been magnificent - the House has so many advantages and 350 people are quite a crowd for Plymouth. What a shame to put in the Paper the death of his son whom everybody lamented here & were delighted with a mixture of indignation however to find it was not true. I have most agreeable letters from Arnie, Lizzie & Fan, in fact all the world but Will, who is very negligent in that way seeming to forget everybody but himself. It is not right in him and very unlike his sisters - I hope however he'll mend. Today I put on whites but was glad to change - the weather is by no means settled down yet & I question if you have not it as warm with you as we have here to our feelings at least. We have got Prince George of Cambridge[48] here - he will than proceed to Naples - a very fine young man. We have likewise the great Sir Moses Montefiore – the dear Sheriff of London - a very clever gentlemanly man - Lady Montefiore - a Jewess - they too dined with us as every body does passing - no joke for the poor Admiral. We are not likely to go to sea for a month yet and I believe we shall leave Lady Stopford and the Young Ladies to fry on this

---

48 Prince George of Cambridge is the grandson of George III who lived with William IV and Queen Adelaide (now Queen Dowager) for many years and spent 6 months travelling before returning as a military officer to England and Ireland..

My Dearest Margaret...

23 June Malta

A fair wind always accompanies us wherewill and hopes the day is now approaching when it will carry us to England - we arrived here on Monday evening the 17th on the 18th the ladies went on shore and on the 19th we all look up our old quarters from whence I am now writing but on the arrival of the Packet we start for the Levant though what we can do is not yet clear to us. All is doubt as yet about the circumstances of hostilities between the Sultan and his rebel Pasha - we shall have no finger in it unless Russia begins her insidious policy of helping the Sultan by way of getting Constantinople the Key of the Dardanelles and encroaching by degrees upon our possessions in India - but I rather think all that will be settled in the Cabinets & expect much such a Summer as the last which was a very agreeable one - Palmer is quite sensible and all you say about his unhappy Father - but says he is away at present & hopes he will keep so. He is the same invariably steady good servant as ever & I never was more comfortable in the respect. Poor Mrs Hillard how she must be grieved about that blackguard son of hers who was on board the Royal Adelaide. He was here with Blount in the Hermes and <u>run</u> from her at Marseilles where he was taken up and is now in Prison till he can be brought back but that is not the worst of it - it appears he forged two Bills for £20 each and the Merchants (Christian is one) are to prosecute when he is brought back which will in all probability make a Galley slave of him with chains about his legs for life - what a sad case! I have written his father that his only chance is to take up the Bills which I fear he will have some difficulty in doing besides which the Boy is over head and ears in debt in fact a regular Scamp who will just go on as before. It must break his poor Mother's heart. How much we have to be thankful for if dear Will keeps clear from extravagance and vice.

24th.

I am again made happy by such a budget of letters from you and Charlotte, Lizzy, Errington, Fan and last but not least <u>Will</u> who has written a very satisfactory one in all respects - taking more care than formerly and in a good and proper frame of mind which is such a comfort to me before sailing on my distant campaign. Alexander has behaved very well in making such seasonable

1839

presents to him & Fan as well as thinking of poor Tom's[54] widow which is a great relief to me - I am sorry to hear his health has suffered so much but he will now rally I hope. Tell Mrs Mends I am very happy the matter is made up between Capt Mends and Dr Stilon in the handsomest manner. We all drank Tea on board Wm.Mendes's ship - the two families met, Capt M and the Doctor shook hands on meeting as if nothing had happened and we passed a most pleasant Evening. Thank God this will be our last trip to the Eastward as I have no doubt you will hear of our Successor in a few months more and we may expect him next April and May. You will think it a bad sign but it is not Captain Fanshawe tells me I must really have a new pair of Epaulettes and a new Undress Coat. If my Tailor in Fore Street is sure of my measure I wish him to send me one of good cloth made in his neatest way and a pair of real good Epaulettes they are so apt to tarnish here - and in the event of my being in the Levant he will direct them to the care of J.B.Collings Esq, Malta Dockyard. I am annoyed at this expense with my time so near expired, but little Crikey Fanshawe wont let me go shabby if I wished it. God Bless you dearest Margaret & give us a happy meeting - is the prayer of Your Affectionate Husband John Loudon.

26 June Malta
Addressed to Miss Fanny Loudon

You little rakish Girl - so you have been doing it nicely in gay London - with uncles and aunts & brother and I suppose by this time you have settled down quickly by the side of your <u>sedate</u> sister at Brompton. I hope you found Will improved & steady in his conduct. It was very kind in Uncle Alexander[55] to make you & Willie such a seasonable present as I have no doubt it was to each - Mamma will now be glad to see him. Will made me laugh at Aunt Eliza being anxious to pay him attention - He's a knowing fellow, Will. I am in great doubt about Mama's movements but her present plan is feasible to keep Willoughby at Plymouth till within a month of his return to College & then go to Chatham together. I am sorry you are disappointed in your French trip - but

---
54 Tom Allen, gardener at Greenwich and servant to Nelson, died in November 1838 - a subscription appeal was made for his widow.
55 Alexander Loudon, John's brother.

My Dearest Margaret...

think you will find your anticipation of never seeing it, wrong. We must not have all our good things at once - they would surfeit. I see Mrs Blount & Miss Clavell often, they are very well and very happy - a brace of fine children & a House like a Palace - and much esteemed in Society. I often wish I would have had Mamma here but that could not be, & for 3 months of the Summer at Least, she would have been overpressed with the heat - every body panting. We shall leave it however I expect tomorrow for Alexandria and other parts of the Levant where we go to keep the Peace with our Constables Staff & shall not be back in all probability till Oct or Novr but we shall receive & write Letters all the same & I hope to have your nice descriptive ones as usual. God Bless You Dearest Fran, Your Affectionate Father John Loudon.

To Fanny 29 June
Many happy returns of the day to my darling Fan. It is the Admirals Wedding day - and we meant to keep it together at a great feast of Fish in honor of St Peter by an Invitation from the Archbishop but the poor Admiral having a slight derangement of the Stomach has been prevailed upon not to go - His son James & I set out in his Caleche & distanced 8 miles where the Dinner was given in an hour. There we met the Governor & the Heads of Departments and sat Down at Three to a sumptuous Table of 20 people & to a dinner such as I never before had partaken of - Soups, roast, broiled, boiled & baked all fish in different shapes even the Jellies were fish the vegetable marrow and other vegetables stuffed with fish - being what they call a jour marigee - Wines Sherry Madeira Port Claret Champagne. After dinner we witnessed the beautiful Service in the Cathedral & then Horse races which offered us excellent mirth as they ride without saddle or bridle & lash away with two whips - the arms up like John Gilpins - We had no Ladies at the Dinner Party but plenty at the Races - at 6 we left & having a monstrous fine animal we passed everything on the road & got back at 7. Thus I spent your Birthday I hope I may spend the next with you. God Bless my dear Pet my Love to dear Arny & Liz & I have not time to write them & believe me Your affectionate Father John Loudon.

1839

1 July Princess Charlotte Malta

My Dearest Margaret

Here I am once more embarked for my last campaign I hope. We sail tomorrow morning for the coast of Egypt & Syria. I suppose we shall do our best to keep the peace between the Sultan and his Rebel Subject the Pasha. I am rather glad we are leaving the heat of Malta which is becoming rather oppressive and many diarrheas are going about, but thank God I never was better. On Saturday our dear Fan's birth day the Admiral & myself were asked to a State dinner of the Archdeacons at Civilia Vecchia the Metropolis about 8 miles in the Country - it was the Admiral's wedding day. He wished much to go but as he had a slight diarrhea Lady Stopford prevailed upon him not to go. James her Son and myself went however in his caleche & met the Governor and the Heads of Departments at their Clerical dinner which was all fish disguised in every possible way. We had Turtle Soup & Fish Soup, fried red mullet, boiled fish like cod, vegetable marrow stuffed with chopped fish innumerable other disguises of fish. Lobster Claw, Prawns, Shrimps Fish Jellies etc and lots of Sherry, Port, Madeira, Champagne & Claret. It is given once a year on St.Peter's Day by the Head of the Church to the Heads of State & knowing them all I felt very much at home seated between Bishop Lamb and the President of the University. We then went in the Church for afternoon Service where I had spoiled a New Coat nearly 40 years ago by standing under a Chandelier with wax lights - From that we adjourned to the Horse Races where they ride without Saddle or Bridle but with two whips which afforded us much amusement. It was also very amusing to see the Peasantry in their Sunburnt condition & Holy day suits. The women display all their wealth in Earrings and other trinkets & the men in Silver buttons - one country bear I saw in his new velvet Jacket with half a dozen rows of Silver filigree earrings as buttons dangling in great state but he seemed half as harried as his finery & crawled behind backs the more the others made room for his display. We left the place at 6 & were back at 7. Our dinner is regularly at 8 but I had enough for that day with the Priests. James had a curmurring[56] all yesterday but I was moderate & rather felt the good effects of a light meal.

---

56 Low rumbling in the guts.

My Dearest Margaret...

Long in now Willoughby is with you and I hope does all he can to make you comfortable - I hope he will make much of his time & take advantage of Charlotte in his French. Poor More - your favourite More is dead - one never thinks of these people going - and of a Lumbago too which nobody dies of.

9 p.m.

I am just come on board again with the Adml having dined as Lady Stopfords Guests. Tomorrow morning we must be off. God bless you dearest Margaret is the prayer of Your Affectionate Husband John Loudon.

Note for Charlotte

Dearest Charlotte - You must enjoy yourself now thoroughly with dear Mamma & Willoughby to keep you both in spirits - I dare say Jack feels himself in Commission again. I long to hear how you go on but as we are off I fear it will yet be some time though the Confrance brings our Letters. God bless you dear Lot.

Note for Willoughby

My dear Willoughby though I wrote you so recently I cannot leave this without conveying my good wishes to you & prayers for your welfare. I am sure you will not deceive my sanguine hopes for your welfare. God bless you My dear boy. Let me hear often from you and believe me ever Your Affectionate Father John Loudon. Capt Mends, Moresby & all your friends even Mahon ask kindly after you.

12 July Off Cyprus

My Dearest Margaret

I am now off the Island I was at nearly 40 years ago but we do not go on shore and are now waiting orders for our further proceedings. The Pasha of Egypt has beaten the Sultan and dispersed his army, and as if evils were never to come single the Sultan is dead[57] & we are waiting the Steamer now in sight to see what our orders may be. Affairs in the east seem drawing fast to a

---

57   Mahmud II died on July 1 and was succeeded by his 16 year-old son Abdulmecid I

1839

crisis whatever that may be and we shall soon see what part in the Drama Russia will perform. The Successor to the Throne is a boy of 17 & the people about him much in the Russian interest but it is quite impossible to speculate on these things at present. We left Malta on Tuesday the 2nd -passed Candia with a fair wind and arrived here two days ago where we are now Cruising ten miles off this beautiful Island. The weather cannot be finer nor were we ever in better health & spirits.

6p.m Our orders are come which take us to the Dardanelles.
16 July

Still off Cyprus which we were off without landing - the Confrance is now in sight with our Letters & all will be bustle immediately. The Turkish Fleet has joined the Pasha of Egypt - a strong Party is formed at Constantinople against the Captain Pasha in the Russian interest & I should not be surprised if they call in the Russians who want nothing better. The great object with the European Powers is to prevent the Ottoman Empire being broken up and then Russia coming in as a friend to add it to her already immense dominions which would give her the control of the Mediterranean. Marshal Soultsums quite warm on our side and we are now going to the Mouth of the Dardanelles off Troy where we were last year & where we shall meet the French Squadron about the same number as ourselves & see what is to turn up. As to Turkey and Egypt the affair is up - our settlement with most probably be with Russia but all at present is in the dark. As to the weather it is magnificent in fact we never think of asking what kind of a day it is for they are all alike - beautiful.

10 am.

and now I have been made happy by your delightful budget - unhappily the Steamer goes off immediately & I am full of proclamations to the Admiralty - I am much gratified to find Willoughby seems to be going on so well - God grant that he may think seriously of his time for he has more to lose to begin doing something for himself. I am sure he has abilities if he could only apply them & if he does not now he never will. I shall write him from Basika Bay when we arrive. His letter is a good one & encourages my best hopes. I have read Willoughby's College account there too

My Dearest Margaret...

they look sharp out but he has not sent me the amount of what he has drawn on my Bankers to compare with theirs & shew me how he goes on. I have very pleasing accounts from dear Eliza & Arney & I rejoice to hear Fan has had such a pleasing season in Town. Poor More - that pretty head & soft smiling face of his - all his magic notes - gone like the snapping of his fiddle string. As to your trip my dearest Margaret to Chatham I like your plan of going a little before Willoughby's term commences because it would not do so well to leave such Young House Keepers together. Charlotte should go with you I think to assist you there and back but you will arrange that together - whatever you do I know will be best. We are now off for Basika Bay[58], whence you will receive my next. God bless you dearest Margaret & with Love to Will & Char & kind regards to all our good friends. I am Your affectionate Husband John Loudon.

27 July Princess Charlotte, Paros

If I am poor by my Bankers Account (£181 in debt to them) I am rich in the receipt of your dear & Affectionate Letters of the 16, 19 & 28th of last month which I received in the 16th of this off the Island of Cyprus - and I assure you that though no doubt disheartened at the many heavy pulls at my purse things which I had anticipated when I made up my mind to sacrifice my own ease & comfort to meet them it was quite a balm to me to peruse your kind supporting feeling on the occasion & I assure you I profited much by your affectionate advice. We know the worst of Lizzie's expence & it is not more than when she was with us. Our own need not be more than usual. The Girls Allowances ought to serve - were you to see the family of the Stopfords you would say so - always proper, nothing new fangled or fine - the principal change is a Ribbon - frocks and gowns I never saw such care in - in fact Lady Stopford is quite a pattern in good plain taste and economy & nothing she thinks so vulgar as fancy; management & care they are all up to & always nice - our only heavyweight must be Willoughby & that I do not begrudge if only he knew the value of it & did his best to make a proper use of it but I am obliged to limit him to £200 a year including clothes, travelling & everything & when I

---

[58] on the coast of Asia Minor between Lemnos and Texedos

1839

lose my present salary I must bring him to £150 which with Liz is £200 a year from our Income and if we part with Jack and Jones we shall not have much to regret in them or the old cart. I agree with you visiting is the most expensive of all modes of living, the hand somehow or other is always in the pocket & fictitious wants arise on every side - kind <u>friends</u> constantly recommending what they take care not to want <u>themselves</u> but recommend <u>themselves</u> by it to their tradesmen. Willoughby will now find it necessary to look into his own affairs - examine all his Bills & avoid employing the Cambridge tradesmen who look upon the students as their game. He should get all clothes in Plymouth and London & even his groceries - who would think of his consuming £3.14.9 for Sugar and Tea in the 6 weeks from 5 Feb to the 24 March & in the Christmas quarter of 1837 (his first one) £4 - altogether since he first went £12.2.7. for groceries alone the last 6 weeks not included. I wish you would get him to explain these things to you - but this kind of information he is never ready to give in fact I scarcely think he knows himself or cares about. I have taken the trouble to abstract all his college accounts and it appears that with so much care of the body there is no time to think of the mind - but the different items are so mystically worded that it requires one to be initiated to get at the truth - there is last 6 weeks for instance to 24 March (for the last account of all I have not yet got called the Midsummer Quarter) - Commons £2.15.0 Buttery £3.5.3. Butler £2.6.0 Cook £6.3.5 in all £14.9.8 & Groceries as before £3.14.7 = £18.4.5. for 6 weeks. The expenses of Education are nothing only £2.10.0. a qr & 40 Guineas which I give extra to Mr Beatson to get him Honors in Mathematics if I can - so that you see there must be much imposition some where.

   I am just recovered from a sore mouth which I think you experienced once - the pain of I hardly think any can be greater . Capt Fanshawe remarked my right eye much blood shot - the Doctor said one of the small blood vessels had given way and applied caustic to it tying it up - this kept me some days very uncomfortable as I believe you know I see very imperfectly with the left in fact if any thing happened to the right I would neither read or write - not even distinguish a Letter - what a sad thing for your Belamour to have come home so. Thank God in about a week the absorption took place, the pupil was not affected but the

My Dearest Margaret…

Doctor thought it best to exclude the light & not to strain it. He recommended a purge of my usual dose of calomel to assist the absorption and keep the bowels open but from the weather or the draft I know not it did not act as a purgative but showed itself in my mouth, tongue & gums in the most uncomfortable manner - no toothache like it. Thank heaven all is right again & every one says I am looking clearer and better than ever. Poor Capt Mends is much disappointed at being the first picked out to go home but he will not be immediately paid off. He is much pleased with Willie's Letter in fact the fellow knows the way to peoples hearts well & has a quick discernment of character. I wish he could turn his knowledge inwards at times & examine well his own & be upon his guard against its failings none else will look out for him - if he does not for himself on the contrary that social turn of his is apt to lead him into any temptation or trap that may be laid for him. Seven & thirty years our fates have been linked together on Monday for better or worse - through many wars we have got much to be thankful for & I am sure you will agree with me that our children are a great blessing to us for which we never can be too grateful to the Almighty - and such I feel for the blessing of my Partner thro' well and woe for life, my never failing comforter & best counsellor whatever happened to me. May God Almighty continue his blessings to her & may the remaining years decreed for us to pass together be crowned with joy here & happiness hereafter. Believe me my Dearest Margaret Your ever devoted Husband John Loudon.

As soon as we have completed our water we start for our old quarter the Plains of Troy - all is peace at present. Every day now tells thank God.

4 Aug Princess Charlotte Basika Bay, Dardanelles.
We are now nearly 5 weeks from Malta & Have so far had a pleasant cruise among the Isles of Greece but have not landed on any of them. The French Squadron are here 6 sail of the line, we are 7 and looking for the Powerful, Implacable and Ganges every day as we hear they have left Malta. Your old friend Charles Napier I suppose will cut a caper among us but still my man will keep him to his bearing. The weather is here much pleasanter than at Malta in fact I am glad to put another covering on Bed at times.

1839

You cannot fancy how kind Capt Fanshawe always is to me - in fact he seems quite unhappy when I am not in his cabin and teazed me as much as a certain Lady did about my eating - nothing but plain meat, no sweet bread nor greasy made dishes. We are all very happy & the Admiral in excellent health. Mrs Duckworth, Annie & Miss Stopford at Constantinople where all is quiet. We are much in the dark as to the part we shall have to act here. I understand some proposals are sent to the Pasha of Egypt & we shall have to wait a fortnight for his answer. The Turks and Egyptians we care nothing about but if John Rusks[59] is suffered to have a finger in the Pye I should not wonder if we have a box but he will think twice or he will have an old horse about his ears. Poland & her Patrons the French & us - Sweden has a crow to pluck - Moldavia & Wallainia are sick of them - the Caucasians would then be in great force in fact they would be in a Hornets nest & I have no doubt the European Powers England, France, Prussia & Austria will at last be roused. The Turkish Admiral our old friend the Captain Pasha had a narrow escape with his head the faction in power which he says is sold to Russia having sent for him on the Sultan's death to consult upon the state of affairs and just as he was stepping in to his Boat to go he learnt his head was to be taken off and away he went to Mahomet Ali the Pasha of Egypt to come with him and arrange the Government, being acknowledged the only fit man to do it - things you see are thus in a very unsettled state - but no movement seems making at present by Russia tho all suspect her. They do say the Sultan was poisoned by an ice-cream. I scarcely believe it. He drank hard & had been very ill for some time. But this Khosrou[60] is a wretch - You should read Slade & Urquhart.

I wrote dear Will a long and I fear he would think almost an unkind Letter by the Talavera but it all proceeded from excess of anxiety about him - perhaps I expect too much but he occupies much of my thoughts & all my anxiety is now about him & his success in life poor fellow which I fear occupies little of his own at present - all is sun shine now - it will be for him to take advantage of the opportunities which have been afforded him. I am glad Fan enjoyed herself in Town & it was very nice in Willoughby to make himself useful to her while he was there. I fear we were too soon

---

59 Russia
60 Khosrou is the Grand Visir (or Prime Minister) of Turkey

My Dearest Margaret...

in Willoughby travelling he had not been enough initiated in his College studies - was not fitted for travelling - having no knowledge of French and upon the whole it might rather unsettle his mind than prepare it for severe study. All the Plains of Troy are now spread out before me & we might suppose ourselves & the French laying along the shore the old Greek Fleet & my good Admiral old Agamemnon but in place of old Priams Palace we have the Castles of the Dardanelles with 320 Cannon grinning along the passage - no fear of them however so long as the Russians are kept out. I am writing upon short warning - we only anchored here last night & are now sending a Steamer to Malta to bring our Letters which we shall receive as regularly as ever only 8 days later - the great drawback is that you will have mine smoked - a greate nuisance - I am obliged to limit my allowance to Willoughby to £200 a year everything included & have written my Banker to that effect. I find it impossible to go on otherwise so he will have to avoid all unnecessary expenses which I was obliged to do all my life & thought it no hardship as you know. I fear I shall not be able to write Lizzie but I will try - love to dear Charlotte & Will & kindest regards to the Daviess. God bless you my dearest Wife and believe me ever your most affectionate husband John Loudon.

13 Aug Princess Charlotte off Troy
We got a great accession to our force by the Powerful, Ganges & Implacable & the Daphne 18 Gun Sloops making 16 as beautiful Ships of the Line as you ever saw - the Castor Frigate, Dido, Hazard, Beacon & with a line of Battle ships under Admiral Lalande - the fields of Troy never were so well lined even in the days sung by old Homer. The French and us all on the most friendly terms - dining with one another daily - & ready for anything our Ambassadors may wish - but I have no idea we shall move further up than we are towards Constantinople where all is quiet & the Admiral & myself are going up tomorrow in the Confrance to call upon Lord Ponsonby our ambassador & see as near as we can the actual state of affairs - we shall be away about a week or ten days & our Headquarters will be in the Confrance or Carisfort now there. Our old friend the Captain Pasha I fear is a Traitor & has run off with his Fleet to the Pasha of Egypt to whom it is however of no use but rather a burden. The Captain Pasha and the old Prime

1839

Minister Khosrou have long been at daggers drawn, as well as the young Sultan whom it is said the Captain Pasha's Mother tried to poison when an infant in a milk posset - but being suspected it was given to a slave girl who drank it and died. Achmet the Captain Pasha was sent for on the death of the Sultan, but either having or pretending to have a hint that his head was to be taken off he ran away with the Fleet. You may have heard of Captain Walker who went on their service he returned to Constantinople where he has the same employ under the new Government as under the old. Mrs Duckworth, Annie & Miss Stopford are all at Constantinople where they have taken lodgings for a month and are much amused. We shall see them in a day or two as we set off tomorrow morning. I am not given to fatigue myself now in sightseeing though I could not resist going to a high Town we see from the Ship in the middle of the plain which gave a most splendid view of the magnificent scenery round. Young Acland, Willoughby's travelling companion has made a Panorama of it from the same point & I am told all Oxford is quite interested in it, he will besides make some thousand Pounds by it - this is to travel for some purpose & Acland was a Capital Draftsman among his other qualifications. I wrote dear Willoughby rather out of humour by the Talavera because I saw Marks of great carelessness about him but his last Letter careful & well written has much redeemed him & replaced him in my good opinion. He has however much before him this winter if he do not distinguish himself I shall begin to despair. If you are going on your visit I think I see you setting about it & hope you will have a fine day to go on board the Steamer. I suppose the Chatham folks are gone to the Brothers at Colchester. The Adml is in excellent health but I led him a dance the other Evening through Scotch Aromatics as he called the thistles which pricked all his legs & we were not able to accomplish my Tumulus after all as we set out too late & he walked so slow & heavy after dinner - but he was no worn worse next day. I am sorry to hear poor Alexanders health is so delicate[61]. I wrote Sturlez the other day by the French Steamer, having received a very kind Letter from him & I was more sure of a Letter finding him than my Brother. Our time is now drawing fast in & I may take leave of Troy Greece & all these far famed scenes

---

61   Alexander, Loudon's brother, died in September

of former grandeur of which the most stupendous are still left but I shall gladly bid them adieu & return with a light heart to my own dear Partner & happy House. God bless you dearest Margaret Your affectionate Husband John Loudon.

31 August, Rhadamanthus from Constantinople. Basika Bay
I have had a very pleasant time here and certainly never saw so beautiful a spot - I am obliged to tell you - My dearest Margaret - that I was obliged from the force of circumstances to mount a Horse & fall into the Procession with the Admiral and a party about 20 going at a snails pace on the Sultans stud to the Mosques which as a special favour the Admiral had a Firman or order to see - that of St. Sophia was a Christian Church & many relics are left notwithstanding the Mahometan acts to alter or deface them - we then saw the Seraglio or Palace & a most beautiful spot it is almost like those we read of in oriental tales but I have very little time to descant on these matters as the moment we get through the Passage of the Dardanelles which we are now in this Ship starts for Malta & I shall be all bustle on my return on Board getting ready the Despatches. I have enjoyed myself very much though the outside beauty alone pleases, the streets are horrid but the Houses, though all of wood, very comfortable within. I dined twice with the Ambassador - we had an audience of the Grand Vizir ten days ago Khosrou Pasha, & yesterday of the Young Sultan himself a Young Man of 17 marked with the Small Pocks but having a good expression. I could not help observing the Stage effect with which he was prepared to receive us - reclining on the Corner of a Sopha with a huge mantle spread out along the Sopha so as to give a greater extension to his figure. Many compliments passed through which he was assisted by the Seraskier, or General of the Army, his Brother in Law who took us through the splendid apartments of the Palace & entertained us with Coffee and Sherbet. The small Coffee cups of the finest China in stands of Gold with sprigs of brilliants.

But now you will say what are you doing with two Fleets of near 20 sail of the Line at the Mouth of the Dardanelles - nothing - The Admiral tried hard to get the Turkish Government to ask us up - but it says no - the five European Powers are all united to preserve the integrity of the Empire and it would only breed all blood with

1839

Russia to see us at Constantinople & serve no purpose whatever - they are willing to give Mehemet Ali the Inheritance of Egypt in his family but he is determined to keep Syria as well & that would make him too formidable a Vassal. The Admiral's friend the Capt. Pasha has astonished us much by joining him, but not against Turkey to which both of them profess the great fidelity as well as to the Sultan - their mortal enemy is Khosrou Pasha the present Visir or Prime Minister who they say would betray the Country to Russia & that there can be no safety or tranquility while he remains in Office. Mehemet Ali is 70 & Khosrou 80 years of age - the latter was a slave bought in the market - the former a dealer in Tobacco & both had befriended & opposed one another during their whole lives. I suspect we shall have to demand the fleet to be given up which he had no right to receive during the Truce that had taken place. But they can be of no use to him & will not in the least change the determination of the five Powers - four of which at least consider it a European question & that Turkey should not fall into the Hands of any one great Naval Power which would lock us out of the Dardanelles & Black Sea & control us in the Mediterranean. I fear however it will yet be a tedious question as no two entirely agree as for coming to blows I see no likelihood of it whatsoever. I should say in addition to the other was this - the Captain Pasha was not many years ago a Waterman on the river whom the late Sultan saw & noticed. I saw too the end of all his greatness - His Body on a temporary scaffold under a Tent till the ground is prepared for his Mausoleum. He was a great favorite with the Franks but not so with the Musselmen whose prejudices he has broken in upon. His death was caused by drinking which many of the Turks are too much given to - but the works he has left behind him will establish his character as one of the most enlightened Sovereigns who has sat on the Ottoman throne - This I feel is a very unsatisfactory Letter I will write you soon. I hope more to the purpose - Perhaps you are now at Chatham & so give my love to our dear Charlotte - I was rejoiced with the accounts of Colchester Dear Charlotte I hope will keep all right during your absence and Willoughby I trust will resume his studies with fresh vigour.

My Dearest Margaret…

1 Sept 10 am
Just returned on Board with the Admiral & Capt Fanshawe & glad to get back after nearly three weeks wandering - all well. My faithful Palmer always with me keeping every thing in order - I am now ready for my Epaulettes - God bless you My dearest Margaret - Love to all Your Affectionate Husbd John Loudon.

8 Sept Princess Charlotte, Basuki Bay
Here we are still a noble fleet of 18 sail of the Line doing nothing but ready for anything. The Plains of Troy never echoed to so much firing as we make in exercising at Marks & so forth and a more animating sight cannot be seen than this wood of ships by the shores of the most picturesque country in the world. The weather too is delightful not a bit too warm & almost every other day I take a walk to some ruin or tumulus & come off regularly to dinner. Yesterday I had a very pleasant short walk with the Admiral for I must not take him a long walk. We have plenty of game too but I do not go on shooting expeditions - enough for me to praise the sport by making my mark in the Teal, Wild Ducks, Partridges, Snipes & Quails at table. We have lost today a fine young man whom Willoughby I am sure will much regret a Mr Overden who always attended the Admiral & family in the Barge - at the time liberty was given to see Constantinople there being no opportunity of a vessel in and a few more went by land - a journey of 3 days in a hot sun & with no accommodation by night. Soon after his return he was seized with a brain fever three days delirium - he breathed his last today at 12 o'clock very much lamented.

We have another sad case poor Sir Wm Haste one of our Lieutenants in the last stage of consumption in the next cabin to mine & coughing & wheezing in such a manner that it is quite painful to hear him. I have persuaded him to write his Mother who is now in Naples not aware of his dangerous state & it is very sad to see a young man hastening to his grave without I believe the least idea of it though he is as weak as water & his lungs very much affected - with a terrible noise at times from the tubes being shut up. Such is man - a machine - or at most a bare shadow. I wonder if Willoughby is still with you & if you are yet at Chatham - Whatever you do will be right for me. I had a nice walk James Stopford to day over 12 miles of the plains of Troy. We landed at 11 & came off at half past 3 at 5 we all dined with the French Admiral Lalande and met Prince Joenville who had dined here before a very nice young man & much improved in appearance and manner since I saw him at Plymouth. I am now winding up the day by writing you. I wrote Willoughby under strong feelings on the receipt of my Bankers Account - I have more reason to be satisfied with him since & his last letter pleased me much God grant he may turn out well for no expense or care has been spared upon him & did he know my anxiety he would strive to do his best. How happy I am to have such daughters of whom I am really proud and all my accounts from Chatham make me quite happy. This goes in such a way that I cannot write dear Liz as it is by a French Steamer directed to Collings. Lou is not married nor likely as far as I know - she is a sweet girl & a general favorite - but she won't have the rich merchant with a Palace to put her in. I wish <u>Fan</u> were here for him - she would ride in her own Carriage & laugh at Papa & old Jack. Love to dear Will & Charlotte. Your affect. Husband J.Loudon

13 Sept Princess Charlotte Basuki Bay
Yesterday brought me a rare treat in your dear letters by Gorgon, as well as the Coat and Epaulettes which were beginning to be wanted as I find myself among so many Great folks, at present Turks, French and all sorts and as you say I ought to think a little of outside appearance which go far among strangers. Capt Fanshawe is a good Mentor in that and many other respects -a regular male edition of you. You would laugh to see him give me a slap on the back when stooping & give me a look at table & set up his own head according to your former use and want. He is indeed a good natured fellow or he would often be put out at my short feisty manner to him. No! No! Johnny it won't do, ye shant make me angry I dont mind you you know! and so on we go. We are still here waiting orders - one says yes and the other no, so that we scarcely know what to be at. My own opinion is it will all go off quietly. We are very cordial with our French friends at present & I think the French Government the wisest of the two - the Turkish Fleet is of no use to Mehemet Ali but a burden to him to support them & he would I think be glad of a pretext to get rid of them - they are very discontented - the whole is from the hatred towards

My Dearest Margaret...

Khosrou the Grand Visir - were he to resign there would be little further difficulty - but what I most fear will be dissension in the Cabinets which in the end may involve us with Russia, although she has too much to lose to go to war if she can help it. We had no instructions when he came on the coast - and the victory by Ibrahim Pasha, the Sultan's death & the cessation of hostilities with Mehemet Ali's offering his duty immediately to the young Sultan so changed matters that we had no idea of interfering with their family arrangements if we had ever been in the way - in fact it might have led to the destruction of the ships we were ordered to protect - at least so though the Admiral when I asked him if he did not mean to go to Alexandria. I wish, however, it had been otherwise. He thought too well I fear of his friend the Captain Pasha.

I am sorry dear Charley sent the Atlas as I fear she will miss it but we shall soon be all together again & all will be right. The new Epaulettes are beautiful & will make me quite a Dandy but the Coat though very nice I am sorry to say is rather too large for me so you will see I am not fitted out nor ever will be I think - but I am better perhaps than if I were of too full a habit. I am sorry the Talavera was ordered back as she had letters for you all - & a long one to Will - whom I am obliged to restrict to £200 a year I fear it will be a difficult task to give him a proper idea of the value of money till he comes to earn it himself & that I suspect he will not do for many a day. - in fact he appears to have an antipathy to all severe study, which I think he may not have reason to repent as there is no road to distinction without it particularly in the Law - but we must hope the best. As to travelling again he must not think of it till he can do it at his own expense.. My Dear Lotty will excuse me not writing her separately. I am very busy & the letters are smoked at Malta but I am delighted with hers and Willoughbys which are both very clever & characteristic. Palmer continues the same steady fellow as ever. I hope his Father will see his error & reform.

1839

14 Sept
    The vessel just going - all well. A fine French frigate the Bellepoule just arrived for Prince Joinville[62] - Willoughby will be sorry to hear of poor Overdens death. He had gone up to Constantinople by land & with the sun & night damp I suppose was taken ill & died delirious. God Bless you my dearest Margaret Your afft. Husband J Loudon.

23 Sept Princess Charlotte Basika Bay
    Here we are still knowing as little what we are to be about & perhaps less than you do in England - However we form a brilliant Squadron French and English 20 Sail of the Line. The Rhadamanthus our friend Capt Wakefield joined yesterday from Malta bringing me your valued Letters up to the 2nd. - you may imagine what a treat they are in this monotonous place - for one cannot feed on Troy for ever. I have had several excursions over the Plains - the last with a very pleasant Party Sir Henry Barnard, Lord Rokeby and Mr Kay who was Secretary to Lord Melville & a great friend of Sir Wm Burnetts. They have travelled over Egypt and my old ground the Holy Land and left us yesterday to pursue their route by the Seven Churches. I suppose by this time you are at Chatham & enjoying dear Liz & Errington's company which I too long for very much. Poor Will how sorry I am for him but your concluding paragraphs give me great hopes. I fear much he is too careless of himself. I must say I was mortified he has taken such a dislike to Mathematics for which I laid out so much money thinking he excelled in that through his friend to whom I am paying 40 guineas a year. However he must just take his chance - & God send all may turn out well. It was a great disappointment to poor Capt Mends to be turned back at Gibraltar & again ordered back but the most unpleasant part is a Court Martial on Lieut. Hennah who he has brought up from a boy & who had come to high words with him about a point of duty - a sort of Lovers Quarrel & neither would give in, the consequence is a Court Martial of which I am to be Judge & Advocate tomorrow. I wish them both well out of it. My health I assure you dearest Margaret never was better &

---

62   Prince Joinville, son of Louis-Philippe, the King of France, joined the Jupiter under Admiral Lalande at Toulon in March 1839, returning to Toulon at the end of December.

every thing comfortable about me - still I yearn for my dear Home - nothing like home. I have generally a very idle life but it comes in great bustle at times & such is the case now. In two or three days more we shall be quiet again. Will you make my excuses for not writing my dear Charlotte Liz & Arney & Fanny this time - I really have much in hand - I get on very well with Young a supernumery clerk who has been always with me and young Couch who is very clever and useful, eldest like dear Eliza - no small praise - What a treat & compliment to Errington to be at the Duke's Banquet - Brougham's speech was superb.

30 Sept Princess Charlotte. Basouki Bay

You will think it odd to receive 2 letters from me at such distant dates by the Talavera but such is the uncertainty of things at the present moment that the Talavera was ordered back to join us after she had got as far as Gibraltar on her way home & still more odd she brought Admiralty Letters by the Packet from Malta to order her home again - certainly our Ministry hardly know what to be at. The Turks will not consent to our going up the Dardanelles for fear of giving offence to Russia & we cannot molest the Pasha of Egypt whose ships with the Turkish Fleet are snug in the Harbour of Alexandria. So here we are doing nothing with the French Fleet assisting us. We are all very comfortable however & generally healthy except Willy's friend Mr Overden who died very suddenly of over fatigue & Willoughby Lake who is now down with a bad cold. The weather is much changed & I am to put a coverlet on my Bed tonight - many are now wearing blues. My health never was better I have had two heavy Courts Martial but what would I not do for my family. The first day I wrote 8 hours without moving off my chair - 64 pages which I have just finished copying fairly to the Admiralty. It was upon Lt Hennah of the Talavera charged by Capt Mends with neglect of duty disobedience of orders & disrespect. It was not proved & he was acquitted - pity 'twas ever brought forward - our old friend Agassid whom you remember a midshipman with me in South America wishing to go home has changed with him & goes home in Talavera. He is now married to a connexion of the Tuckers of Trematon Castle[63] & says he will

---
63 Near Saltash, Cornwall

1839

call upon you & say how he left me. I need not say it will please me your paying him some attention. Willie owes something to all the Pembrokes his former ship Capt Mends had been most kind & we never can forget his attention to Will. I suppose before you receive this Willie will again be at College - I hope he will profit by it though I begin <u>not</u> to be sanguine. The festival at Dover must have been superb. How the Duke must have felt but he must have hardy nerves for nothing puts him out - through good report and evil report he is still the same imperturbable Duke of Wellington. It is odd that Errington should be working away as Judge Advocate at Maidstone & I here. My last was upon a drunken engineer of a Steamer who was broke - this extra work gives me £10 but it is a severe fag - what will one not do for ones family - enough of that.

I think with pain of our long separation & pray God to continue his unmerited blessings to us to shed his merciful bounties on our evening rays so that we may make up for all by gone evils by a happy close of life together - but I must not yield to my present mood - a few months more will soon turn over & I know the grass wont grow under the feet of our successor - such a man as Sir Robert is not to be met with & I am as comfortable with him as I can be away from my own home - still home is home. If I can I mean to go over the Plains of Troy with Captain Mends & Captain Austen but I fear I shall have too much work. 10 Sail of the Line 17 in all is no sinecure for me. Yet all goes easy & light & I am my own master more than I ever was in my life. We have much amusement here with your old acquaintance Capt Napier whom I am very partial to as a downright honest independent man - but very restless & anxious to do something right or wrong. We have a very nice fellow in Captain Sharpe and another in Knox - in fact all the Captains are most worthy excellent fellows - Griffen too looks well & comes often to see me but he has not the tact to make himself liked. I would have sent Batson his Bill but he has not made my coat well & I shall deduct what it cost me to make it fit.

1st. *Oct*

Not a word of News. Capt Mends is just going he will tell you how he leaves me. I hope dear Will is recovered again but I much fear he does not act prudently - in fact I am far from easy about him. I had a long letter for him by Talavera but I fear it was rather

My Dearest Margaret…

severe & as she brought it back I do not send it. I am my dearest Margaret your ever affectionate Husband John Loudon.

21 Oct Princess Charlotte, Basika Bay
I have just received your dear Letters & Charlottes and thank God you are all well - I am really glad you did not take that fond but mad trip to Chatham at so late a season. It would have thrown you out terribly besides risque of discomfort of all kinds & I am sure Lizzie could not be do unreasonable as to feel disappointed, more particularly as you are to meet soon in your own snug dwelling. Poor Willie I hope his Boils are really over and that there is no fear of a return. His health is delicate & the worst of it is he does not think so & will not take care of himself. We are now on the point of moving to Smyrna where we have a snug anchorage now the wintry weather is coming on for when matters will come to a settlement we know less than ever. We ought to have allowed the Sultan and Viceroy to have settled their own affaire & it would have been done long ago. It is said the 5 powers have different views and that the French and us do not quite sail in the same boat but here we are on the most cordial terms[64]. The Admiral and all of us dined with the French Admiral on Saturday and a very nice pleasant Party we always have there. You will now soon see Capt Mends my most kind & steady friend. I have a Letter from him saying he leaves Malta the 25th. We learned the news of Sir Thomas' death a while ago & I have now a Letter from Jessop with the particulars. My good Admiral expects the appointment certainly & it would be of great use to his large family, but in these jobbing times he fears it will be given for some party purpose & I am much feared about my countryman Fleming whom all the world knows to be a cunning fellow of great weight with the Scotch Lord and Sir Charles Adam. Even if Sir Robert gets it I do not expect to be home till Spring though I do assure you nothing would delight me more than to be with you by Christmas, never on any account to leave my happy fireside again. It affords me many a pleasant hour to think of the happiness there awaiting me, though we cannot hope to have the delightful Evenings again in the midst of all the dear Girls - but I must not go on with this.

---

64 French support of Mehemet Ali was to cause diplomatic problems in 1840.

1839

I shall not forget your Commissions be assured & I am pleased things look so well up as to one coming home but the Admiral is not sanguine as to Greenwich - nor am I to tell you the truth. We are off for Voulca tomorrow & I think the Admiral will not be long from Malta. My Admiral has had a ride with me over the Plains of Troy & was highly gratified - the poor worn out Horses of the Country at a walk but very sure footed - & we were going in the Zebra Commander Stopford's Brig the other day to a famous ruin of a Town built in honor of Alexander the Great but the weather got rough and we gave it up.

22 Oct

The Hastings has at last joined us making us 11 Ships of the Line the Benbow Belleisle & Edinburgh are daily expected making 14 but the Minden then goes to Plymouth & the Pembroke to Portsmouth leaving 12 Line of Battle here. We start to morrow for snugger quarters at Voulca where we were last year but no Malta for us I fear for sometime - God Bless you I must close this indeed I write by patches - I shall scrawl a few lines to Charlotte. Ever your Affectionate Husband John Loudon.

My dearest Lottie. I cannot help taking up a part of dear Mamma's Letter to thank you for your very nice Epistle which accompanied hers though you appeared to be busily occupied with your young & amiable friends the Bresners and dear Georgie of whom you give such pleasing accounts. I assure you your Letters are so pleasing accounts that they always set me a laughing & my frolicsome friend Captain Fanshawe who is very curious torments me to tell him what is the matter. We go on in the same happy way on board as ever and dull as this place is we make it out well but to morrow we change the scene to Voulcah our old quarters till this tiresome affair is ended, or we receive fresh orders. I am glad Mamma wisely staid at home. Twas so like her that I was sure it would be so & she did right to let well alone. God bless you dear Charlotte Your affect Pa J Loudon.

1 Nov Princess Charlotte Voulca

My Dearest Margaret

As I was rather hurried in my last from Basika Bay I am determined upon being beforehand this time as when the Packet goes all my bustle comes in at once. This is a spacious beautiful Anchorage very superior to Basika Bay which is not safe in Winter & as I see no possibility of our going to Malta till this tiresome affair is settled we lay as snugly & comfortably here as in any harbour in England. We have delightful walks in the Country the most rich and beautiful I ever saw & the only regret is to see so fine a country almost a desert - you may walk for miles and not see a single creature - there are two or three wretched Greek villages & at about 6 miles is the Town of Voulca on a fine elevated situation but like all the rest dirty & miserable within. The Admiral, Capt Fanshawe, James Stopford & myself rode there two days ago & were well received by the Governor a gentlemanly Turk who entertained us with Pipes, Coffee & Sherbet and showed us the New Hot Baths he was building, which are very fine particularly the Ladies Part, quite distinct from the Gentlemans - the saloon of which is fitted up with Divans all round for the Ladies to gossip & take their refreshments. It is to be ready in 8 days when the Admiral is to have due notice. The Horses are like lamas most tractable & sure footed & never exceed a gentle trot, 4 miles an hour. I feel quite set up with the considerate view you take of my mounting at Constantinople & I assure you I use the greatest caution when I am obliged to do so with the Admiral, never by chance using speed in fact the Horses here are small, not strong, & have no vice, nor are there any roads over which they could gallop, all being pathways among shrubs and bushes which the whole country is covered. You will not catch me riding at Malta.

Our last accounts take away all hope of my poor Admiral having Greenwich at which he is sorely vexed & disappointed for it is just the place for his large family & was besides his Birthright but it was a sad break in on the old custom when Sir Thos Hardy got it over the head of the old Admirals & altho it was excused on account of the man, it made a bad precedent & there is no such excuse for Admiral Fleeming whose services are nothing but serving himself & who never saw a shot fired in anger. It will be a sad disappointment to Lady Stopford & her Daughters tho I believe she wisely thinks it may be all for the best as he had the chance of being Vice Admiral of England which he could not then take but this is all well enough when the Grapes are sour. I am very sorry for it for her sake.

1839

5*th*. Nov

Dear Willoughby's Birth day poor fellow I hope he will now think seriously of life & apply himself to take his part with credit. He is yet too fond of pleasure but let us hope the best. Your dear Letter up to the 10th of last month was a great treat to me & I rather wanted it at the time as I was worried about a Court Martial to sit the next day (yesterday) upon a young man, a Mate of the Castor, for being off deck in his Watch. It was unlucky for him the Captain came on Board unexpectedly at 3 o'clock in the morning in a shore boat from Smyrna & found not a creature on Deck, the Mate in charge below, & the quarter master & sentries either off deck or asleep. I tried hard to get him off but Capt Collier said he could not punish the men & let the Officer go free, so there was nothing for it & the young man expected to be dismissed the Service which he said would break his mothers heart already half broken. She is the Byron's sister and Leigh (for this is the young mans name) Lord Byrons nephew, his Father commanded the 10th Hussars in the Peninsular War & his Grandfather was the celebrated circumnavigator Admiral Lord Byron - so we never know what is to happen to our posterity. The trial came on yesterday, 13 Post Captains & myself as Judge Advocate in full uniform - great curiosity in a Fleet of about 20 vessels small & large in the Bay. The poor young man with his sword taken from him and laid on the Table & the Provost Martial with a drawn sword beside him - a tall fine looking strippling of three & twenty, ten years in the service, four of which passed for Lieut. He acknowledged his offence but the Evidence was gone into that the Court might judge of the degree of the offence. He had lain down on the top of his Hammock but with all his clothes even his cap on & started at the instant he heard the bustle of the Captain on board - alas too late - "Go down below Sir this is the last time you shall do duty in the Castor or any other Ship" when called upon however yesterday at the Court to speak to his character he said he was a zealous efficient attentive officer except on that occasion & that he had not before found fault or had any complaint of him - the Court was then aloud to deliberate - I am sworn not to divulge any individual opinions, the youngest member gives his first & so up to the President Commander Parker & I assure you the fair & impartial good feelings I have always perceived among them (&

My Dearest Margaret...

this is the fourth Court Martial I have attended) is beautiful & does them great credit. The opinions given, I draw up the Sentence which they all sign. The Bell is rung "Officer of the Court" a Lieutenant in attendance appears - the Court is open - Prosecutor and Prisoner with the drawn sword by his side, the Witnesses & audience rush in making a muffled sort of bustle, you hear a sort of rushing noise - "Judge Advocate" says the President "call over the Names of the Witnesses". That done I stand up at the foot of the Table, the poor Prisoner by me, all in suspense, & here is the provoking part of it, that I have to read three pages of nonsensical form - Titles of the Admiral a yard long, names of 13 Members, Preamble to an Act of Geo IInd & then comes "the Court finds the Charge <u>proved</u> & judges the Prisoner to be severely reprimanded & incapable of promotion for 2 years - what a relief - he expected to be dismissed. I dont know why I should always identify myself with every body's ills but I felt so worried for two or three days that I could hardly sleep, it only happened on the 30th last month. God bless you dearest Margaret your affect. husband J.Loudon.

20 Nov Princess Charlotte. Voulca Bay

Last night the Packet brought in your welcome Budget as usual full of kind and good feeling and of that piety and trust in Providence which bears us in the midst of all our ills. I am sadly disappointed at Sir Robert not getting his Birthright but our comfort is that he is so much disgusted he cares not how soon he is superseded and I have even great trouble dissuading him from going to Malta as he says there is nothing for us to do here. I do believe he will go next week leaving the squadron under Commander Parker, but I shall do all I can to keep him at his Post a little longer for although we can do nothing without orders our being on the spot ready to strike a blow when necessary and if any mischance were to happen in his absence he would never get over it. Besides we are as comfortable here as at Malta but he does not think so. The French are with us and all Cordial as ever. You may well suppose I have had enough to do with 12 ships of the line and many changes besides a Squadron of upwards of 40 Sail in the Mediterranean. Young Couch and another being all my help but they are very valuable, quick and industrious and my work is only heavy at times. I am obliged my dear Margaret to write you by patches as I can. I suppose if I have had one I have had 100 openings of my door and half the Captain's officers of the Squadron besides the Admiral sending for me every minute so you must not expect any very connected matters here. You will now soon have one dear pet Liz and her worthy Husband with you saying nothing of my dear Fan whose morning feats quite astonish me. I am sorry for Willoughby's mishaps, poor fellow, I fear something is wrong and am very anxious to hear but he never writes. We must just as you say hope the best having done our duty. It was very fortunate he was in such a good quarters so there are few evils without some remedy. If the Doctor's protegé young Norman of Talavera calls be kind to him on the Doctor's account. He is a fine youth himself. I congratulate you on getting rid of that clown Jones. I hope your present boy will answer your purpose though he must be rather awkward at first. Old Jack is the great drawback for a new Servant - I wonder the old brute wears so well. I amuse myself very much in my solitary cell thinking of you all round your cheerful fire in Durnford Street and wonder often how one can give up the liberty and superiority of ones own fireside for any other consideration whatever but the thought of a Provision for ones family conquers all. Here I am at no expense whatever. You will now see my good friend Capt Mends &, when you do, remember me most kindly to him for he is a kind friend and will tell you long stories of Will. The weather is now pretty cold and I am glad of Winter clothing which we have had these two months. We are all very happy but I shall be truly so when I once more get alongside my dearest wife and the chimney corner. God Bless my ever dearest Margaret your affectionate Husband John Loudon.

Enclosure to Charlotte
My Dear Lotty
 Reading as I always do with a hungry appetite dear Mama's Letters first, yours be it known to you come in like a nice dessert after a rich feast for there is always something to please the palate after the Gizzard has had its due. Still the subject in your last was sad sad & I hope it will be many a day before you have to touch upon such another. Poor Alexander after all his cares & all his striving it comes to this at last - still he had the consolation of not leaving his offsprings to the buffettings of a cold heartless world. I

My Dearest Margaret…

find Peter Joseph is his Executor & hear he is to return to Holland for the purpose. It showed great confidence in him on the part of Alexander & I have no doubt he will execute his trust as becomes him. How odd he should preach in the Church I first attended & well I remember the Pew under the Gallery I used to be put upon with my back to the Minister & my face & restless legs to my poor Mother who gave me many a look, many a shake of the head & many a pat for not sitting still - a sin I was often guilty of - all - all now gone. They have treated my poor Admiral scurvily - it was his birthright Greenwich - Then such are the Whigs - a merry Christmas dear Lot, your affectionate Father John Loudon.

29 Nov Princess Charlotte, Voulca Bay
My Dearest Margaret

    We are exactly in the same situation as when I wrote you a week ago & have not a word of news but the weather is beautiful & we enjoy our walks on shore very much which we take almost every after noon. The Admiral at our head walks like a Trojan. I went yesterday to the pretty town of Voulca about seven miles off & from the heights over it saw the towering hills of the Isle of Samos, off Ephasus on the otherside. I never beheld a finer prospect or a richer country but wretchedly inhabited and no wonder under the late Turkish Laws. The Governors buy their places and then reimburse themselves by the most arbitrary exactions on the people but a new law has just been published putting an end to such arbitrary conduct & establishing every man's right of life and property and laying down an equal system of laws for the whole, rich and poor, Turk, Jew & Christian. The Country is all a Jubilee for this Charter of Liberty & I think in a few years more this fine sand will again revive from the deathlike sleep at present. It is a very odd circumstance that a Party of four of our officers went to visit Ephasus a month ago & about a week after their return they were all seized with Fever & one is at the moment despaired of, Mr North, Willoughby knows him. The others were not expected to recover but all now in a pretty fair way. The rains had set in and they were caught.

1839

Sunday 1 Dec.

We had yesterday St.Andrews Day Captain Napier & Captain Houston Stewart with a Highland Piper playing the Pibroch[65] & other Scotch lilts round the table to the disorganisation of our Englishman's ears but yet it was a melancholy one to me so long away from my own fireside. I thought of you deeply & had your health drank by all the Party - another thing keeps me down is a Court Martial tomorrow on one of Captain Napier's men for Mutinous Expression & shaking his Superior Officer which is death. I fear the fellow will run great risk of being hanged. One thing my health is excellent & I only hope to be early back to you never again under any inducement to leave my dear Home.

3 Dec.

I had a hard days work yesterday from 8 till 4. The poor man was condemned to be Hanged & I had the pain of reading the Sentence. The Article of War is like Admiral Byngs there is no alternative. The Court were very reluctant but could not help themselves. We found, however, the poor man had some years ago fallen from the Rigging of the Naiad and hurt his head & upon that they recommended him to mercy. I have just drawn up a Letter from the Admiral to the Admiralty with the sentence & backing up the recommendation commuting the Punishment to Transportation or in such way as their Lordships may think fit. The State of this Squadron not requiring so severe an example I should be distressed if it were not granted. In fact these Courts Martial worry me & I have nothing to do with them in Malta & need not here unless I like. The £4 for each is dearly won. How soon spent without thinking of it I hope there will be no more. But why inflict my cares among your happy Christmas circle - I have only one more on hand two Deserters from Griffens Ship the Ganges - I expect this will be trifling & then I hope Goodbye to them. The Admiral is very anxious to get to Malta poor man & we have much ado to keep him back. I trust he will have permission soon from the Admiralty & then he is safe.

---

65   Traditional music for Highland bagpipes.

My Dearest Margaret...

Tues 3 Dec 9 p.m.

Our Packet goes in the morning and I am so busy preparing for a Court Martial on two fellows of the Ganges who seemed to have intended to desert in an American Merchant man, that I shall not be able to write as I wished to dear Lizzie & Arney but hoping they are now with you one Letter must do for all. I know not how it is everybody tries to make me happy & yet I am not so, for I repine on being so very long separate from you though it was meant for our Children but I begin to see that his is all nonsense for the more we do for them the more they may expect though I do flatter myself this is not the case with ours. The Admiral is the same nice man as ever but dreadfully sick of our present work. I would not have him commit himself however on any account. Capt Fanshawe quick as a Brother, in fact nothing is wanting to make me comfortable except you. God send we may be soon together. I have been dreaming about dear Willie - glad when I awoke. I suppose he is with you when you receive this which I suppose will be about Christmas. What a happy fireside - I think I see you all - Your dear self on the Armchair and your happy faces around you. I see no end to our work but we lie snugly though we have not the Malta or any other society of any kind & the finest views fade without that. I want none - no. 44 is meat and drink to me. Capt Lawrence is not quite well & his sons conduct I fear is mainly the cause of it however he begins to rally. What a sad thing it is for a Father. I am now longing to hear from you. God Bless You dearest Margaret My Love to all about you. Ever affectionate Husband John Loudon.

on the outside of the envelope in another hand.... My dear Mrs Loudon. Don't you listen to the good old man - he is just as well as ever, only bothered with a couple of Courts Martial and has not had his glass of whiskey tonight because I have been dining out Rodney a merry dinner. Lord! a Glass of whiskey I have not tasted one but on St Andrews day when Captain Stewart and his Bagpipes were on board.

20 Dec Princess Charlotte Voulca Bay

Your dear letters of the 20th with Charlottes and Harrys & Willoughbys and Erringtons and Elizas and Fannys are all come to hand together, and in this Bay too; many leagues from the world. You may well judge of the delight all this has given me - to think you are all in the old House enjoying these Christmas times so happily together adds greatly to mine. Both Capt Fanshawe and myself have been doing all we can to keep dear Sir Robert at his Post & I even ventured to write Miss Stopford not to tempt him to Malta till he could go with flying Colours - He heard from them to day - what they said I don't know but he is not going in. Indeed I have a Letter from Miss S saying thay dare not wish it - but it is a great disappointment to the Ladies who came out lately to be all the Winter with their Husbands - Mrs Houston Stewart & Mrs Reynolds. We are not however to be pitied & I would rather wander about this beautiful Scenery than be in Malta. The Admiral Capt Fanshawe James & I take a Saunter of about 3 hours every day. I have just been at Smyrna to a Ball given to the Archduke Frederic of Austria & a very gay but crowded concern it was - about 300 Ladies Greeks Armenians & Franks which they call the English French Italians Germans all handsome but the Greeks and Armenians I am sorry to say cut the Franks out all to pieces. I dined that day with the Consul who Ready asked me the moment I arrived to meet their new Turkish Governor & the Heads of the Government after which we adjourned to the Ball which was so crowded that there was no room for dancing. At half past 11 I came away Captain Napier kindly took a Room for me inside his own in the Swisse Hotel & we stopt 2 days together when I returned on board & he went with a Party hunting the wild Boar, very Common in the woods here. The Admiral did not go but sent me up in the Dido which waited & brought me back - which I was more glad to do than to go for it is a dirty stupid place & I wonder it is ever clear of plague being in the middle of a swamp and stuff'd with all kinds of rubbish, dirt & filth. The Streets too cutting your feet to pieces. I have still a due regard to my promise & indeed am a great Coward become - for when Captain Napier bespoke me a Horse & he & Capt Stewart & Austen mounted for a Country Excursion I walked good 12 miles & Captain Townsend of the Tyne kept me company - a walk we both enjoyed much.

 I wrote you in rather a dull mood on the 3rd. I was low on pronouncing Sentence of death upon a Fellow Creature but I got the Admiral to back the Recommendation for Mercy before he read the Minutes, but he said if he had read them first he would

My Dearest Margaret...

not have recommended him & if the Court had not recommended him to Mercy he would have ordered the sentence to be put in immediate Execution. It was certainly a hard case but I hung upon his once having a severe wound on the Head & I have written Sir William Parker privately to keep the poor Creatures neck out of the halter & send him away as a Convict for life. On this gay occasion of the Queens Marriage[66] I should be sorry to see such an exhibition among us. The two seamen Griffen brought forward for desertion & whom as Judge Advocate it was my Duty to assist were acquitted, though I believe they were let off too easy . But I am sick of Courts Martial I hope we shall have no more. I have just got the Admiral to refuse one today & I have likewise told him I dont mean to worry myself any more with them - let those take it that like them. It is dearly earned money and a Secretary to the Commander-in-Chief of 43 Pennants has enough on hand without it.

It was very thoughtful of my poor brother Sandy to give the Legacies he did - £80 to my Sister Marys 2 Daughters - £80 to James Drummond - £80 to Thomas's 2 Daughters & £250 to Joseph as Executor - poor fellow I could have wished to have seen him once more as when we did see him formerly he appeared always to be under a cloud - James & Thomas & poor Betsey now all gone & in a very few years more - where's the difference? But how thankful ought we to be dearest Margaret for being thus spared, renewed as it were & blessed above all other blessings in our offspring, so dutiful so well disposed so everything we could wish them to be, & how it cheers me to think they all give you so much happiness when life otherwise has very few attractions. I declare it is the thought of that keeps me up under the unspeakable privation I have so long submitted to for the sake of our Children's welfare. I see no conclusion to this warfare but I do not think there is any danger of our coming to blows - we are all two wise for that. God bless you My dearest Margaret how happy I fancy you may it long continue & a little of it soon come to my share. Your ever affectionate Husband John Loudon.

---

66 Queen Victoria was married on February 10th., 1840.

1839

25 Dec Princess Charlotte Voulca Bay Xmas Day 1839
Again dearest Margaret Christmas shows his old frosty face but a more beautiful day than it is here I ever saw. Fine clear dry weather & just cold enough to make exercise pleasant. I can see you all happy in dear 44 and fancy you thinking of, if not writing at this moment to me, and about 5 o'clock drinking my health which you may well believe is quite returned. This is the third away from my dear home and I have great consolation it must be the last. The Admiral has just sent to know if I will take a walk - away we go - and again on Board at 4 o'clock - Ship's Company have the Lower deck set off in beautiful style - Admiral followed by all the Officers walks round - tastes their pudding all standing Hats off with 3 Cheers and God Save the King played as he walks round - I have seldom seen anything more improving. Our own dinner came after and I am sorry to say it has been very dull - hardly ever passed a more stupid one and between the Admiral, Captain Fanshawe and myself I scarcely know who was the most stupid - I hope and trust the next one will make up for it - very different was our dinner yesterday on Board the Benbow with Captain Houston Stewart. I never passed a merrier. He had a Highland Bagpiper such as Capt Skene had, who generally accompanies him whenever he goes to dinner. You would laugh to have seen how he tickled the Frenchmans ears when he first struck up the Pibroch strutting round the table.

29 Dec Sunday
Took a long walk on Friday with Capt Henderson from the Gorgon and saw more of this fair country than I had done before, going over a ridge of Mountains to the seashore on the other side, very near Teos where Anacreon[67] was born - the people were out tending their vineyards and plowing their cornfields - all very civil to us offering us Coffee and Wine but the Turkish Villages are much cleaner and neater than the Greeks - with pretty little Mosques and Minarets. Their burying grounds generally under Cypress trees with small upright narrow Headstones full of Inscriptions, the males having the figure of a Turban and the females not. These tombstones are even by their houses - by the roadsides and about

---
67 A Greek lyric poet.

My Dearest Margaret...

their public walks and Gardens and seem to be as familiar a sight as the abodes of the living. Nothing I ever saw so impressive as a Turk at his devotions. It matters not where it is and how many there may be near him he seems wrapped up in one only thought that of his prostrations and prayers to the deity - without looking to the right or left.

31st. Dec Hogmanay

Our fine hills are now covered with snow & I am glad of a good stove which I am sitting by with Capt Fanshawe my tormentor and best friend. I am very much pleased to think dear Lizzie is getting over her sea sickness - for it is a dreadful suffering for her poor thing although she always tries to conceal it not to give pain to others - part of her general character - dear Girls - I see no immediate hope of our going in to Malta - the French have something in hand now with Algiers which may relieve us a little from some apprehensions afloat about their designs on Egypt - but I hear they have given the Algerians a threshing though that will not avail them much as those savages disperse when hard pressed and rally again when not expected. As to your wants I assure you Port Wine is to be had better and cheaper in England than here with all the trouble and expense and accidents and English Duty when it arrives & I shall not be able to get any unless we touch at Oporto. Here we pay no duty - very different in England & we drunk light wines of the Country at 8d & 10d a bottle. It is very tiresome for the poor Admiral to be kept out in this way and nothing really to be done but he now puts on a determination not to compromise himself. I am now at the end of the year & I wish you & I all our remaining ones together. I hear Sir George Cockburn is likely to relieve us & I shall be very glad to see him - though were it not for the thought of dear Home I have had nothing to complain of - Good Night!

1840

Quarantine in Malta again - Captain Napier - Palmer leaves - waiting for orders - sulphur mines - Napier - problems in Syria - Isle of Thasos - Alexandria - landing in Beyrout - the Mountaineers - attack on Acre - Captain Napier makes terms with Mehemet Ali - birth of grandson

1st. Jan 1840

My Dearest Margaret

Another morning wakes us, may it usher in a prosperous year for us all say I. It is a fine hard cold morning with a beautiful sky in fact the climate here is particularly fine and very enjoyable but I could wish it a little warmer at present. Little Louisa Collings has just sent me half a dozen pair Worsted Socks, very acceptable & bids me take care & keep myself warm. She is a dear little child and the nearest to my Fanny I know in everything. She is so pleased when Fan writes to her that I hope she will often & Collings is a very nice friendly fellow himself, Mrs Collings as excellent Stepmother to Lou - well perhaps she has no children of her own. I am again as usual in a bustle sending a Vessel off to Malta - which causes a great sensation through the Squadron - God Bless you all is the Prayer, My dearest Margaret Your affectionate Husband John Loudon.

9th. Jan Princess Charlotte Voulca Bay

Still here you see but I begin to think we shall have permission by the Packet which we shall have on Sunday to take part of the Squadron to Malta to recruit & relieve the rest for there is nothing at present going on to keep us out. In the meantime we have nothing to complain of having fine mild weather and abundance of all sort of good things Beef, Mutton, Pork, & Wild Boar, Poultry, Eggs,

My Dearest Margaret…

fine Dutch Butter, Stilton Cheese, fish such as Soles, red Mullet & a variety of other sorts - Wild Ducks, Widgeons, Teal, Wild Geese, Swans, Turkeys prepared in all ways, Partridges, Wood Cocks & Snipes. What could we desire more and I assure you the Geese are better than Swans as far as eating goes. Still everybody sighs for Malta except myself & I prefer this fine Country a thousand to one. I think I told you Doctor Allen was come out here. He is now appointed to Haslar Hospital[68] and goes home again immediately. He says Sir Wm Hargood was very poorly and gives a woeful account of Jeffrey. I see poor Collings of the Admiralty Office is dead. I fear you will be now thinking of parting with dear Liz and Arney as well as poor Will who I hope will take the most direct road to his College as nothing is dearer than travelling even the most prudent way you can.

16th. Jan

I just learnt poor Sir William Hargood is dead - poor man! Allen tells me he fully expected it for he was worn out. Thus my three friends Sir George, Sir Thomas & Sir William have passed in one year - only a little further on the road we are all going & so goes the world. I expect now to be in Malta in 8 or 10 days more. I have sent four of our Squadron already - & the Admiral expects to go tomorrow if the Packet we are looking out for do not order us to remain for nothing whatever is going on in this freezing Season. The weather is much colder than I expected and we have frost & snow from the high hills around us. I shall be glad to find it a little milder for I can scarcely hold my pen.

19th.

Happy day I have had a real treat in all your dear Letter of the 18th last month with all the happiness of your fireside before me. Would that I were once more by your side where all and every thought of mine has ever dwelt. Thank God the time is now drawing nigh for such a blessing. My poor Admiral is rather disappointed at not going into Malta which we were all ready to do when the Packet arrived and put a stop to it till Sir John Louis comes out to relieve us which the Admiral had written him to do

---

68 Haslar Royal Navy Hospital in Gosport.

1840

so that in a month hence we expect to pass 6 weeks in Malta of which 3 will be in quarantine but Lady Stopford and the family will be with us. The Admiral though looking very well requires certainly a change of scene & some relaxation and by the time he is all to rights at Malta I hope his relief may be on the way from England for I long much to revisit my dear old Durnford Street & the most affectionate of Partners. You would see by my former Letters I was very uneasy about a poor seaman condemned to be hung. He had no Counsel but me. I saw his case was as bad as could be. It fortunately occurred to me to ask him if ever he had been wounded on the ship - he said he had fallen from the Rigging once. I made the most of it. He was recommended to mercy & I wrote a Letter from Sir Robert enforcing the recommendation but fearful of the worst I wrote Sir Wm Parker and after many a restless night for I feel I am getting nervous I have the pleasure today to communicate to the man that the Queen has been pleased to commute the sentence of death to transportation for life. The man goes home in the Rodney. Commodore Parker was President & a kind hearted man as he is he could not get over the positive clause in the Act and the man was condemned to die - but with a recommendation to mercy - nothing but this saved him for his conduct was very bad. Dear Will! I have a strong Fathers feeling for him and with a Father's prejudices perhaps flatter myself he will yet make his way in this life for though he may not answer my hopes & expectations in the Book way I have pretty plain proofs that he is not deficient in making his way in the world. I am always amused with the manly stile of his Letters - and as he is now at an age to judge for himself I shall desist hammering into him all my wise Laws of which he does not yet see the value. His last letter is a very good one & shews some thought. You must not begrudge postage in certain cases. Remember me most kindly to Captain Mends a most kind & worthy man. Ever my dearest Margaret Your Affectionate Husband John Loudon.

16 Feb. Fort Mannel Quarantine Malta

Sir John Louis made his appearance at Voulca on the 9th (last Sunday) just at Breakfast time and the Admiral put himself and staff on board the Gorgon steamer and started at 2 o'clock - we arrived here in 80 hours being 670 miles on the Wednesday

My Dearest Margaret...

Evening. Lady Stopford had the Apartments all most comfortable for us and next morning we were on shore in our quarters and Lady Stopford and three of the Young Ladies put themselves in quarantine leaving 3 to keep house with their Brother Robert who commands the Zebra and Cousin Edward who commands the Confrance. Lady S. all kindness, the Admiral invariably the same and in fact I am, if I could feel myself so, as one of the family. The Duckworths as usual all kindness they come every day but we are under guardians and must speak at a distance - the time is shortened to a fortnight & we get to our own house on the 26th. The Princess Charlotte was to leave Voulca on Tuesday morning the 11th and may be here tomorrow as the Carysfort frigate which sailed on Monday the 16th arrived here this morning and having a fair wind.

There is nothing earthly doing in the East a great deal of braggadocio[69] which I am confident will come to nothing. If the Admiral is not relieved we shall return I expect in about six weeks time to our old station but I trust the weather will be settled. We are not anxious of the alliance with Russia and I hope Mr. Brun is broken off. So you have had gay doings getting our young Queen a Husband and our people here are looking for something to rejoice them upon the occasion as there must be a promotion. The Election after all against poor Mr Dawson - I hope his day will yet come altho' Ministers seem to have a large majority. The greatest treat I had on leaving Voulca on the 9th was your valued packet of the 16th Jany only 4 weeks for such a distance - 2700 miles for 2/-. We must not begrudge postage now though I think you look rather gloomy at the charge[70]. I thought the 4d. a good charge at once but it will require time to make such a full answer. In the course of a short time however it will cause great activity in the manufacture of thin paper - give great Employment and till well from stopping the abuse of franks - all will now tell - people will write who never wrote before and those who did will now do so much oftener & this will make people better friends, at least so I think.

---

69   Swaggering
70   The new universal penny post service was inaugurated on 10th January 1840. Now cost depended on weight, not the number of sheets and distance.

1840

Parting with Lizzie must have been trying to you. I am rather glad you keep Charlie and Fran yourself for the Winter as she has now plenty of friends and cannot be lonely with a husband like Errington travelling without a good real object is both expensive and uncomfortable. Willoughby shewed some signs of grace in setting off to his time for in sooth he has now little to lose if he thinks of doing anything for himself. You will most likely see a friend of mine Lieut Nowell of the Vanguard who has married the Young Marchesa Testaferrata, as unsophisticated a girl as I ever saw. The Marquis and Marchioness (her Father and Mother) have a numerous family and are like most of the foreign Noblesse not rich but they are excellent plain unassuming people and having always shewn me the greatest attention. I am anxious if the Vanguard touches at Plymouth you should be as kind to them as possible. He is not only an excellent young man but clever and has painted me a picture of the Flagship saluting the French at Tunis very much admired. I have several friends in the Rodney Dr Allen has changed to the Vanguard as she goes direct to Portsmouth. Dr McArthur no relation to our Doctor but a most respectable man takes charge of the Figs and I wish you to show a good face to him as well as to Commander Shepheard of the Rodney who will call upon you with a letter. I don't know if Captain Parker (Commodore I beg his pardon) & be sure you call him so if he calls. He has the most agreeable creature of the world for a wife a nice clever family & stands himself high in his profession - but till you know him he has an odd manner. We are all comfort as usual and our newcomers all most agreeable men particularly Captain Houston Stewart of the Benbow who has brought Mrs Stewart now in delicate health and talks broad Scotch a most agreeable woman. I think she was a Maxwell. Poor Sir Fredk Maitland died at Bombay after dysentery - only a few days ill. Lady M comes home by the Cape. I have just seen Mr Ogilvy his Flag Lieut who has just brought the Despatches by the Red Sea. Thank God my good man holds up capitally as does his Secretary - though the latter is most anxious to revisit his own dear home but he could wish to do so with flying colours not a birky draggling home with his tail between his feet - no fault of his if he do. Your friend Captain Napier is the life and soul of us but he is sadly anxious to get us into a row. He and I are on capital terms but he was

My Dearest Margaret...

nearly taking the ... the other day at not being made Commodore when Parker was ordered home and a Rear Admiral sent to relieve the Admiral while he went in to recruit here. It was all explained however & blew over but he had written a letter to be superseded. When Princess Charlotte arrives Captain Fanshawe will leave Mrs F on board - all to themselves.

19th. Feb

No Packet yet I must send this in the morning at any rate and as I shall be overwhelmed with business I shall close this tonight - I am sanguine as to the new rate of Postage - the old abuses were most preposterous. God bless you my dearest Margaret and send me soon home to you is the prayer of your Affectionate Husband John Loudon.

Note enclosed to Charlotte.

How does this economical world agree with my dear Charlotte - the one-eight part of a penny allotted to Lotty and a hard - very hard lot it is - thank you dear Char for your lively & enlivening little note - marriages and giving in marriage all gaiety & rejoicing and long may it continue. I did not suffer your Birthday nor Lizzie's nor the wedding day to pass unnoticed - of that you may be well assured. Princess Charlotte is come in, a week more and we have possession of our house. James Stopford is made a Commander - a matter of rejoicing to all the House and I have presented him with a pair of Epaulettes. Sir R and Lady Stopford overwhelming me with thanks.

Note to Fran

Thanks my dearest Fran for your short pithy note. I must now write you on a corner - but you don't want many words from a Father who loves you - dear Lou has got a had cold from coming across the water to see me. She is poor girl quite a hothouse plant but exceedingly pretty. Her father is a very superior man, he always begs I will not forget him to your Mamma and you - remember me kindly to Georgie, Lady Eliot and Mrs North. I left him quite well - but the Lawrences don't suit your affectionate Father.

1840

9th. March

Better My Dearest Margaret half a loaf than no bread. I have scarcely a moment to acknowledge your dear and welcome letter of the 18th last month - as we are all hurrying off the Hermes for Woolwich tomorrow morning. You will wonder that Palmer is going in her. He has latterly taken a fit of thinking himself unhappy though not with me and us I would not wish to keep any one as a favour I have got him discharged into the Hermes. I must say he has served me faithfully and honestly and saved me many a shilling in my washing accounts. He has given me a most correct list of everything agreeing perfectly with the one I brought out & I even if not that I think him as too lofty a disposition for his station with the three servants he is the most perfect young man in principle and conduct I ever met with - I am sending off 3 ships at once - the Ganges to the Squadron, Zebra to the Ionian Islands and Hermes to Woolwich with distinct orders. We hear nothing yet of our successor. I have written to Eliza and sent her a Bedside Rug - a little coffee and a few anchovies. I shall write you by the Rodney which sails in a few days but don't expect anything as we shall soon be home ourselves. Will is very sparing of his writings as usual.

God bless you dearest Margaret my love to Lot and Fran Your affectionate husband John Loudon.

14th. March Malta

We are still in suspense as to a successor but I hope it is now all settled and that we shall be with you in summer. My health continues excellent and it is all a fudge as to the Admirals he is quite well and in high gear. The affairs in the East are as stupid as ever - we are making a great man of Mehemet Ali & I think it a thousand pities we did not allow them to settle their own affairs - which would have made all smooth before now. I scarcely think we shall return though our successor is not yet named. I see Will perseveres in not writing - not a good sign because where theres a will theres a way and I'll answer, for if his reading is not so hard as to prevent his writing - if his thoughts led that way. I trust at least your own fireside is comfortable with such dear daughters - god bless them - I see by my Banker's Book for the last 6 months his damage is £120 and all yours together £170 making about £600 a

My Dearest Margaret...

year and with the Estate say £670. But of course it may be more or less. I know you must be exposed to much expense - I did intend sending you a carpet but as we are coming home soon ourselves I think I can manage the Duties better - I am thinking of getting a larger Turkey carpet for the back bedroom but am not sure of the dimensions - Give my love to dear Charlotte and Fanny. I wish them well over their bridesmaidships. Believe me my dearest Margaret Your affectionate husband John Loudon.

18 March Malta

Here we are still as much in the dark as ever and we can expect nothing by the Packet having received later orders over land than she can bring. The Admiral and his Secretary are both quite well however and we are enjoying such good things as Malta can produce before bidding it good-bye for ever. I have had several excursions some pedestrian and some on the carriage (but none on horseback) with the young ladies - Annie Duckworth is an excellent rider and the others have been taking lessons except Miss Stopford who has not mounted since her black-eye. Capt Fanshawe the same as ever and Mrs F very kind but deaf for which she uses a trumpet. James Stopford who was a midshipman when we came out is now Captain of the Zebra at Corfu and Robert who was 8 years Lieutenant commands the Phoenix at Voulca Bay. Lou Collings pretty as an angel but very delicate - she took a water excursion with us in the Alecto to Gozo about 18 miles yesterday but the day was showery and raw. I had charge of her and the young Stopfords. Mrs Duckworth was sea sick and some of the others a little so we had a good set out - returned to dinner. I told you Palmer had left me. He was to the last the same steady and most attentive servant he had ever been but was not content with the society of the other servants. I recommended him to Blount in the Hermes who took him as assistant to the steward on his passage home. I was sorry to part with him but I never could lay myself under an obligation and Palmer required putting in his place occasionally. The one I have now is far behind him but willing and I am assured honest. You will have the Rodney with you about this time. Commodore Parker is considered the first officer in our service, an odd little fellow, his wife a most amiable woman and a most clever family to whose education she devoted all her time. Sir Wm Seden her brother will likewise call upon you. Dr.McArthur too a very superior man and Lt Scott very accomplished and friendly - all asked to take home anything I had but as this ship will be going home very soon I did not wish to give you the trouble and vexation you had by the Rhadamanthus with the Custom House. I shall not forget your black tea but Lady Stopford cannot drink the tea of this country and always sends to Twinings.

[cont] 19 March

I have just received your dear letter of the 27th Feb with one from Will - which shews he has a knack at least of making friends if not brilliant in his studies though I do not despair of his setting to with a will when the trial comes. These boils are a sad drawback to him poor fellow but I trust they will soon disappear. He seems to have got rid of them by his riding and rough exercise with his friend Joscelin. Would he only beat a little law in his head his aptness to make friends would almost ensure his success in the world - but it is no use boring him we must now hope the best. Our fate is as great a mystery as ever as no successor appears yet to be named. I see this Postage snibs me of dear Charlotte and Fannys ... but they were frying other fish at the time. Our weather delightful but the Maltese are afraid of the want of water. God bless you my dearest Margaret. Our time thank God is nearly drawing to a close when I shall be made up by your smiling face and my dear girls and Will for all our pains. - your affectionate husband John Loudon.

[cont]

My dear girls- you see how this Penny Postage treats us - but you and dear Liz must reap the advantage of it I have a long letter from her and her swain in their usual affectionate style - I have just received it 8 a.m. of the 19th and our mail for the Admiralty starts at 12 so that I have not much time to spare and must conclude with love from dear Lou who is very delicate. Your affectionate Father John Loudon.

31 March

This completes my three years and most fervently do I hope our successor is now appointed and preparing to join for it is indeed a most tiresome absentee. There is absolutely nothing going on

My Dearest Margaret...

here - all just as well here as in the East. I scarcely expect it will come to anything after all and Mehemet Ali may laugh at all the 5 Powers who are more likely to quarrel among themselves than to hurt a hair of his head. - as for England I think we are crazy. The weather is at present rather cold but very pleasant with exercise. It we what we call a Scirocco[71] & everybody had headache more or less, even I who am not troubled with such things. I dined with Collings on Sunday Mrs Collings was laid up in bed and Lou had it slightly but the wind changed and we were all well. Poor James who had the Zebra got her on the rocks at Corfu, carried off her rudder and part of her false keel but the rudder is replaced and the false keel when she comes back be put to rights - but it was a bad beginning poor fellow. The Master was in fault who had been there often. I am just going to sit down to dinner with 20 people - a very common thing here. Last Tuesday I dined with the Christians and in the evening we went to a party at the French Consuls where we met the famous French painter Horace Monet and 5 pupils who had been travelling in Egypt and the Holy Land and were dressed like Turks with long beards and red caps; French men can turn into anything. I was vexed to hear Willys boils had been troubling him again but hope they have at length taken their leave of him for they are not only painful but break up his studies & God knows he has no more time to throw away. I only hope for his own sake he will not trifle with himself any longer. I have nice letters from our dear Liz and Arny they are quite delightful and I am sure they are a happy couple. Should Hermes put into Plymouth I am sure you will be glad to see Mr and Mrs Blount and Miss Clavell for they are nice people and have been most attentive to me. The weather has been terrible at sea and the Asia was very ill treated by it on her way back to Voulca but I think it is the last puff of Winter. We receive the news so quick through France that we do not look for anything new by our own Packet. We have had London papers in 8 days and once on 7 - think of that - by way of Marseilles. The talk is now that Admiral Fleeming is to relieve us and keep Greenwich into the bargain or to be kept for him - but that I think would be carrying the joke a little too far.

---

71 A Mediterranean wind which comes from the Sahara.

1840

1st April

Our work is coming double quick upon us. The Phoenix is just come from Constantinople and the Squadron at Smyrna - but not a word of news. Bad weather and the Powerful struck by lightening which shivered her Foretop Gall mast. Tomorrow we have to dispatch the Packet for England and one for Corfu and on Saturday we send the Bellerophon to Voulca - plenty of work this but not too much - Our Packet is just arrived but we have not yet received our letters - they are now come. 5 o'clock p.m. & very happy they make me to find you are all well and in good spirits - but not a breath from the Admiralty as to our successor though it appears by common report to be that Arch Scotchman Admiral Fleeming. I see the Vanguard arrived at Portsmouth on the 6th so you are not likely to see Lieut and Mrs Lowell.

God bless you dearest Margaret is the prayer of your affectionate husband John Loudon.

Note for Charlotte

Thank you dearest Charlotte for your nice spiritual and affectionate letter. We are all as gay here as Lent will let us and I should have escorted Lou Collings to a Pic-nic of about 60 people given 10 miles in the Country (Boschella) but have too much to keep me at home. I can easily fancy the entertainment Capt Sharpe must have given you with his witch and warlock store is such as used to make my hair stand on end when young & firmly believed by my old Granny - poor woman - the Witch of Endor was a real and true witch!! Love to dear Fan and the Davies - our affectionate Father John Loudon.

I thought well of the Epaulettes and there was no end of the sensation it made but I considered I should not want them and my second washed look as good as new & will serve my time.

12 April Malta

Still at Malta my dearest Margaret though the startling news we received by the Queens Messenger very nearly took us to Naples and I really wish the Admiral had not been persuaded out of it which he was when all things were partly on board and we ourselves ready for a start - the Bellerophon only went on with the little Inseur and

My Dearest Margaret...

the Hydra but if the King[72] continues obstinate we shall certainly oblige him to give up the monopoly he has established in Sicily of the Sulphur Mines against the interest of the English who in the faith of Treaties sank a great deal of money in the mines which they had leased for years and are in a manner excluded from the benefit[73]. Ld Lyndhurst's speech in the House of Peers on the 2nd March has awakened the energies of the Government on this act of injustice and we are ordered to seize and detain all Neapolitan and Sicilian vessels we may meet within these seas till the King gives it up. He is tremendously violent fancies himself another Bonaparte - most probably will invite a trial of strength. Our very appearance off Sicily would throw it into a state of revolt but that we don't wish as we cannot support them and the poor people would of course be sacrificed. He has thrown in fifteen thousand troops into it already from fear of the people. I am rather anxious about it because if that hot-headed fool should fire a shot at any of our ships it would not only bring on a war but the Admiral might get blamed for not going in greater force. I hope however it will be all well. Mrs West will most likely call upon you, the wife of the Commander of the Volcano steamer. Unfortunately she is very deaf a sad drawback, but she kindly said she would call. I received my Bankers Account all right now but the London people make sad mistakes which might be very serious if I were not to look after them - of course you receive the rents regularly which are some help to you. Willoughby has his recess for a short time I suppose he passes it in Town - or perhaps with his friend Joscelyn again nearer Cambridge this travelling being very expensive. I had a delightful letter from Lizzie and her soldier just as the Packet was leaving this so I had not time to acknowledge it then but shall by this Packet. She is indeed a treasure & he in all respects worthy of her. I sent them a rug for their bedside and would a carpet but it is too cumbersome for light infantry movements.

16th.

This is the day we close our dispatches and the Packet is now getting her smoke up. I had a very nice letter from Blount who

---
72 The King of Naples
73 England depended on sulphur for many aspects of manufacturing such as dyeing, bleaching, gunpowder and medicines.

1840

fortunately touched at Plymouth and took Charlotte or Fan he does not say which to Chatham a very nice chance for her. I have always met the greatest kindness from both Mr and Mrs Blount and this adds greatly to it. She is a capital sailor's wife full of spirits and makes no difficulties about anything. Blount was afraid of her not holding out for the voyage and a man here Dr Stilon said she would risk her life if she went but she took her chance and all is well. I expect to be back in a month or six weeks. Our Neapolitan concern is vexatious in so far as it is neither war nor peace - for if we detain their vessels they will naturally keep ours out of their Ports - I hope it will be won as it is very nagging and the Admiral does not know whether he goes too fast or too slow. Besides I hear there is a split in the Cabinet about it. Give my love to dear Lotty or Fan whichever it may be - God bless you dearest Margaret your affectionate husband John Loudon.

26th. April Malta

I still write in great uncertainty with regard to our outbreak with Naples. The worst of it is there are some who think he[74] is not so much out as we suppose, not having actually broken the Treaty though very unjustly towards us but that is not our affair here and we are taking his poor peoples vessels and ruining their trade to punish him. We have four here just now and 2 coming and the Talbot and the Zebra are doing the same at Otranto - our small vessels are called in from the Levant and coast of Spain the Bellerophon and Benbow Tyne and Jasene or Iasene with the Hydra are off Naples and in the Streights of Messina and the Implacable and Princess Charlotte are ready when fresh orders come out that may require them. Your dearest letter of 26th March was very consolatory to me in the midst of all this perplexity and I was delighted to hear such good accounts of you all. The girls were going on board the Hermes. I did not know then one of them was so near taking the trip to Chatham - which was a kind act on the part of the Blounts. I am rejoiced to hear Willoughby has taken to his studies and hope that he has done so in earnest. The weather is perfectly delightful just now between winter and summer. You know the orders are to change our blues for whites on the 23rd April even in England, but

---

74 The King of Naples.

My Dearest Margaret...

I assure you we find it cold enough for blues - and although Capt Fanshawe who as always beforehand has put them all in white on board the Admiral and myself continue our winter wear. On Friday night Mrs Christian gave a grand rout[75]. The Governor, the Admiral's family and 120 more were there. I came away with the Admiral's family, Mrs Duckworth and Annie at 2 and the Ball did not break up till 4. The young Miss Christian divided the prize of beauty with our Louisa Collings who looked more of heaven than one of this earth poor girl through all her beauty she does not look as if she had a long tenure in this world. She calls me her second Papa and Fan her sister. Her stepmother I think a most excellent friend to her and so far as I see fulfils a mother's duty with great solicitude for Lou's happiness checking any vanities which might arise from the attentions she is constantly receiving but which really don't appear to change her. This is not much of a marrying place.

You will be glad to hear that I do not miss Palmer in the least. My Maltese boy who speaks English and Italian I thought awkward at first but he is very quick and very clean and very attentive. Blount recommended him he is the son of a respectable man on the Dockyard reads and writes and takes as much care of my things when once he knows my ways and wishes as Palmer, more he cannot tho I still look to see all is right. Poor Palmer had taken some dislike among the other servants and in fact I had to bring him round a little once or twice for his stiffness of manner and consequence among them but he was certainly very superior and perhaps awakened their jealousies. I observed the last row was between him and the cook who wanted him to carry from the Galley here to the cabin our pudding and Palmer would take the pudding and two tarts or pies at once thereby touching the cook's nerves for the healthy condition on the table. The steward brought it before me on a board of green cloth and I gave it against Palmer certainly - I had no wish to keep him against his indication. You know it is not my way to do that and I thought the Hermes a good opportunity. I fear very much my dearest you have taken to heart anything I may have said about money matters. I assure you I am quite satisfied with your good management. I know well to what

---

75 A fashionable gathering or assembly – much used in the early 19th. Century.

1840

expenses you are exposed therefore do not make yourself uneasy about that. I wish with all my heart I were by your side again - all the sulphur in Sicily should not take me away again and the poor wretched vessels are coming in fast, very miserable work this but we must obey orders.

29th.

It never reigns but it pours I have recd by the Cyclops and Packet all your dear Letters of 1st and 5th and 9th with weighty ones from dear Charlotte, Fanny and Eliza as well as a very well written one from Will who I see is going to Chatham. I am glad you embraced so good an opportunity for Fanny. We have just received orders to suspend seizing Neapolitan and Sicilian vessels until the result of the French mediation is known - the convention is to be held at Paris and if we do not find that it terminates favourably in 3 weeks we begin again but I hope it will for it is not a creditable warfare and I quite grieve at the poor creatures we bring in. I have not time to write to Charlotte in answer to her spirited epistle. Austen gave us all at dinner an amusing account of your firmness in not listening to all the flying reports about the Admirals health and return in which you are right. God bless you my dearest Margaret your affectionate husband John Loudon.

To Charlotte and Fan.

I thank you dearest Charlotte for your entertaining billet. You put me in the drawing room, the garden and the stable. I fancy I see your lame old Bear Dash - old Jack and all the old scenes of no. 44. Not a word of our successor but he may be getting his sword and cock'd hat ready for all that. I am anxious to be again with you - for I never can look for my 12/- half pay which by the bye is likely to be only on paper for some time. Dear Fan must be ready to jump over the moon - I am quite pressed with business just now - Naples, Corfu and our own Packet - God bless my dearest Charlotte is the prayer of her affectionate father John Loudon.

Enclosure

Dr.McArthur presents his compliments to Mrs Loudon & begs to inform her that he has this day sent to the Customs House two drums of figs addressed to her and which were given by Mr

My Dearest Margaret...

Loudon in charge of Dr. Allen & subsequently transferred from him to Dr. MacArthur. Rodney. Thursday 30 April.

11th. May

Your valued letter of the 25th reached me yesterday morning and would on the 9th had not the Packet been kept back close to the Island by a strong easterly wind. I received at the same time a nice letter from Eliza on her recovery from her fearful enemy the pain in the chest. She is indeed very delicate and the climate of England is not favourable for her but she has the best Doctor and the best substitute for Mamma in her worthy prudent and firm husband and at present it was almost providential that dear doctor Fan was with her. I hope and trust she is by this time quite set up again and as for me I thank God I have not had the least symptom of cough or cold for the Winter and are all now all in whites again with heavenly weather neither too hot nor too cold. You will have heard poor Jessup has lost his youngest daughter Nora poor man he seemed consoled by writing me the following day the 28th April as he did on the death of his wife. This silly affair of Naples is not yet settled and if it is not in 3 weeks we have orders to begin again. The Bellerophon and Benbow are still there and it is not unlikely we shall go ourselves in the Princess Charlotte. The King of Naples is an absolute fool and may not see his error till he has war about his ears - though the Admiral has given orders not to molest the poor inhabitants when they can possibly avoid doing so. A fortnight of the 3 weeks is already expired but our mail through France is due on the 13th and I am pretty sure if the affair is not adjusted orders will come to extend it[76].

We are worried too in the East as affairs will never be settled there with Lord Ponsonby at the head. He has taken a woeful side against Mehemet Ali who is on his part equally inflexible and the interference of different Governments has obstructed the settlement of the dispute which was on the point of taking place between themselves when we were there last year. Mutual jealousies only keep the fire alive. Mrs Duckworth and Annie are leaving us on Thursday in the Packet for England taking Henrietta Stopford with them for change of air - they are all delightful people and

---

76 As a result of the blockade and helped by French mediation, Napier notes that the King of Naples "was brought to his senses" (Napier 'The Syrian War, Chapt.II).

1840

will create a sad blank amongst us here. Do not lose a moment in seeing them and tell them how much they both have of my prayers and wishes that all thats good may ever attend them Henrietta too is the most amiable quiet even-tempered girl in the world & I hope her health which I take to be much like my Fans will be benefited by the voyage. I am sorry for this break up for really it has been to me like my own family particularly of late that we knew one another better & become freer. I am glad to find dear Will is at Chatham for the sake of Erringtons good advice & I do think he begins to consider seriously his situation in entering a Profession which he must look to not only for fame and honor but for his daily bread, indeed with his turn of mind I think it is the fittest he could have chosen for connection is one of the most necessary steps to rise by - & when he finds perseverance lead to wealth he will I know persevere.

14th. May

I am now come to the end of my tether. The Steamer is come from Marseilles and not a word from the Admiralty. The Confrance is dispatched to Naples to communicate with our Minister - and I just find we are to start for Naples on Saturday so that all will be bustle and hurry. I rather think the Ladies will go with us & even fancy the Admiral will take them to Corfu & then go on alone to Naples but this is only fancy though I had a hint of it a few days ago - Poor Mrs Duckworth has got a bad cold and cannot well go today as she intended and the news of Lady Duckworth's death may alter her plans. I meant to write to Dear Charlotte but am much pressed for time - with affectionate regards to her and all your circle I am Dearest Margaret your affectionate Husband John Loudon.

21 May Naples Bay

Here we are again after 2 years absence from this really magnificent place, but under rather different circumstances though we still keep up appearances and hostilities have not yet broken out. Our Ambassador remains and all our people go about as if nothing were the matter. It is not a popular quarrel and I hope it will soon be settled. Many of our English Merchants even think their Countrymen wrong and that there has been no infringement

My Dearest Margaret…

of our Treaty - but that is nothing to us who have only to obey orders. We left Malta on Sunday morning the 17th came round the west end of Sicily and anchored here just now where we find a French 3 Decker the Ocean with Vice Admiral Rosamils flag and 2 Decker La Corvette - an American Sloop of War and we have here the Princess Charlotte, Bellerophon, Implacable, Benbow, Carysfort, Tyre, Phoenix & Confrance a beautiful sight giving life to this splendid scenery. I hope it will end well.

    When I think of it I do not miss Palmer in the least. My present servant is a Maltese boy but well up to his business and the son of a very respectable man in the Dockyard - exceedingly willing and of good principles. He has soon got into my ways and I find him more useful in giving my messages because he knows the people better - but I shall leave him behind when I go home. You will have heard of Lady Duckworths death. Mrs and Miss Duckworth had taken their places in the Steamer to go home but Miss Duckworth having been seized with a cough and pain in the chest, they could not go and now they have heard of poor Lady Duckworth's death they will wait till they hear from Sir John when they are likely to meet at Paris. Before we started on Sunday morning I found a pretty little Note on my Desk with Mrs and Miss Duckworth's best wishes and an elegant Gold Pencilcase as a Souvenir - was it not pretty? My dear Charlotte the Admirals youngest daughter presented me with a handsome large Dollar Purse of her own working and one of the Marquis Testaferratas young daughters, sister of the one who married Nowell of the Vanguard, with a clasp silk and gold purse and Nowell before he sailed presented me with a painting of the Princess Charlotte and Squadron in Tunis Bay. If my dear Charlotte would kindly make one of her famed Reticules for Charlotte Stopford she would do me a most particular favour - for indeed all the family are most kind and attentive to me and I am most comfortable with them. What are you about in England that you do not relieve us? I assure you I long most terribly to be at your side again, I think I shall make much of it and send my Books to the deuce for though they have been agreeable always to me, yet they have occasionally kept me from better company, for which I owe them no thanks - very different here - they beguile the time. You would be disappointed at receiving almost nothing by Rodney - but I know the Custom House frets you and what I may have I will

1840

bring myself. I heard from dear Liz and Fan up to the 27th April - Willoughby with them - not given much to writing honest man - I hope he begins to think and to study - but my greatest anxiety at present is for poor Lizzie's health which is still so delicate. I shall now close this and if I have an opportunity I will enclose a few lines more as the postage is now by weight. The Admiral, Capt F Glanville our Flag Lieutenant and myself are again on shore and I would write dear Lottie but fear to swell the postage - God bless you both and believe me with great anxiety again to be with you. My Dearest Margaret, your affectionate husband John Loudon.

24 May Naples.

We are on shore at the same hotel we had two years ago - the Crocelli - Yesterday being the Queen's Birthday all our Ships were dressed in Colours and fired a Salute which made a famous racket in Naples Bay and in honor of Her Majesty the Neapolitan Men of War were all dressed in their gayest colours and the Batteries fired a salute, after which their Admiral came off and waited upon the Admiral to compliment him upon the occasion. In fact we are all here as if nothing was the matter only these Forts and Batteries are in a state of readiness to give us a warm reception as they think but which would soon come tumbling about their ears but I am in strong hopes it won't come to that. They are very complimentary and civil and yesterday they dressed their Ships in Colours and fired a salute with us in honor of the Queen's Birthday. We all dined with the Minister Lord Palmerston's brother - the second time I have dined with him since we came in the day before yesterday. I had an excursion round the coast to Baia - & I am not surprised the luxurious Romans fixed upon it as a watering place - it is covered all round with remains of Temples, Theatres, Baths and other buildings and where art and nature contended in forming the most delightful spot you can imagine - but all hollow within and in one night a mountain rose from the water which is now covered with vineyard and looking so delightful that you would suppose all was right under but the whole of this beautiful Country is like a painted sepulchre and may bury the Inhabitants in a moment. I have been much tempted to go to Rome which I can do in 36 hours but cannot be spared at present. Our Chaplain and two more set off tonight. With all this my dearest Margaret I sigh for home

My Dearest Margaret…

and hope our successor is now picked upon which you will know before we do. The weather is most delightful here and my health good because I do not fatigue myself. I declined a Party today to visit Pompeii again but shall still go over those extraordinary Remains when I have more time I can do it leisurely. The Admiral's family being all left at Malta we expect to be there as soon as this affair is settled - only Capt Stewart's wife of the Benbow is here with lodgings on shore and this breeds some jealousy with others who were refused - as the Admiral does not think it right to be carrying women about under our present circumstances. He had some idea of taking us in the Hydra Steamer tomorrow to see the famous Ruins of Paestum. Gold Bless You dearest Margaret your affectionate husband John Loudon.

7 June Naples

Here we still are but things seem to be in progress of an arrangement and the Admiral is impatient to return to Malta - for he finds it expensive and inconvenient living on shore here at a hotel and one foot as it were on shore and one at sea. We have partaken of all the good things going however - have dined four or five times with the British Minister and gave a round of Dinners on Board and on shore. On the King of Naples' Birthday we fired a salute and dressed the Squadron in colours. We dined with the Minister afterwards - then attended the leveè at half past eight and then went to the Operà which was a splendid sight so magnificently illuminated and the King and Court there - but all eyes seemed to be turned upon my dear Admiral in apparent admiration of his noble appearance. It was certainly curious for the Neapolitans to see the Admiral and the English officers among them enjoying all these amusements with these Bull dogs lying close in to their Batteries and ships and ready to open them if the King did not undo what he had done which we have now reason to think he has done, and I expect the news from England in a day or two which will send us back to Malta. It is not true that the Admiral has asked for another year - but I know not that to think of not hearing a successor named. I shall be very much disappointed if we remain and if so you must really make up your mind to come out for this absence is dreadful.

1840

I suppose dear Willoughby is with you by this time. I am glad to hear a good account of him from Errington and Eliza. He is now arrived at a time of life where he must stand or fall according to his own exertions and I shall therefore not offer any further incentive to study. If he does not now think and act as becomes one who has his own bread to make he will bitterly feel his lost time but I hope otherwise and that he will yet distinguish himself in a profession which has raised more to honor and wealth than any other. I am glad to learn the boils are gone and trust he will have no more molestation of that sort. Charlotte and he will go on well together in music and French and I hope that his vacation will not be lost. It is a great reading time to those who are eager for University honors. I am anxious about dear Eliza who seems to improve but slowly. I trust the air of Colchester will be of service to her, but if not she must come to you without fail and as soon as possible. It was quite right Fanny going with her and we must not grudge any necessary expense, which that is - for it is only idle or thoughtless expenses I find fault with. You and I never indulged in that way, indeed we should not have been able to bring up our children as we have done if such had been the case. The Admiral is sending Lady Stopford and his four daughters to Corfu for the warm months - Henrietta is gone with Mrs D being in delicate health. I find my situation both with them and the Admiral much more to my taste than formerly and am infinitely more at my ease - in fact they are much changed for the better. I am here alone as it were with my very kind Admiral with whom I joke or consult seriously upon a footing of the most perfect freedom, go about visiting all the curiosities in town and country together as he has his carriage by the day and in all respects feel quite at home. I can find nothing at Naples but what is very dear everything even to the sea water being enormously taxed for instance a black silk cravat for which they ask 12/- has a tax of 8/- or two thirds. How can a country thrive in that way. Gloves are the only cheap article I know of (about 10d. a fair pair and 8d. inferior). I met a Mr. Martin here who married a daughter of Sir Francis Colliers. He made himself known to me as having been at a gay Ball given by us in Durnford Street - that one I suppose when we had the two houses.

God Bless You Dearest Margaret is the prayer of your affectionate husband John Loudon.

My Dearest Margaret...

Enclosure to Lottie

My dearest Lotty your letters always give me good spirits even your Dutch Paintings of the interior all so graphic that I fancy I see all your message before me - dog, cat, old Jack and Mr.Bumkin. The garden scenes and little flashes of Charlotte's esprit giving life and interest to everything she touches upon. That puts me in mind of the studio here which I will attend for months - the most interesting objects for every taste ancient and modern - old Pompeii vividly in the stucco of its walls shewing the freshness of yesterday and the most beautiful taste in their fresco paintings - with their utensils their everyday customs, habits, dresses, ornaments in gold, bracelets, earrings in short you enter their houses as it were a guest of 2000 years ago. I may fancy them now living and offering you a hearty welcome but I cannot enter upon so all absorbing a subject. So, Charlotte, await till I come home. God Bless you believe me my dear Charlotte, your affectionate father John Loudon.

22 June Malta

You would receive in this a letter from me from Naples overland through France on the 8th. Since then we received orders to liberate our detained vessels as the affair between us and the King of Naples was in a fair way of being brought to a satisfactory conclusion upon which the Admiral and I set off instantly in the Confrance Steamer and arrived her in 46 hours on the 14th leaving the flagship to follow us which she did on the 25th and are all again expecting to join the Squadron at the mouth of the Dardanelles taking Lady Stopford and four daughters to Corfu where they are to pass the Summer heat till we call for them on our way back, for here it is getting very hot. The Thunderer joined us on Saturday the 20th bringing our old friend Mrs Barnard. Lady Charlotte Berkeley having arrived in the Cyclops repenting very much her folly on ever leaving England. She was told she would see her husband at least every 6 weeks - we were away 6 months last time. However she has him with her for 5-6 days when he must go to the Eastward with us and the Bellerophon. Many of the ladies are talking of going to Smyrna where the Plague is never absent and our Mrs Reynolds is already there. Great jealousies all about preferences but all in a lady like way and I nearly fall into disgrace occasionally from not telling them when and where the ships are

1840

going or coming back. I am very glad you allowed dear Fan to accompany Eliza and Errington to Colchester because it would do her own health good as well as keeping dear Liz in countenance among her new relations, however kind and Fanny will not run away with money foolishly dear girl. I suppose Willoughby is with you but I know very little of his proceedings. I trust to hear he is not neglecting himself for whoever does not move in a race must be left behind. I get through my own duty here by regular attention to it and though I have only two clerks for the service of 36 sail, 11 of them of the Line, I get on very well without hurry or confusion - certainly Capt Fanshawe is of great use to me and the Admiral himself has a head turned to business and we go on most pleasantly. I am sorry to hear Knox is so unpopular among the sailors at Plymouth for he is a good officer and a sailor's friend. We still continue comfortable here and they all know they cannot else be friends with the Admiral. I wonder you did not see Mrs Parker because she and I were great friends and he promised to call but he has been torn to pieces by gout and rheumatism in fact a general break up.

23 June Tuesday

I had a most pleasant evening with the Collings and Lt. Hoseason of the Alerto Steam packet who is making money and a lover of Lou's and I think there is no objection on her part or her fathers. He has a house furnished and all looks promising. The Report now is that Sir Chas Adam is to be our relief and that he will come as soon as the Session of Parliament breaks up which I take to be next month or August and I don't care for the cold season when you have a good fireside ready for me. Willie and Charlotte will keep you amused for a few months and he may enjoy his cricket and his flute and yet keep up his studies. I am not aware how many terms he has yet to serve nor what credit he has attained in his College only I hear what is not over palatable to me that he is certainly not a reading man - however this must now be left to himself as I can do no more than what I have done.

25th

I just received your dearest letter of the 4th with Charlottes and one from Liz with a little one from Errington according to custom. I am sadly grieved at Willoughby's boils. You have done right in telling him to consult Brodie but my own idea is that he must submit to a gentle course of caloniel and then all will be right. We are off to Corfu and then the Dardanelles on Saturday. I have hardly a moment to myself in all these doings but you will hear again by next Packet as we are going first to Corfu with Lady Stopford and the young ladies - many thanks to dear Lottie for her nice letter - I don't begrudge dear Fan her trips for I know she will be as prudent as possible. God Bless You Dearest Margaret is the prayer of your affectionate husband John Loudon. Poor Mrs Goldsmith I fear in a [sad] way and Miss Goldsmith quite a leper with mosquitoes.

5 July On Passage from Malta to Smyrna

I wrote Willoughby on dear Fanny's birthday off Sicily. We put Lady Stopford and the young ladies that day on board the Phoenix Steamer commanded by Capt. Robert Stopford and they would get to Corfu on the 31st or at least the 1st. of this month. The wind has been light and partial ever since. We were off Athens yesterday and have today got through the Dora Passage an important point between Negra Point and St.Andrews so that we reckon upon being with the Squadron in two or three days more. The weather is perfectly delicious and the scenery about us is always fresh - only think of 12 Pillars as white as snow standing on a Promontory looking over the sea which have stood there for 2300 years connecting the heroic age of Pericles with the present forlorn state of Greece - and the islands of undying fame clustering all around us. The sea like glass and such a sun as sets over Attica still in view but sinking in the distance.

6 July   Voulca Bay

Here we are again my Dearest Margaret after a beautiful passage through the islands - we found here Admiral Sir John Louis and five ships & right glad they all seem to welcome us back - Capt. Lawrence has come on board to see us and I am glad to find his health greatly improved for he was far from well poor man when we left this. Capt. Worth & he got on very ill together I believe.

1840

8 July

Sad doings in Syria - the Druzes in a state of revolt against Mehemet Ali - but as it is no business of ours we cannot interfere. The Pasha has sent 13 Frigates with about 15000 troops to Beirout to keep them down but as they have possession of the passes or the Mountains of Lebanon it is thought the Egyptians will be cut in pieces in detail. They commit great irregularities in the Town however & their officers are afraid to punish them - an Englishman or a man under English protection was murdered in the streets - a Frenchman was attempted to be assassinated. A Council was sitting upon the murderer of the Englishman but the French Consul was laughed at when he sought redress & immediately struck his flag & retired to Alexandria. We now have Capt. Napier your old friend there and another line of Battle Ships and the Castor with Austin in the Cyclops to protect our countrymen. Three Turks were caught attempting to run away with a Frigate to Constantinople and were drowned in the night from fear of punishing them openly.

9 July, Thurs.

The time crawls on. The Hastings in going out this morning on a short cruise has got ashore on a reef of rocks & although she is in no danger she will most probably have to be sent to Malta to get repaired. It is a passage something like between Drake's Island[77] & Mount Edgecombe but it has been gone through by a 1st rate and the Pilot thought it safe. The Admiral has been very kind and considerate to me and has offered to give me 2 months leave from Malta if our relief don't come out, which I will gladly avail myself of - but I can hardly think we shall be kept out so long. So we hear Cpt Sharpe has married again to Miss Erskine - a good compliment to matrimony - I was not surprised at it.

12 July

Very hot but a nice breeze. I have not been on shore yet but think myself better on board. My health excellent and no want of appetite. Is it not odd that all my former complaints of indigestion have disappeared and I have not even had one twitch since I went with Sir Wm Hargood - nor any other but old age which I cannot

---

77 In Plymouth Sound.

My Dearest Margaret...

keep off more than my neighbour but it creeps on very gently and I should not perceive it if my teasing neighbour Capt Fanshawe did not call me old Johnny - but one comfort I tell him is that he is getting on himself.

17 July
I have just received your dear letter of the 14th and 19th June. I am glad you are all so well and Willoughby again at home. Poor fellow he had a rough passage and I am in hopes soon the railroads will soon take the place of steam. I have not a single thing to send you by the Belleisle. Capt Nicolas will call upon you. He has been very kind to me always and offered to do all in his power for me but I hope and trust to be soon with you myself and bringing myself to you will be content I know. I am always charmed with Charlotte's notes.

God Bless You All - your affectionate husband John Loudon. Affectionate regards to dear Will.

29 July Princess Charlotte Isle of Thasos
This is a day[78] my dearest Margaret never to be forgotten and the first thing I do is to set down and have a chat with my dear wife whom many as my wanderings have been I have never forgotten one instant of my life - four of these days have already passed over us since we last parted and this I pray to God may be the last we pass separate from one another. We are now besides three full years on the actual station having taken the command from Sir Joshua Rowley at Mahon on the 30th of July 1837 - and excepting the dreadful sacrifice of so long an absence from my home and family I must say I never passed any portion of my life so much to my own satisfaction. Being tired doing nothing at Isouda we took a cruise among the islands and passing by Mount Athos and Lemnos which Charlotte will point out to you we anchored off Cavallas a romantic Town at the foot of a range of hills where Mehemet Ali was a coffee-house boy, and then a tobacconist being born in the neighbourhood. It is the very Neapolis where St Paul preached the first Christian Doctrine. Europe about 8 miles over the range of steep mountains and the most beautiful and extensive

---

78   33rd. wedding anniversary.

plains I ever beheld bounded by abrupt and lofty mountains where the Battle of Philippi was fought and where the two heights which Brutus and Cassius seated themselves before the Battle all yet seen. The Town of Philippi is commemorated to this day by the ruins of a church which I take it that pious woman Helena the mother of Constantine had built on the spot where St Paul was imprisoned and the Earthquake shook the prison and opened its doors. We set out at 3 in the morning, got there before the sun got hot - reposed under the shade of a grove of trees by a fountain of water like ice till the heat was over and returned in the evening. Next day we moved to this island which we all allow to be the finest we have ever seen. So green with trees and rich cultivated valleys and the mountains lofty and fantastic in their shapes clothes with wood to their very tops. A valley here is covered with marble tombs, many of them with great inscriptions to the inmates, rich and great no doubt among themselves but unknown to history. A very strong Venetian Fortress commanded the Town when they possessed the island but an earthquake destroyed it in 1742 nearly 100 years ago and now there is no town near to defend. There are 10 however on the island and the day before yesterday I went to the nearest and principal one 5 miles off which gave me a good idea of the country and the people who are all Greeks and miserable enough but have all nature's beauties spread out before them. The Admiral wanted to go from my description but I told him the road was rather abrupt and Capt Fanshawe has just now set out upon the Expedition with Captain Berkeley leaving the Admiral in my care till his return. But he must travel in the heat of the sun while I set off at 4 and rested in the shade by a fountain as usual till the cool of the evening. This island was celebrated for its gold and silver mines of which there are no traces now. It belongs to Mehemet Ali - an odd thing in the heart of the Sultan's dominions but the Revenue is all paid by his order for the support of a school at Cavallas and he is an immense favourite all over Turkey.

 The insurrection in Syria is quelled but I see nothing approaching to a settlement of the question and I fear from the wrongheadedness of some of our diplomatics there will in the end be a fracas between us and the French who evidently favour Mehemet Ali and wish him to reform Syria. He will now have increased his army by eighteen thousand men whom he sent to Syria on pretence of

My Dearest Margaret…

quelling this insurrection - a most extraordinary man. Our friend the Grand Vizir is deposed but I yet see no change. The Admiral is managing pretty well, he has sent the Phoenix commanded by his son Robert to Corfu for the ladies whom he will send most likely to see Constantinople - then while away the time till October when if nothing occurs he will return to Malta and there hopes to find his relief, who all the world say is to be Sir Charles Adam. Tell dear Charlotte that the bag will be a beautiful wedding present to Miss Duckworth now Mrs Douglas. Lady Stopford made me a present of a very neat Polygraph[79] machine which she sent for a purpose and James has just now brought me a piece of Brusa[80] silk from Smyrna for a Dressing Gown. I do not expect Fan will be yet with you. I have no doubt she will benefit by her trip. I wrote Lizzie last and as the Postage is cheap you can lend one another and perhaps may send her this. We expect to move back to Smyrna in a few days to be more in the way. God Bless You My Dear. My love to dear Will and Charlotte, the dear girls at Ridgeway and kindest regards to Lady Elliot. I am ever your affectionate husband John Loudon.

19 August Mitylena

I fear my dearest Margaret this will be a shabby little letter in return to your nice Budget of the 18th last month which I received here just 4 weeks after it was written. Lady Stopford and three daughters arrived here 3 days ago and all obliged to be packed off again today for Malta as we are off for Alexandria and the Coast off Syria. The Benbow has just joined us and we are sending her to Commodore Napier with 5000 stand of arms for the Syrians. We are off at 12 o'clock and poor Lady Stopford has just bid me Good-bye - Ay! says the Admiral you and Mr Loudon always together and I meant to write dear Lotty but fear my letter wont be worth receiving. I shall write from Alexandria and my letter may arrive as soon as this. Monstrous hot and I perspire terribly but it keeps me healthy though thin. God Bless You your ever affectionate husband John Loudon.

---

79 The polygraph machine is likely to have been one of the machines being developed to copy writing.
80 Bursa (Brusa) was the source of most royal silk products, importing raw silk from Iran and China, and supplying kaftans, pillows, embroidery and other silk products for the royal palaces in the Ottoman Empire.

Enclosure to Charlotte
Dearest Lottie. I devour every word of your interesting epistles. I wrote Willoughby by this and hope what I say to one is understood for all. I am now in the Land of Song and Classic Lore but malheureusement have not much time to profit of it though I have had several trips on shore before the Admiral is up at 5 o'clock in the morning and back to breakfast. I took the young ladies up to the top of the ridge which looks over a splendid Lake in the interior which strikes abruptly on the sight. At our feet surrounded by another girdle of hills with spacious groves on the margin of the Lake and looking back we had the romantic town and castle of Mitylene with the Royal Princess Charlotte and smaller vessels and the lofty hills of Anatolia bounding the prospect on the East. The country houses look very pretty being white full of windows and perched up as it were through the trees which they partially out top. But we must leave it and away we go to Alexandria. They are making a terrible noise over my head now. Kindest regards to all. God Bless You Dearest Lottie your affectionate father John Loudon.

23 Aug Princess Charlotte 60 miles from Alexandria
My Dearest Margaret
We left Mitylene on the 19th - the day I wrote you with the Phoenix. Poor Lady Stopford and her three daughters started at the same time and have got to Malta I expect today. It must have been gratifying for her to be in her eldest sons vessel and meeting the Zebra commanded by her second son James who was a midshipman when we came to the station and her husband's Flag flying at the main of this ship as Commander-in-Chief in these Seas. The next day we saw a ship behind us firing guns and found it the Benbow with the Zebra having intelligence to communicate - Lord Ponsonby saying the French Ambassador had made an official Representation to the Sultan that France would oppose by all the means in her power any attempt against Mehemet Ali - although there appears to be a little bullying in this it is necessary for us to be upon our guard and we are getting our ships together. The Admiral is sorry now for sending the Belleisle home but we shall still go on following our orders and if France acts the Traitor the fault will be hers, not ours. I expect Mehemet Ali will keep in

his ships without giving us the trouble of shewing our teeth to keep them in and after that we expect to go on the Coast of Syria where we have now 5 Line of Battle and the Castor and a Steamer besides the Asia, Implacable and Hastings, should the two latter not be wanted up the Dardanelles to protect Constantinople in case of Ibrahim marching upon it. The French Squadron of 8 Sail of the Line we left in Voulca Bay. the weather is very pleasant and we have had a delightful passage so far all in good health and spirits - come what may. It is like a weight off our shoulders to get the ladies back though most agreeable to have them under other circumstances. Tell Willoughby his friends the Austens are left pretty much as they were at Athens and the old Lass bitterly regrets being such a fool as to have left Malta - vowing she never will be persuaded again by anybody.

24 Aug Monday

Just arrived at Alexandria and a curious sight to me to see the places so familiar to me nearly 40 years ago. The Lines occupied by our Troops on the day of the Battle of the 21 June 1801 in which Sir Ralph Abercromby was mortally wounded are now before me (Aboukir Bay - Nelson) as if nothing had ever taken place upon them - but all life is the Town and Port - fine Houses, Shipping, Flags and Pendants streaming in all directions. We shall know more immediately - 12 o'clock anchored. Col. Hodges our Consul came off - things look gloomy - the French give Mehemet courage and he certainly will not bend - he would be nothing without the French however. Beautiful weather here but very hot. Very odd to be put in quarantine at Alexandria where there are a few cases of Plague still and we come from a healthy quarter.

26th.

I must send this off - though I have very little to add - I see no hope of an adjustment but as little chance of hostilities unless France takes the shameless part she threatens. We have letters from Commodore Napier at Beyrout where he is very active and is stirring up the Mountaineers again according to orders - but they are afraid unless they saw greater help at hand. I have just received a very kind note from Capt Lyons reminding me of old times and of your kindness to them - hoping to see me. He has

1840

employment of some kind at Cairo but is now here. I don't know if I mentioned that Lou Collings has another disappointment in Hoseason - which I almost expected would be the case when I heard his sister was coming out. Collings is in a great rage with him. The Pasha I understand is very anxious to see the Admiral and if he goes I shall go with him - but I hope he will not put us both in the Pyramids. If so I will set you and Charlotte about his ears and he will then be glad to let us out. We are lying a mile and a half from the Town and a very uncomfortable rolling sea we have. My affectionate regards to all.

Believe me ever   My Dearest Margaret   your affectionate husband John Loudon.

10 Sept Princess Charlotte off Beyrout

The plot thickens and where it will end God knows. I fear not well. Mehemet Ali is I believe by this time declared a Rebel another named Pasha for Egypt and another for Syria - so says Lord Ponsonby[81] the prime mover of the whole. We have Napier here too - brave as a lion but both too violent - much more I think than was intended. I fear my Good Admiral is a little led from his better judgement by them. Walker who was on the Vanguard is now a Turkish Bey and a Rear Admiral in charge of a Turkish expedition of 5375 troops in a Line of Battle Ships, a Frigate La Corvette and 24 transports - they are all landed with about 1000 marines and English Sappers and Miners and Artillery at a post when they hope to rally the Mountaineers who were in insurrection but subdued. To cover the landing we have been firing shot and shell among the Egyptian troops all in arms outside the Town and I fear have killed and wounded a great many by the shells we saw burst among them - they have not fired a shot but if they get at the Turks they will repay them well. You never saw a more beautiful Town than Beyrout of its size hid among trees and gardens, rising gently from the water. I fancies Lebanon farther back but it rises close to the sea and more towering bluff looking mountains I never saw with villages on their sides and passes and up on top like eagles Nests - but rather bleak. Walker Bey fired a salute on the landing - had we not kept the Egyptian troops at Bay at least 10000 men -

---

81 Lord Ponsonby the British ambassador in Constantinaple 1832-41.

My Dearest Margaret...

the poor 5000 Turks and our own marines could not have effected it and if we withdraw our marines and the Mountaineers[82] dont join, they will I fear hardly be able to keep it.

I am more and more rejoiced Dear Margaret you did not come to Malta - a right jolly Scotch Lassie very much of your build the wife of Dr Martin of the Hospital we left in the best of health but the heat was too much for her and I have just heard from Collings of her death. She has not been a year on Malta - poor woman much respected. I really am much encouraged by dear Will's letters. There is a manliness and a style of good sound sense that give me hope of his distinguishing himself in the business and affairs of life - whatever he may have shewn at school and college - this often happens. He rates his abilities too low and forgets that nothing is acquired without close and steady application. They never forget me at Chatham and the more I hear from them the more I am convinced that Dear Lizzie's lot in a Husband has been a prize God Bless them both. Fanny is I suppose again with you altho poor Liz will miss her much. Tis of no use speculating any more about our return for Lord Minto has written the Admiral privately that they are so well pleased with his conduct that they are not to relieve him till Spring when another will be sent out. But when we shall leave this I know not for matters are very gloomy at present. How strongly I wish myself at your apron string again. Captain Fanshawe laughs me out of my susceptibility when everything does not go right or as I wish it and says I have been spoilt. You know my little pettish hasty temper I am sure I have said a hundred times worse things to him than I ever did to you but can never make him angry "no! no! Johnny you can't make me angry - I don't care what you say I know you don't mean it" then he takes me up in his arms for he is as powerful as a horse and squeezes me with my feet off the ground that I cannot but laugh and all is right again. A Captain is a solitary being without a companion. God Bless You and Charlotte and Fan, believe me Dearest Margaret your truly affectionate husband John Loudon.

---

82 The Mountaineers were armed insurgents who supported the Turkish cause against Mehemet Ali, amongst them many deserters from the Egyptian army.

1840

17 Sept Princess Charlotte, Coast of Syria. Beyrout
Although I have a long letter on my desk for you and a longer one for Willy giving him an account of ourselves since I last wrote you on the 26th August, I take the opportunity of the Ambassador's Bag at Constantinople to give you the heads of all the occurrences. I went on shore with the Admiral and Capt. Fanshawe at Alexandria and saw this mighty Pasha who was very unwell with Will's complaint - Boils. He was very affable but declined entering upon Politics - He invited the Admiral however to dine with him next day but was too ill in the morning and sent an excuse - two physicians sat up with him a night or two after. He would not come in to the Sultan's terms however and away we came - leaving the Asia and Implacable to keep her man of war from coming out, and on the 8th instant we arrived at this ill fated place Beyrout then in all its gaiety and freshness - now alas a spectre of what it was. We found the Turkish troops - about 4500 and Napier all ready to make a landing. We saw the grounds about the Town all bristling and glittering with muskets and bayonets all ready to appoint the troops and our marines about 1300 making 6000 in all were under weigh. The Steamers all covered with red Jackets and the Turkish Transports 24 in number with red caps to divert the Egyptian troops from the place of landing. The ships threw shot and shell which stirred up the dust amongst them and protected the only road from the Town to the Position we took up which is a small ridge about three quarters of a mile long well protected by our ships and surrounded by deep ravines. - about 5-6000 Mountaineers the finest fellows I ever saw have come in and received Muskets and many desertions have taken place from the Egyptian army. With all this I am not sanguine. Winter will soon be on we are on an open stormy coast and our marines are on shore without shelter. The Admiral seems determined to leave it on the 28th on this month and, if we do, the poor creatures I fear will be sacrificed as they are afraid to come in in sufficient numbers to defend themselves - but I trust something will turn up ere that. The Egyptians are advancing and an attack is expected which we are in good hopes of repulsing and if so there is then no fear. But it is an awkward kind of warfare and I am heartily sick of it - not because there is danger but that there actually is none and we have been killing away unmercifully upon people who do

My Dearest Margaret...

not return us a shot. The people of this country are enslaved and would gladly rise but the time I fear is gone by. The villages are all guarded and hostages are taken from those of any influence so that their children would be put to death if they were to return to their allegiance to the Sultan.

The weather is terribly hot and I dread going to bed as I perspire so much but a fortnight more will cure that. I think it a great misfortune we were not relieved as this business will not do us any credit, I fear. The Admiral would do very well himself but he has too many advisors mostly against Capt. Fanshawe and myself. I must confess this business is worrying me terribly but we are into it and must get out as we best can. I cannot write our Dear Chathamites this way but have as long a ballad as my time will allow for them by the Piquet. Young Elliot quite well - we had severe loss the other day attacking a Roman Tower which they thought the ship's guns had cleared - a party of marines marched up to it and a volley from some loop holes below killed 5 marines and wounded 16. Young Adair grazed in the leg. Dear Gifford of the Cyclops severely wounded - our Party obliged to retreat and the Pilot thoughtlessly left the flag which Sidney Grenfell gallantly ran back for and brought away - the next morning the Tower was evacuated. The day after another Fort was taken defended by 500 men - the Mountaineers, 250, volunteered to take it with the assistance of the Carysfort and Cyclops - the Great Guns roused them out, the Mountaineers followed up, killed many, took the Fort and one of them in their own homely way brought Capt. Martin a present of a head as a trophy. Capt M reproved that brutal warfare and offered a Musket and a Dollar for every wounded man they brought him.

God Bless You My Dearest Margaret. Tell Willy I am very well pleased with him.

20th. Sept

I received your dear letter of the 30th Aug and my dear Lottie's very entertaining one about the Bazaar and Launch - which amused me much in my present far from comfortable state of mind. God Bless you Dearest Marge, Your Affectionate John.

1840

23rd. Oct Princess Charlotte, Beyrout

Though I rather think you will receive this and my former letter together yet I cannot miss this opportunity of a Steamer going to Malta to let you have one of a later date assuring you I am quite well and everything going on favourably - the Vanguard arrived yesterday and brought me a rare lot of letters from you all up to the 25th of last month. Sir David told me he never was more astonished in his life than when he came to Malta and found you not there. It might or might not be the case... I was truly sorry to hear poor Will was so ill - but I trust Dr. Isbell has given him a thorough clearing out and that he is now at his studies. It is certainly most unfortunate for him at such a time but health is the first object and so far it is a matter of rejoicing to me that the Doctor had taken him in hand. You must have had an overflowing home for a time but your birds of passage dont stay long. I have a nice little correspondent in Henrietta Stopford who has written me a most entertaining account of Annie Duckworth's wedding with Captain Douglas at Berne on the 19th Sept. and I am sure all who knows dear Annie will wish her much happiness. Little Charlotte writes me all the news of her family in Malta and with your dear despatches and the Chathamites which are quite delighted I am like the Post Horses in the Stage Coach taking a drink of water - so refreshed in this dreary absence of mine. We have got hold of the old fox of the mountains and sent him voluntarily however to Malta. It was two of his mens heads I saw bleeding on pikes at Gezzar Pashas Gate when I first saw him 40 years ago. He is about 88 - dark strong features with huge bushy white beard and whiskers like the Greats of Abraham and other patriarchs in the bible. In fact you would think you were living among the giants of those days - Dress and manner decidedly the same.

We shall move soon to Marmorice Bay - a place of great security where bad weather comes on- but I trust this affair may soon be settled - Mehemet Ali's subjects even more disconsolate at Alexandria even than here and were they sure of support they would rise against him immediately - the sick left here when the troops retired were wretched and it was degrading to human nature to witness the apathy with which their very companions passed them by when panting and dying of thirst and exhaustion and would not even offer them a cup of water - or throw them a rag

My Dearest Margaret...

of a covering over them though pitiably entreated with accents of despair to do so. One poor wretch I saw worn and dying by a stone wall under a tree not a bit of flesh on his legs - his head leaning on his breast, the tremor of death upon him - nobody heeded him. We gave a piece of money to his fellow soldier passing who took him on his back as if he had been a dead Jackass laughing and hitching him up as his spindle shanks dangled on the ground and away he trotted I believe to the hospital. But the steamer goes. God Bless You Your Affectionate Husband John Loudon.

15 Nov Princess Charlotte Beyrout
You will receive my rigmarole letter My Dearest Margaret by the Phoenix and had I more time I would not have sent the first part of it. The Fortress of St.Jean d'Acre had a formidable appearance and had they pointed the least bit lower much mischief would have been done. They killed 18 and wounded 41 but the shot flew principally among the Rigging. Lieut. le Mesurer died of his wounds and that gave the Admiral an opportunity of making Genniss who is expressively grateful and I am glad of it. The poor old Java was almost blown in the air and the fire left smouldering after it blew up another magazine of live shells which killed and wounded several people - particularly poor Captain Collier among the latter who was carried on Board with a broken leg - I confess I did not like it the day I went on shore. The fire was burning and the live shells quite exposed. I did not like sauntering so long near it but as they did not wish to hurry off though I was right glad to go. We left St. Jean d'Acre on the 9th and got back here on the 10th. The Admiral is now easier in his mind and his spirits better. We are not in such a hurry neither to leave the Coast which is not so formidable as it looked at first. There is now nothing more to do but to keep up the courage of the Mountaineers and to dispirit the Egyptians who are concentrated in Ibrahim's camp about 25 miles in the plain near Balbeck. The whole Coast of Syria is now ours and if the French dont strike in[83] I expect fully to be with you very early in the Spring. I have had a very hard and uncomfortable time of it for the last 3 months but thank God I have kept my health and get through. I shall not be able to write our Chathamites

---
83 The cooperation, if uneasy, between France and Britain since Waterloo was threatened by the attacks on the Syrian coast, as Mehemet Ali had been encouraged by French support.

this time - you can send this to wish them a merry Christmas or rather that you spend it altogether. I thought last year I should certainly have been with you this. Nothing can be more beautiful than the weather is now here - and we begin to wear blue trousers though it is not cold - but now and then showery. I hear Thiers is out and Soult Prime Minister of France but that the mob are fractitious. They are aching for a return to their former lickings and we shall not be unwilling to give it if they bully too much. Their late conduct has been underhanded and very unworthy of a Great Nation. They have done all they could to oppose us here sending emissaries among the inhabitants to tell them we were to take the country for ourselves, and that if they held out France was bringing an immense Fleet and army to support them. In fact the poor old man Mehemet never would have given us this trouble but for their promises of support. How they can get out of the scrape I don't know - certainly not with honor or credit.

Thank you again dearest Margaret for your mindfulness of the Flannels which are proof against the hardest winter. My light Deal shirts have done their work well and never wear out. I never had such a bargain. I leave them off now for the Winter. I hope dear Charlotte's cold is well again and that you are all happy in the old quarter where I fancy I see you by a good fire and you in your magisterial chair by the window side of it. Would I were with you. I hope Errington will assist you through Christmas I can hardly expect poor Will unless he has kept from College. I dined yesterday with the Archduke Frederic the son of the Great Archduke Charles who fought the French so well in the time of the Revolution. He is a fine young man - commands an Austrian Frigate and very brave.

God Bless You All your affectionate husband John Loudon.

Many thanks dear Lottie for your good readiness to work another Bag to my Dear Annie Duckworth as a wedding present. I preferred the original colour to Lady Stopford.

22 Nov Princess Charlotte Beyrout

A Merry Christmas to you all. My Dearest Margaret. You see we are still at the old quarters and now every thing smiles upon us. The weather is heavenly. Ibrahim Pasha has retreated we hear back to Egypt if he can get there and all Syria may be said to be won back for the Sultan. No French war likely though we all now were

My Dearest Margaret...

prepared for it and we have reason to think Egypt may be given up to Mehemet which would be a good thing for us as few if any are so enlightened among the Musselmen. I see Admiral Fleming poor man has had but a short career in Greenwich Hospital[84] but Lord Minto has so many family connections that my Admiral is not even now so sanguine. How delighted you must be to have all your circle round you although I am absent you know I am well and every thing going on well. We shall go to the snug harbour of Marmorice whenever it blows which it never seems disposed to do under our stupendous mountains. We are close to the shore. I take a walk occasionally among the mulberry trees which this place is famous for as well as its raw and manufactured silk but it is very coarse and I think dear and bad in quality. The dress of the Mountaineers is flowing and exactly like the old patriarchal dress you see in the pictorial Bibles. I don't think it has altered since the time of old Abraham, and as little have their manners. It was close to this Lady Esther Stanhope ended her days leaving behind her the white horse she had bought for our Saviour to ride to Jerusalem upon the commencement of the Millennium. By the by the Egyptians have been turned out of Jerusalem and we sent a fine old Turk with a bushy grey beard to be Governor of it a day or two ago. I send you a plan of our battle. The Admiral and staff were on board his son's steamer which peppered away famously and enabled him to see the double attack on both sides - that on the South was the smartest though the Batteries looked the most formidable on the West, particularly a large Cavalier on the South West Corner. It was thought to be shell from the Gorgon - the steamer on our left which blew up the magazine - but for that we might have lost a few more lives but the place must have been taken all the same. It is worth your turning to the Story of the Crusades. St. Jean d'Acre has always been a charnel -house - 120,000 buried in one year at its siege and 4 or 5000 butchered in cold blood by Richard I and Philip of France - very holy wars!! I can hardly tell you what sensations I had when when I first saw its towers rising out of the water as we approached and the same cupola and minaret I had left nearly 40 years ago with Mount Carmel jutting out in the sea on the other side of the Bay. My old friend and

---

84 Admiral Fleeming died after a short period as Governor of Greenwich Hospital.

fellow traveller Catapago the Austrian Consul was still alive but had fled to the Convent of Elias and I regret I did not see him - the only one left of our party except Mr.Cripps the Member.

The reason you were so long in hearing was our want of means of sending to Malta, having use for all our steamers to carry troops and assist in redeeming the Coast. They were most useful and efficient in every way[85]. God Bless You All is the prayer of Dearest Margaret your ever affectionate husband John Loudon.

1 Dec Princess Charlotte Beyrout
You will be glad to hear that our labours here are drawing to a close. Commodore Napier has conceived a convention with Mehemet Ali which I have no doubt will be confirmed though it would just as well have been let alone till he had authority to do it - for one of the Articles is that Mehemet shall withdraw his troops from Syria whereas we have driven them out - at least Ibrahim is beating his retreat on the Mecca Road through the desert and is cutting up sadly by the county people and desertions - all the country is now free - but state that Mehemet Ali is now to restore the Turkish Fleet a soon as the Great Powers give him Egypt then which they cannot do better. For to give him his due, he is the most fit man to have it and very soon now I shall be with my dear wife and sheets, at my own fireside again. The change has been very sudden here in the weather. I am glad of flannels. Snow on the mountains and real Plymouth weather below. The Admiral and all our party were to keep St. Andrews Day yesterday with Capt Houston Stewart of the Benbow, sheeps head broth and haggis but there was no moving out of the ship. In a day or two we are going to Marmorice about four hundred miles off near Rhodes where there is snug anchorage and then for Malta. You cant fancy how the Egyptians abuse the French for their conduct in this affair. They have neither behaved well to them or us, deceiving both, but they have only exposed their own crooked underhand policy. Mehemet would have accepted our terms but trusted to them and they were pretending to make common cause with us when they were giving them information of everything we intended to do - well!!. Let politics alone. I fancy I see you in your Lady Margaret's Chair

---

85　The speed and manoeuvrability of the steam-powered ships, landing troops and supporting the ships of the line, contributed to the quick success of the operation.

laying down the law to your riotous subjects in these Christmas times, all waiting your nod for the amusements of the evening. What would I give to be with you where I hope Errington is by this time and perhaps Willy, though it is a long journey for such a short holiday. I live upon your thoughts of all this - for otherwise very little enjoyment comes to my shore. I am now obliged to close double quick - the steamer is starting for Constantinople - Napier I thought to have exceeded his powers and the Admiral will not ratify his convention very wisely I think. God Bless You all and a merry fireside is the prayer of him thats far away. Your affectionate husband John Loudon.

3rd. Dec Princess Charlotte off Beyrout.

I wrote you only two days ago by Constantinople that all was well. Commodore Napier had taken upon himself to make terms with Mehemet Ali and altho' nobody would be more happy than I should be at an end to this war, yet it is an interference not justified, even by the Commander-in-Chief, far less a second in Command with no authority but to obey his orders from the Admiral. He is reluctantly obliged not to sanction it. We have just come through a danger greater I think than St. Jean D'Acre. Yesterday morning a tremendous gale came on and having no protection a rolling sea came in which dismasted some and drove on shore ten or eleven small vessels. We rode it out famously but it was frightful to look at. Though now more moderate it is sad to see those poor vessels lying wrecked along the shore - though I am in hopes there were not many lives lost as their crews are in tents and going backwards and forwards on the beach. One poor vessel had gone down at her anchors in the night, very close to us, and part of her upper works separated from her main body. She is just seen in a level with the sea full of water - but no boat can yet go to her and not a creature is seen - such a gale has not been seen here for ten years. We are all off to sea.

1840

5 o'clock, Sat. 5 Dec.

We are now sailing beautifully along the coast of Cyprus its hills covered with snow and are on our way to the snug harbour of Marmorice where I hops to have a little rest for I have had a fagging time of it these last three months at Beyrout and Acre. If Sir John Ommanney is here I should not wonder if we return to Malta but we have yet something to do ere we finish our work properly. I fear this has no chance of reaching you by Christmas but may by the New Year. I hope it will be a happy one for us all.

7 Dec.

I received yesterday your dear letter of the 4th Nov. written the day after our action. I am delighted Eliza and Fan are again with you - what a happy fireside - I can fancy it but it must be rather as anxious time for dear Lizzie who it seems wont let me off from scratching a Grand Papa's brow.[86] Poor dear if however what you all wish to come to and Errington writes me the very day we were fighting that he confesses he wished a baby. He was right in sending her by land and Fan came in for a good thing by her companionship. I have sent Errie £50 extra this year in anticipation - for Mrs Blount let the cat out - and I shall open my heart for Lizzie by letting her keep the £20 as Grand Papa's present for his Grandson or daughter as it may be. But I dont mean to encourage such doings every year - let them look to that! Poor Will - his ill health just throwing him back than getting through his studies at College losing the privileges as he did at school, but I must say nothing only hope he has recovered his health. I suppose he will not underestimate such a long journey for the short vacation and will pass his holidays in London. It is now raining here like Plymouth. We have just sent Capt Fanshawe to Alexandria 200 miles off in the Magicienne to offer Mehemet Ali Egypt if he gives up the Turkish Fleet and I think he will. We are now authorised but Commodore Napier was not. He is useful but difficult to keep in his place. How much this weather reminds me to thank you my dear for your care of my body and shanks, in mindfully sending my flannels. I assure you I find the good of them when the snow is all around me. I am still doubtful about the Admiral

---

86 First indication of Eliza's pregnancy.

My Dearest Margaret...

We have had a quiet Christmas - only the Admiral, Commander Jones (Capt Fanshawe gone to Constantinople with Mehemet Ali's proposals) the Flag Lieutenant Johnson, son of Mr Johnson the Secretary in the Dockyard, Mr Kitson, the Parson and myself and all the healths of all our families and absent friends were drank in champaigne. Glanville is gone as happy as a bucket at his promotion which I rather think some of his people will call and tell you. I mentioned Ginniss being Lieutenant and think the Admiral has behaved very handsomely to his wife's family. I am getting rather fidgety about dear Eliza but trust in God she will be as lightly dealt with as the Queen. Good night God Bless You all.

1841

The new grandson - Malta - letter from Lottie - Napier's honours - Willoughby's extravagance - Malta - futures

1st. Jan.

Another year begins upon us my dearest and thus we go on. We have had a week of most delightful weather and the Admiral and I have had a pleasant walk every day in the most pastoral scenery you can imagine shut out from all the world in beautiful valleys surrounded by rocky hills and thickets with herds and flocks grazing and only a few shepherds huts and barking dogs to keep us in mind that it is inhabited. The sportsmen are all in their glory and our table is well furnished with partridges and woodcocks. Were we merely to think of our living we could not be better any where but that is a very poor consideration and all our longings are homewards. I can fancy you this evening again thinking of the absent, and I hope Errington is by his wife's side to bear her up for the evils he has caused her. God send all may go with her, poor dear girl. How happy shall I be when all is well over. I dont know what weather you have but here it is raining as it never rained before at Plymouth or elsewhere. I long to hear of Willoughby and how the holidays have fared with him for I hardly think it would be worth his while to come such a distance to Plymouth. I am vexed at his hardly ever giving any account of himself.

7th. Jan.

When we have no opportunities of sending our letters away what can we do but write on - such is my case but we have the arrivals today of Sir John Ommanney and Sir Watkin Pell in the Britannia and Howe but not a scrap from home, I expect. However in 5 or 6 days more a rare Pacquet by the Locust and an anxious

My Dearest Margaret...

arrival it will be about poor Lizzie. However we must not make up our minds to whatever may happen and I am trying to put my mind in training - poor dear girl she absorbs all my thoughts at present. We have sent Commodore Sir Chas Napier, your old reading room acquaintance, to Alexandria to assist in giving up the Turkish Fleet. It may do good and will shew at least there is no jealousy on the part of the Admiral.

8 Jany 11 p.m.

I must now close for the steamer starts at daylight and I want sleep. I am in hopes the affair will soon be settled but we shall hear in a few days. Sir John Ommanney is arrived with the Howe in company we are now 16 sail of the Line with 3 three deckers - too much for poor me. All I long for now is to get home and God send it soon. I am very anxious about poor Eliza poor dear - it will be the best of news I can get to hear she is well over it - a friend of mine Mr.Dornford called today to tell me he saw them all well at Chatham. If a young Syrian called Antonio Arniuny calls do pay him attention for I have a high opinion of him. He is going to Cambridge to study for the purpose of educating the people of the Country who are all very ignorant and is patronized by Lord Francis Egerton and other people of consequence and the University educates them gratis. Good night - alls well I hope, God bless you all is the prayer of Your Affectionate Husband John Loudon.

Affectionate regards to Errington.

23 January

My Dear Grannie

So Lizzie has made us old in spite of ourselves - I forgive her and only hope she has made a good recovery and that the new grandson gives you all proper amusement. I am very anxious tho about this but shall not hear I fear till I get down to Malta, which will be next week as the Admiral means to start in a few days more leaving the Squadron in charge of Sir John Ommanney and then I trust we shall bid farewell to the Mediterranean. the business is all over and well ended.

I received a rare batch of letters from you all on the 18th up to the last of December and a pretty winding up of a most eventful

1841

year it is. I am sorry dear Liz is not likely to suckle the young soldier but she must do as her Mammie did before her. I had a very good letter from Willoughby who always wipes off any angry feeling I have for his silence by his sensible letters when he does write. I long to hear from him again as this is an anxious time both as regards his health and studies. I fear Arney will be soon leaving you now but he will leave his wife and child to keep you in countenance till Grandpa comes home. That mad boy Fanshawe amuses himself now by calling me Granny - he is not likely to be one himself the mores the pity. I tell him my only annoyance will be his haunting me when I get home - no use my sky parlour he would clamber up outside like a monkey If the young grandsons nose is small you must pull it out when you can for when he grows up it will be a ticklish thing to do. All is going on well in Syria and Egypt and the long affair is at last I hope ended - and sick and tired I am of it. The poor Zebra - James Stopfords Brig is still on shore at Acre and small hopes of her getting off but he is in good spirit and cannot be blamed. The papers I see talk of what they know nothing about and puff the Commodore at the expense of the Admiral but as he says each will have his right in the end.

24th.

The Locust was off double quick but I am almost glad I can now inform you that this moment we are enjoying the glorious sight of the Turkish Fleet standing nobly in 12 in number, 2 three deckers, five 74s and Frigates - a most exulting sight and a proud winding up to all our labours[88]. I know not when I was so elated - for these ships have been always a heartsore to me and now all is decidedly settled before Sir Robert goes off the Station or even to Malta.

3rd Feb. Malta

I was cut short by the Locust starting but have now the pleasure of telling you we left Marmorice on the 28th in the Cyclops and arrived here yesterday the 2nd. The Admiral prefers the Steamer and making shorter and surer passages. We towed the Princess Charlotte out of Marmorice but as the wind was foul she may now

---

88 The Turkish Fleet preparing to return to Constantinople

My Dearest Margaret...

be here for a week. You may easily fancy what happy faces we found here. Lady Stopford looks ten years younger and the Young Ladies blooming beyond what I ever saw them and all agreeableness. My favourite Charlotte Stopford quite delighted with Lotties little bag and all admired it very much. Miss Stopford says she thinks a table cover worked with worsted in the same way of a Persian pattern would be beautiful. I shall send Mrs Douglas's wedding present to Corfu as soon as we are out of quarantine, that is in three weeks time, but are very comfortable and I am now sitting in the same room I was in the last year - the Governor having turned the poor Rifles out of their quarters to make room for the Admiral's family. Captain Austen of the Cyclops, one of the best creatures ever lived, gave me up his own sleeping cabin next to the Admirals and took a shakedown himself in the Rudder head - in fact I meet with nothing but the kindest attentions every where.

Your budgets last night of the 16th January gave me quite a luxury of joy - only 16 days from the time you wrote and all well - Dear Eliza over it but delicate I fear poor dear girl she will be some time in regaining strength particularly if that young soldier tears away at her - but he must not be starved and I think I would give him a bottle as you did - it is only for a few months and then the poor child does not suffer. I was delighted with the lock of hair which was much admired by all the Young Ladies and the dear Mamas letter made me almost weep for joy. I think now I may venture to predict our arrival early in May whether another Admiral comes out or not as the Admiral could now leave the Squadron in charge of Sir John Ommanney - his work being finished. I like Arney and Lizzies idea of the Savings Bank for Baby. It may give him an idea of saving when he grows up and maybe he may have a little eked to his stock at times by his friends when they know he has a nest egg.

7th Feby Sunday

Quite a fine sunny Summers day I wish you had it in England - we see the advantage of steamers - the poor Princess Charlotte not yet come in. We have just had Church as we had last year - a beautiful chapel and it is curious to see us all in separate groups according to our different quarantines. The Winter months are here perfectly delicious and indeed all the year excepting July, August and September when the English families contrive to have

1841

cool shady houses by the sea side with refreshing breezes. Malta is now quite crowded with visitors for health or curiosity - all the fashion with their yachts visiting the shores of Italy and Greece.

13th Feby

I had my dear Margaret another rich treat in your budget by the Phoenix and happy am I to find dear Liz and the Pet all going on well though I fear her recovery is slow. She must not hurt her own health and the childs by a very natural fondness for being her own nurse and you will use your influence if you see reason for it. I am rejoiced to find Willoughby has got through, had not his health interfered he would have had a more creditable place but under the circumstances I am very well satisfied and I hope he will shine in the business of life more than he has done as a scholar, as he must depend upon that for his success in the world. I suppose Errington is returned to his Depot. I hear nothing of our Relief but the Admiral will not remain after the Spring.

14th Feby.

I have just received by the Liverpool which had bad weather in the Channel and was late in consequence Lizzies dear letter and yours of the 30th and you may tell her I kissed the mark in which I understood Johnny had sent a kiss to me. All I want now is for her to have more milk or getting him another bottle - for he must not suffer poor fellow. I am glad you make such a play thing of him and every day he will become more amusing. Nothing new for us and I fear the scurvy dogs will bilk the Admiral out of his peerage after all.

15th Feby. Monday

All well but not a word from the Admiralty - Capt Fanshawe has got great credit for his mission to Alexandria and the Admiral is made a Knight.

27th Feby Malta

The time seems long since I wrote you but I have been very busy and see no end to my labours. There has been a great deal more work done in the East and I have had all my clerks at it hard preparing for the Admiralty Mail with the details of all the

My Dearest Margaret…

proceedings in Syria. Thank heaven Ibrahim Pasha is gone by sea to Alexandria with about ten thousand sick men, women and children and twenty thousand have marched by land - the miseries and hardships they have suffered in their route from Damascus was sad - dying by hundreds of fatigue, thirst and starvation, harrassed by the Mountaineers, Bedouins and Turks but Syria is clear of the Egyptians but whether for better or worse is doubtful. I fear there will be sad disorders among the people of the Country. The only man of influence the old Emir Bashir or Prince of the Mountains is here and anxious to get back. I believe the Sultan could not do better than reinstate him - he has a young and handsome wife - a Caucasian - whom he bought for £500 very richly dressed but the lower part of her face covered according to their custom - what a degradation of your sex to think she was a Caucasian slave sent to market yet has the manners of a Lady. We have had a regular round of Parties since we were let out of quarantine - never in bed till 2 o'clock. I wonder how I stand it and yet I am always up and at work by seven in the morning - however we are beginning to fall into quieter habits and shall soon I hope fall into our old family way. I am terribly severe to get up and I feel years getting heavy - we must all bend to our fate and I ought to bless God for sparing me and you thus far. I really did not believe I could have gone through so much. You talk of books - 'tis a long time since I have thought of one having other fish to fry.

A sad accident happened on board the Vanguard after we left Marmorice - a very fine young man Lt.Wemyss of Fife whom Sir David Dunn had brought up and got on his ship only a few weeks was taking a turn of a walze at the wardroom over for a frolic with Lt Cannon, the Band happening to be playing one, when either becoming giddy or tripped up by a ring bolt in the deck they both fell down the hatchway into the Cockpit and Wemyss broke his neck, Cannon much bruised as you may suppose falling through two decks - this makes 18 midshipmen Lieutenants since we came out. One has been very sickly and some cases of plague have broken out but our people have escaped. The poor little Zebra is breaking up - the Master a fine fellow has just fallen a victim to the fever and dysentery. Captain Pring of the Incenstant brought me your letter which was always welcome. He is a very worthy man and I was very much obliged to him for his attention in calling upon you. I

1841

have seen Will Foote who gave me all your news. I am sorry to hear the poor baby grows thin - and should be most happy to pay for his bottle if you would borrow a good one for him. Poor fellow - it is early for him to feel the ills of this wicked world of ours and his Mammie must get over her prejudices as you did for the sake of her child. I hear not a word from Willoughby or his Tutor - but am satisfied under all circumstances with the degree he has taken. His law studies I hope will turn out well - I think it will be more to his taste - but he must fight his way up in this. You will know before us when to expect us I think in May but we shall not certainly go to the Eastward again. I am now sitting by a comfortable fire 10 o'clock at night alone and all my thoughts wrapt up in you at home in your arm chair with all the dear circle round you. How I long to join it. Most of our people are gone to the Opera - I am tired of everything - Capt Fanshawe is come back to torment me I dine with him tomorrow. God Bless You dearest Marge is the prayer of Your ever Affectionate Husband John Loudon.

1st March

All well - no news only our friend Lord Ponsonby presses hard upon poor Mehemet Ali - now he has him down - I shall have a longer letter for you in a fortnight.

Letter from Lottie to her father at Malta.

Dearest Padre. *March 13th*

To commence with the most important personage in the family I must give you some account of your little grandson who you have indeed reason to be proud of. We are all quite fools about him and with all due reverence be it spoken Mamma not the least so and we all want the dear Grandad at home to make 44 the fools paradise. Everything is changed into Baby nothing else thought or spoken of from morning to night - reading quite out of the question for in the midst of the most sublime tragedy or most pathetic story - enter Baby and a death to sentiment at once and then instead of a choice air from Strauss, Flemmel must be played for Baby, no more caps just frocks for Baby. Nothing heard but Nursery Rhymes for Baby, our faces distorted into grimaces and every kind of noise of which the human voice is capable put into requisition to amuse Baby and in the midst of all this Master

My Dearest Margaret...

baby thrives and looks as fat as a little Alderman and crows and laughs in the most engaging manner possible. Fan's face amuses him particularly and a sight of it always excites a laugh even in his most crabbed humour but without any joking he takes more notice than a child of his age ever did before and he surprises everyone by his precociousness. Lizzie is getting stronger by degrees and really makes a very tolerable nurse. At any rate Baby thrives and that is every thing but as I have not too much room I must thank you at once dear Papa for the past two darling notes you kindly wrote me, every word of which were Pearls and Diamonds to me. You do not say whether you think my little drawing like the Princess - perhaps with your usual sauciness you will tell me it has the advantage of being like any ship you please. Never mind I will still write or draw for my dearest Paternoster and with best affections to all friends remain his dutiful child Lotte.

27 March Malta
My Dearest Margaret
Not a word yet transpires about us - the Alexandrian steamer is momentarily expected, the conditions imposed on poor Mehemet Ali are very hard - it is cruel and vindictive. Lord Ponsonby ought to be recalled unquestionably I think - or nothing can save a war. Our relief seems tardy enough but the Admiral will not wait beyond next month. Napier is here in quarantine, bullying as usual - the Harbour full of our ships, Sir John Ommanney still at Marmorice with the Calcutta, Cambridge and Rodney. This climate does not agree with poor Mrs Barnard and most of the Captains wives regret they left England. We have fine weather and all healthy. We have a heavy job before us in the Investiture of Sir Charles Napier as K.C.B. with great parade on board the Flag ship by Her Majestys Commands - dirty beast - a power of dirt under his nails. He is clever and certainly brave but grasping and grabbing all to himself. I am heartily sick of all this fuss. James Stopfords Court Martial[89] comes on too in about a fortnight - but every little thing now worries me and there is never a morning that I dont fidget half asleep, half awake for 3 or 4 hours before getting out of bed. I wish I were once more at mine ease.

---

89   A Court Martial was always held after the loss of a ship – James Stopford's ship the Zebra was wrecked in a gale off St. Jean D'Acre.

1841

28th. March

The Oriental is not come yet, which gives me a little more time. I expect you are now writing me if the young gentleman allows you and so we may consider ourselves as having a tete a tete. My people are all at church and I have for an hour and a half a quiet life. Our rum old Commodore has just asked leave to go to England and I shall be very glad to get rid of him for he is a regular Peter Lowe, delighting in troubled waters and perfectly restless. I have no doubt he will be the idol of the day and that his object is to catch the clap-traps while the iron's hot. I thought I was quiet but am again interrupted in every way. Little Fanshawe has come in to say I must dine with him today - and away he jumps upstairs to ask Lady Stopfords leave. It is impossible to be more comfortable than I am and my time would pass agreeably enough if I were not rather pressed with too much business. As for reading a book I have not opened one these six months. The poor Admiral as much confined as myself and every often neither of us go out of doors till 4 or 5 o'clock and then back to Dinner and dress by 7 - add to which our evenings are lost by large Parties keeping us up till 11 or 12 o'clock. What a different life I look forward to at home. I hope Willoughby is now with you and that I may have a letter from him, for all his letters are good and very sensible. How pleased I shall be to go over some classic lore with him again, though he will now teach me and I shall be at least a willing scholar. All the world are getting mad for New Zealand or Hobson's Place, Capt Wakefield has left the Rhadamanthus and gone out as has Mr Sconces son in law and daughter Mr and Mrs Bunbury. I believe Errington's Regiment there - what do you say? Shall we go with Liz? No go! How happy Lady Dunn is now on board Vanguard.

1st. Mar.

The mail is closing - the Packet from England not yet arrived so that I am longing for letters. I am in excellent health and now I am getting rid of the Commodore I look for a little quiet. Yet he is a very good fellow - only he must be about something he's restless.

My blessing upon all our flock. Kiss dear Baby for me and again God Bless you all, Your affectionate Husband John Loudon.

They are still too hard upon Mehemet Ali and we hear he is putting himself in a good state of defence - but that will not detain

My Dearest Margaret…

us a moment. I see Sir Gordon Bremer is gathering laurels in China and I hope those fellows will be soon brought to their senses[90]. I must now close. I am very anxious about Willoughby. I hope he is at home.

Enclosure to Fan   28th. *Mar*

What can I say to my notable Fan after saying all to Mamma Lizzie and Lotty - By the bye I ought to have dined with Captain Norcott last Wednesday but the trip to Gozo which I mentioned to Lizzie was put off and I mean to dine with him next week if I can. He is a very Gentlemanlike man - quite for the ladies but an old Bird - Fan! not caught with Chaff - Major and Mrs Saumarez are in great odour here and no wonder they are a nice pair, indeed the Rifles will be soon in favour - their Barracks are out of the way a little but they move to this side of the water soon. Malta never was so full of company and houses are not to be got under a most enormous rent. The weather is perfectly beautiful - but the island has always a dry arid look from its rock and stone walls. The grand Emir Bishir or Prince of the Mountains of Lebanon is here and I have had a great deal to do with endeavouring to reconcile him to the Sultan. The Princess apparently 27 - very handsome and he 93 - is a most pleasing little woman dressed in cloth of gold and the richest ornaments is very fond of Lady Stopford whom she calls her Avocata and says she is her only consolation in her adversity. They have finest children I ever saw - yet this fair Caucasian was purchased by the old fellow for £500!   Your affectionate Dad J.Loudon.

Letters from Lottie and Fan   *27 March*

How we wish our darling Padre was here to enjoy this lovely Spring weather. We have had such a lovely March with Baby - a few showers now and then to entice out the blossom. Fan and I have just been decorating the rooms with long kind of flowers from the highly scented Jonquil to the violet - a present from our good friend Mrs Mills who always remembers you in the flower season. Little Capt Harry came to see us yesterday and gives us a famous account of you - your good looks, but no time is mentioned for

---

90   Bremer served as Commander-in-Chief of British forces in the 1st Anglo-Chinese War from 1839-41, during which he took formal possession of Hong Kong.

1841

your return and hope deferred has made our hearts very sick. I am so afraid Lizzie and baby will be obliged to leave us ere you come home and we should have so liked to be present at your first introduction to your grandson, who goes by no less a name than the Pride of Durnford Street. He is such a little darling and knows us all quite well and has managed even in this short time to twine himself round our affections. Even Uncle Willoughby defers to him uncommonly and makes a capital nurse and what will we do when we lose our little plaything I scarcely know. Poor Arney longs to see him again and we must not be selfish enough to forget him although our hearts fail us as the time of separation draws nigh. Jack and Pretty Pretty quite in the background now! We have a short allowance of paper this time so I shall resume my chit-chat for the next dispatch. With kind remembrances to all friends remain ever your affectionate child Lotte. *and...*

My dearest Paps. I am determined the dispatch shall not leave without a line from me tho we're bound down to a very small share of paper. How we long for your return, the delay of which appears interminable and I fear now we shall not be able to present our darling to you as Liz must leave with him next month, so tiresome, we should so have liked to be all at home to welcome you. We want you to make a commission for us viz some <u>small</u> size black silk gloves and mittens, from one I believe to 2 shillings a pair. We have seen some sent to Augusta Foot by her brother and they appear so beautiful and cheap that we should like to have some. We must reserve all the chat of the place for a future occasion. No riding remember for you or any other impudence. God Bless you dearest Paps ever your devoted child Fan

April 10th

Darling Padre. Your last dear letter and every ones reports make us now really fancy that we shall have you with us in the course of another month or two and Mammy already talks of getting chimnies swept and house put in order to receiving her good man. We are longing to keep Lizzie and Baby with us till your return that we might have the pleasure of introducing your little grandson to you and seeing the effect he produces - but I am afraid this would be rather hard upon poor Arney who is already very tired of his solitude. Dear little fellow he grows more engaging every day and

My Dearest Margaret...

we cannot bear the idea of parting with him - such a merry little sprite too - he actually laughs out loud and crows till we almost fancy he is going to speak. The present arrangement is for Willy to escort them at the end of this month when he is obliged to go to Town to complete his term. The influenza has been victimising us both but in spite of that Willy is in capital spirits and plays his usual tricks upon us all and more especially upon poor Mamma who hates kissing as much as ever but is nevertheless obliged to endure -Capt Glanville came to see us the other day and gave us a good account of your looks which with Gods helping we shall be able to judge for ourselves in a short time. Your affectionate Lottie. *and...*

My dearest Paps We need not now grumble at the small space allotted to us as your last letter has put us quite in spirits by telling us you are to be home so soon and how can we express the happiness at the prospect of the happiness in store for us next month. God grant that nothing now may delay your departure from Malta. We hear you are bound for Corfu previous to your return. Our little darling is thriving wonderfully as big as any other babe of 8 months and the greatest of pets. How we shall part with him I dont know - it will be a heart breaking affair. Grandmama quite doats on him and is ever thinking of him night and day. Willy is just now flirting it taking half an hour from his Law for the purpose. I hope he will do well at the Bar - he seems really now to wish to get on, he is very nice with all of us and manages Mama famously - God Bless, your ever affectionate child Fran.

28 April Malta

Still here My Dearest Margaret but symptoms of moving are now making in fact we are packing up. The plan now is to await the steamer which goes today to Marseilles with the Indian mail - which will return on the 13th next month with the latest news from England - then pay a visit to Corfu which will take us a fortnight more when we shall go direct to England - doubtful even whether we shall put in here at all. The Court Martial on James Stopford for the loss of the Zebra acquitted him and all the officers and men with great praise. He will soon be promoted to full Captain. The Admiral has so far been lucky in his family and a happy father

1841

he is, for I never saw such well conducted steady and considerate young men in all respects in my life. I am yet full of work and shall be to the last. We leave Sir John Ommanney in Command and I am much mistaken if they won't miss my dear kind Admiral. they are to give him a Dinner and Ball next week. He is quite beloved and altho Napier seems to carry all before him now there will soon be an end to humbug. You will have received my letters by the last Packet and I fear they will have given you much pain and annoyance as the cause of them gave me. I trust Willoughby will put two grains of common sense into his head and consider his family. Where could he have learnt his extravagance - I am at a loss to know - certainly not from you or I - who begrudged ourselves the smallest extra expense. I ever pinched to make two ends meet after all. But enough of that. I hope my ever dear Eliza and Baby are well and thriving and am delighted she is making a tolerable nurse, though I fear he will pull her down. She must not wait for me as I shall be obliged to go to London and then see her at Chatham. I am now in great glee in the hope of so soon finding myself ensconced by your side in the dear old quarter which I see so often in fancy. God Bless My Dearest Wife and Pets is the prayer of your ever affectionate husband John Loudon. *with...*

My dearest Lotty. Do my dear excuse my very short and hurried scrawl. the mail goes at 2 and I am now at 8 breakfast to take at 9. A thousand things to do and all my Admiralty cases upon my back to pack up as well as I can - you will ask why defer them till the last, but my dear girl they cannot be closed till the last. I long for the quiet and tranquil life of my own 44 and its appendages. Your letters are like a good cool draught to a thirsty traveller. All seems settling down in the East. We are going to pay a visit to Corfu when dear Annie Duckworth is married and on the back of that away we go to England.

God Bless You my dearest Lotty your affectionate father John Loudon.

Nothing but hammering and nailing boxes right and left, up and down. Sweet sounds!

with...

Dearest Fran. Last not least. How are you? I long to see your quiet half saucy face again. Lou, you know, is returned from

My Dearest Margaret...

Gibraltar and again with her father. Her step mother is an excellent mother to her but sadly racked with head aches ever since she came to Malta which does not agree with her. You will have lots of people calling to tell you about me and of course will make them as welcome as you can not giving dinners of course which is never done by Ladies to Gentlemen - unless very old particular friends. Ever my dear Fran your affectionate Paps, John Loudon.

18 May Malta
My Dearest Margaret.

We are at length drawing I hope to the end of our pilgrimage but take a trip to Corfu first which will lengthen our departure a fortnight, for the Admiral is not to wait more than a few days on his return here. We were all ready to turn the papers over to Sir John Ommanney when a private note from Lord Minto told the Admiral he would like the ship to wait till he heard from him, which he would do officially by the next Packet and the Admiral's health is not so good as it was and he is anxious to get home. He has had swelled ankles which is no good sign at his age but the Doctor had put all to rights for the present. We were all packed up and to have started for England as today when this tantalising note put a stop to us, the Packet which brought this bad news brought me your dear letter of the 29th April and 1st.May - only a fortnight in coming and I can picture your feelings on the parting of dear Lizzie and the baby. I hope they had a good passage in the horrid Pig vessel and are now all right again. Willy is of course eating his dinners[91] - I cannot tell you how I long to be again partaking of your fine weather and all the comforts of my own dear home and soon now I must be in it - but unless the wind is against us I fear I shall have to pass your door as we did coming out - and much about the same time. Young Campbell of Ilay was here, and went to a gay ball given to the Admiral by the officers in his Highland costume which was much admired - the kilt looked quite decent. I am still very anxious about Willoughby - but am glad he is sensible of his extravagance and appears resolved to correct it which indeed he must do as we cannot afford it and I shall superintend his supplies. I have been so pinned to my desk, preparing for parting and with

---
91   Entry to the Bar

1841

so much daily business that I have not been scarcily off my chair from seven in the morning till 5 in the afternoon when I take my walk till 7 our hour of dinner and then after my soup and fish and a patty I fear I have very little appetite. Yesterday I dined with Sir David and Lady Dunn upon a bit of fish and roast lamb and made the best dinner I have done for some time.

Matters are not yet settled in the East but I don't imagine our force will be again required. The Commodore Napier has been shewing the people in England what he has shewn us for a long time that he is a regular Mountebank[92] - his imposture from beginning to end - the devotion of the Captains and officers here to my good Admiral is most gratifying. He is absolutely adored by everybody abroad and ashore and I must say deservedly - and the family are the most happy in themselves I ever saw - it is quite beautiful to be among them and I am sure their kindness to me knows no bounds. They wish they had me with them at Greenwich Hospital - but at any rate Lady Stopford gives me the warmest invitations always to see them. Sir Wm Burnet kindly wrote me that the agency of Haslar Hospital would be vacant in July - and I mentioned it to the Admiral who said he would write Lord Minto with great pleasure but thought I was leaving paradise for a swampy bleak place in an Hospital and that he did not think you would like it and so thought I so we want it not though the salary is £400 a year and a house. Something else may turn up - if not we must make the most of what we have and be our own masters. The Admiral would have got me I am quite sure the Storekeepership of this Dockyard but I knew Malta would not agree with you - indeed that you could not live there prevented his applying.

God Bless you Your affectionate Husband J. Loudon. Not having time to write to Chatham tell them I am quite well and shall write a longer letter next time.....

---

92   Charlatan

My Dearest Margaret…

POSTSCRIPT

The *Princess Charlotte* eventually reached Portsmouth on July 19th 1841, from where Loudon returned to his family home in Plymouth. After service in the East Indies, the ship became a hospital ship in Hong Kong, finally being sold for scrap in 1875.

John Loudon never served at sea again, but became a purser in the Admirals' Office in Devonport, Plymouth, and appears on the Navy List as 'still active' until March 1851. Loudon had hoped for a share in the £60,000 Prize Money distributed after the Syrian War and for over two years he persisted in writing letters and making personal appeals but with no success. Admiral Stopford informed Loudon in September 1843, that a Proclamation of February 1836 gave no preference of Prize Money to Secretaries of the Commander-in-Chief. However, he does, in 1845, appear to have been awarded a pension of half-pay from the Admiralty. Loudon died, aged 75, at home in Durnford Street on May 1st 1851, the cause of death on his death certificate being 'paralysis'.

Margaret remained at no. 44 until her death in September 1861.

Elizabeth (Lizzie) had three more children, two boys and a girl, and the Errington family went to Tasmania in 1844 to further Arnie's career. Errington became Lt. General Arnold Errington, Commanding Officer in Malta in 1855. He died in 1890, Elizabeth having died in 1869, aged 61.

Charlotte (Lottie) married an army officer, Captain Knox, and spent many years in India.

My Dearest Margaret...

Frances (Fan) stayed at home with Margaret, as was customary with youngest daughters, and after her mother's death continued living at no. 44, Durnford Street, until at least 1867. By the next Street directory (1873) the house was unoccupied and since then the street has been damaged by war-time bombing and renumbered twice. However it has been possible to identify no. 44 as the present 103, now in flats. Fan died in Australia in 1894, aged 78.

Willoughby, after graduating from Cambridge in 1841 was admitted to Lincoln's Inn on May 3rd 1841, worked hard, was called to the Bar (June 11th 1844) and a successful career followed. In a letter to his son in January 1842, John Loudon forgives him and encloses a 100 guinea draft, hoping for future prudence, as his college education 'cost me £1400-£1600'.

For his services in the Syrian War, Admiral Stopford was awarded the Freedom of the City of London and became Governor of the Royal Naval Hospital at Greenwich, where he lived until his death in 1847, Lady Stopford surviving him by almost twenty years. Of his three sons, all of whom served at some time on the *Princess Charlotte*, Robert became an Admiral and James a Vice-Admiral. Loudon kept in touch with the Stopford family during the Admiral's time at Greenwich.

Both Captain Arthur Fanshawe and Captain Charles Austen were awarded the C.B.[93] for their services in the campaign and both went on to have eminent naval careers.

Napier commanded the Channel Fleet from 1847-9 and in 1854 at the beginning of the Crimean War was made Commander of the Baltic Fleet, where his reputation as a controversial commander continued.

Also on board the *Princess Charlotte* since 1838 and employed as midshipman was William Peel, aged 14, the third son of the Prime Minister, Sir Robert Peel. On his return he not only brought back his first medal for the capture of St. Jean D'Acre, but three orange trees for his mother!

---

93 Companion of the Order of the Bath

Postscript

By the mid 1840s, steam technology had improved to the point that thereafter nearly all new warships had steam propulsion, though they still carried sails. From the 1850s the first ironclad warships made wooden vessels obsolete, as metal entirely replaced wood as the main material for warship construction. The majestic wooden sailing ships of the line had been superseded by the new steam-powered iron battleships. It was the end of an era.

printed by: ORPHANS 01568 612460